THE RISE AND FALL
OF THE
SECOND LARGEST
EMPIRE
IN HISTORY

This edition published in 2013 by
CRESTLINE
a division of BOOK SALES, INC.
276 Fifth Avenue Suite 206
New York, New York 10001
USA

This edition published by arrangement with Fair Winds Press.

Text © 2010 by Thomas J. Craughwell

First published in the USA in 2010 by
Fair Winds Press, a member of
Quayside Publishing Group
100 Cummings Center
Suite 406-L
Beverly, MA 01915-6101
www.fairwindspress.com

10 9 8 7 6 5 4 3 2 1

ISBN: 978-0-7858-3057-3

Library of Congress Cataloging-in-Publication Data
Craughwell, Thomas J., 1956-
   The rise and fall of the second largest empire in history : how Genghis Khan's Mongols almost conquered the world / Thomas J. Craughwell.
      p. cm.
   Includes bibliographical references and index.
   ISBN-13: 978-1-59233-398-1
   ISBN-10: 1-59233-398-2
   1. Mongols—History. 2. Imperialism—History—To 1500. 3. Genghis Khan, 1162-1227. 4. Kublai Khan, 1216-1294. 5. Eurasia—History. 6. Middle Ages. I. Title.

   DS19.C73 2010
   950'.22—dc22

                                                                        2009031087

Cover design: Peter Long
Book layout & design: Sheila Hart Design, Inc.
Photo research: Anne Burns Images

Printed and bound in China

THE RISE AND FALL
OF THE
SECOND LARGEST
EMPIRE
IN HISTORY

HOW GENGHIS KHAN'S MONGOLS
ALMOST CONQUERED THE WORLD

THOMAS J. CRAUGHWELL

CRESTLINE

CONTENTS

This fourteenth century miniature depicts a Mongolian rider catching a stray. Note the stirrups on the horse; they are believed to have been invented in the second century on the Asian steppes, the Mongols' homeland. akg-images

GENGHIS KHAN'S FAMILY TREE

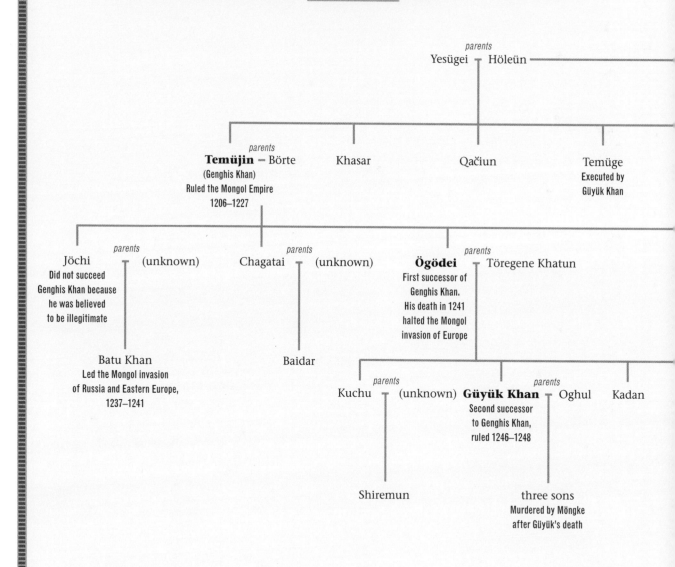

parents
Yesügei — Höleün

parents
Temüjin — Börte
(Genghis Khan)
Ruled the Mongol Empire
1206–1227

Khasar

Qačiun

Temüge
Executed by
Güyük Khan

Jöchi
Did not succeed
Genghis Khan because
he was believed
to be illegitimate

parents
(unknown)

Chagatai

parents
(unknown)

Ögödei
First successor of
Genghis Khan.
His death in 1241
halted the Mongol
invasion of Europe

parents
Töregene Khatun

Batu Khan
Led the Mongol invasion
of Russia and Eastern Europe,
1237–1241

Baidar

Kuchu

parents
(unknown)

Güyük Khan
Second successor
to Genghis Khan,
ruled 1246–1248

parents
Oghul

Kadan

Shiremun

three sons
Murdered by Möngke
after Güyük's death

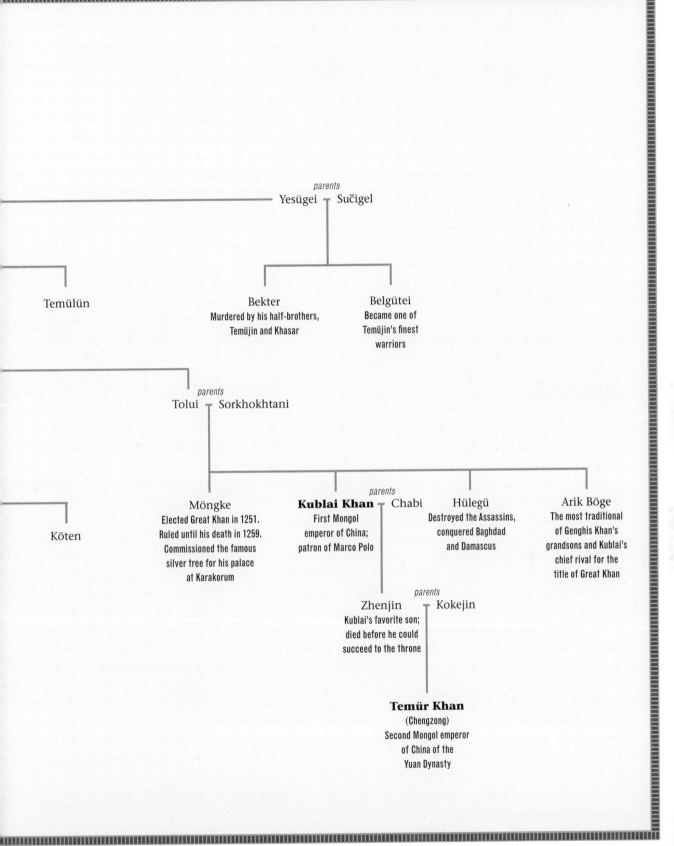

parents

Yesügei ┬ Sučigel

Temülün

Bekter
Murdered by his half-brothers,
Temüjin and Khasar

Belgütei
Became one of
Temüjin's finest
warriors

parents

Tolui ┬ Sorkhokhtani

Köten

Möngke
Elected Great Khan in 1251.
Ruled until his death in 1259.
Commissioned the famous
silver tree for his palace
at Karakorum

Kublai Khan ┬ Chabi
First Mongol
emperor of China;
patron of Marco Polo

parents

Hülegü
Destroyed the Assassins,
conquered Baghdad
and Damascus

Arik Böge
The most traditional
of Genghis Khan's
grandsons and Kublai's
chief rival for the
title of Great Khan

parents

Zhenjin ┬ Kokejin
Kublai's favorite son;
died before he could
succeed to the throne

Temür Khan
(Chengzong)
Second Mongol emperor
of China of the
Yuan Dynasty

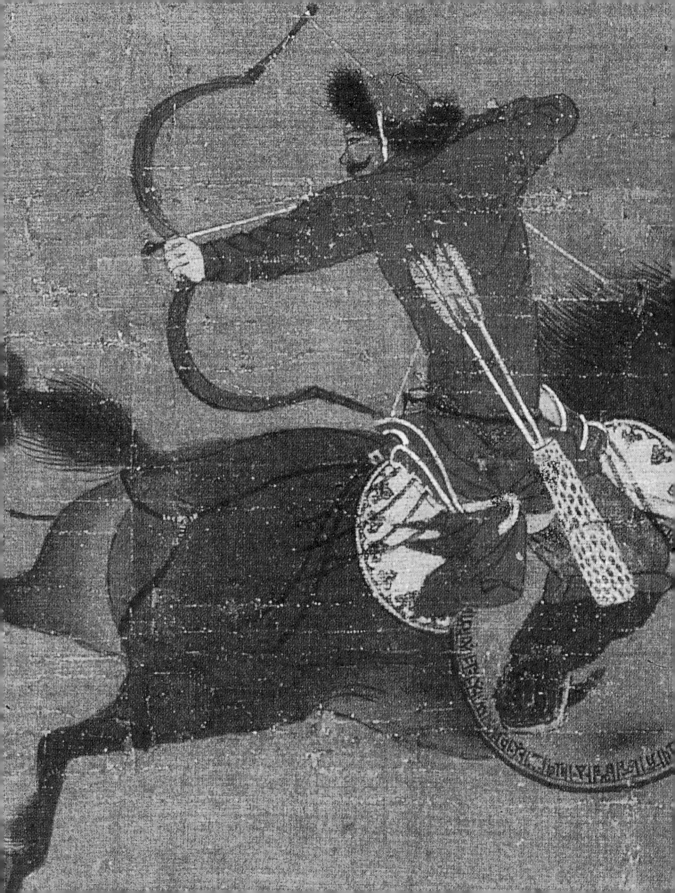

At its height in the late thirteenth century, the Mongols ruled an empire that covered approximately 9 million square miles (24 million square kilometers). It was the largest contiguous landmass ruled by a single emperor in human history.

The second largest contiguous empire was ruled by Russia's last tsar, Nicholas II, whose realm extended over 8 million square miles (22.8 million square kilometers). In comparison, the Romans ruled an empire of 1 million square miles (5 million square kilometers).

In 1300, the world population stood at approximately 429 million, according to world population historian Jean-Noel Biraben. The Mongols ruled over approximately 110 million people, or about one-quarter of the world's population, comparable to the British Empire in the early twentieth century.

DIVIDED AND LEADERLESS

In the twelfth century, there were about 700,000 Mongols scattered across the steppes of Central Asia. They were nomads who lived in small encampments. They had no towns, fortresses, or farms. They had few comforts and fewer luxuries. And they were divided up into clans and tribes that more often than not were at war with each other. All that changed thanks to one man, Temüjin, later known as Genghis Khan.

Genghis was a man of tremendous ambition, great courage, and extraordinary insight. His own clan was weak militarily, so as a young man he began to forge alliances with powerful chiefs. He collected around himself a circle of great warriors of unshakable loyalty. Those Mongol tribes he could not win as friends or allies he conquered in battle. By the time he was about forty-four years old, Genghis had united the Mongols into a single nation and had been elected Great Khan.

At heart, Genghis was a Mongol traditionalist, but he was willing to do away with any custom that threatened to hold him or his people back. The autonomy of the many clans and tribes had kept the Mongols weak, so he united them. The Mongol class system rewarded men of rank over men of talent, so he abolished the Mongol nobility. Nomadic life on the steppes was hard and the Mongols were poor, so

Genghis looked beyond his borders to wealthy nations he would conquer, and loot, and compel to pay tribute.

A NEW CIVILIZATION

As they built their empire, the Mongols showed themselves to be murderous, merciless, and incredibly destructive. They piled up the heads of their victims; they drove thousands of terrified peasants into moats and ditches so Mongol warriors could climb over them to storm the battlements. They reduced great cities such as Kiev and Krakow to rubble. They devastated the rural areas of China, Russia, and Hungary. Perhaps as many as 40 million men, women, and children either were killed outright by the Mongols or died of the famine and disease that inevitably followed in their wake. The Mongols committed these atrocities because they provoked terror, and terrified people are more likely to surrender, thereby speeding the conquest of a region and costing fewer Mongol lives.

Obviously, the Mongols could be cruel, but they were not mindless. Genghis Khan discovered during his very first campaign that the people who inhabited the lands outside Mongolia possessed skills and technology that would be very useful in warfare as well as domestically. And so the Mongols adopted a policy that spared engineers, technicians, artisans, and craftsmen, but they also spared musicians, singers, dancers, and actors. Just as the engineers could teach the Mongols how to construct siege engines to batter down the walls of enemy cities, artists and performers could enrich Mongol life.

Like every other empire builder, Genghis Khan sought power and wealth, but he was unique among other conquerors because he realized very quickly that he could take what was best from his neighbors to create a new Mongol civilization.

THE MONGOL DYNASTY

In terms of imagination and ambition, one could argue that Kublai Khan surpassed his grandfather Genghis. When Kublai came of age, the Mongols counted northern China as part of its empire, but southern China, the home of the Sung dynasty, was still independent. It was rich and possessed fertile farmland, which made it desirable, and it had an eight-year-old boy as emperor, which made it vulnerable. Kublai conquered Sung China easily, then embarked on a series of remarkable innovations that made him almost as famous as his grandfather.

He united China into a single nation, something the Chinese had never known in all their long history. He proclaimed himself emperor of China and founded a dynasty, the Yuan, which was beyond even Genghis's wildest dreams. He built a magnificent new capital city—what is now Beijing—and erected a splendid palace—the forerunner of the Forbidden City. Eighty years earlier, the greatest Mongol khan lived in a felt tent; now the greatest khan dwelt in a palace of marble and gold.

Once the conquests were accomplished, the Mongols imposed peace, the Pax Mongolica, upon their territories. It was said that during these decades of quiet in the thirteenth and fourteenth centuries, a young woman with a sack of gold could ride from one end of the empire to another and no one would trouble her. That is an exaggeration, but it is true that the Mongols did everything in their power to ensure the security of merchants and caravans as they passed through the Mongol Empire. International commerce had become important to the Mongols, and they did not want anything to disrupt it. But more than trade goods moved across the empire: because the Mongol Empire was contiguous, stretching from Korea to Eastern Europe, it was easy for technologies, ideas, and trade goods to move back and forth between East and West; for example, gunpowder came to Europe, and Christianity spread to the Far East.

The Mongols were terribly destructive yet remarkably innovative, and it is because they possessed both qualities that they had such an enduring impact on the world.

CHAPTER 1

THE ASIAN STEPPES: AN INTENSELY HOSTILE WORLD

NOTHING COULD HAVE PREPARED THE POPE'S EMIS-SARY FOR THE STEPPES OF MONGOLIA. JOHN OF PLANO CARPINI WAS A FRANCISCAN FRIAR AND A SON OF THE CENTRAL ITALIAN PROVINCE OF UMBRIA, A LUSH, GREEN COUNTRY OF WHEAT FIELDS, VINEYARDS, AND OLIVE GROVES. MONGOLIA WAS A DIFFERENT AND, TO FATHER JOHN'S EYES, AN INTENSELY HOSTILE WORLD. WITH CLASSIC UNDERSTATEMENT, HE RECORDED IN HIS *HISTORY OF THE MONGOLS*, "THE WEATHER THERE IS ASTONISHINGLY IRREGULAR."

"In the middle of the summer when other places are normally enjoying very great heat," he observed, "there is fierce thunder and lightning which cause the death of many men, and at the same time there are very heavy falls of snow. There are also hurricanes of bitterly cold wind so violent that at times men can ride on horseback only with great effort."

It was Pope Innocent IV who had sent Father John on this diplomatic mission to Güyük, Genghis Khan's grandson, who was about to become the new Mongol khan. In part, Innocent wanted to negotiate a treaty to prevent any more Mongol invasions such as Europe had suffered during the years 1237 to 1242. The pope also wanted intelligence regarding the Mongol military, and insights into how the Europeans could drive back any subsequent Mongol attack. Furthermore, word had reached Europe that it was the policy of the Mongol khans to treat clergy of all religions with deference, and tolerate all

Genghis Khan, seated on a raised dais, greets his four sons, Jöchi, Chagatai, Ögödei, and Tolui. Of these four, only Ögödei would become Great Khan. akg-images / Werner Forman

خواتین او و او را بغایت دوست میداشته چون مال خاتون گذشته شد بعد از مدتی او راپیش چنگیزخان سوق آورده و بهره یوسون مغول او راد رنج آورد
و دیگر خاتون دختر بادشاه دختر بادشاه سکونت بود و چنگیزخان سوقات او را بخشیده و بسیاری از خواتین بادشاهان دختران امرا خاتون چنگیزخان بوده لکن
در عدد خواتین بزرگ نیامده و چنگیزخان را از آنقرار توم ابرم سری نام بود جوحتی نام از سپرستر زمیده بیان فوت که دو ماه مادر در شد معلوم نیست و
بسری دیگر نیامده نام او و اوجان جهان هم درکره کی نامه بود و ما او قته بو دازوم تامار و ماهش معلوم نشده است نازخواتین معتبر چنگیزخان فرزندان خان وجوان جهار پسر
که معتبر بوده و ایشان جهار پسر که لوک می گفته یعنی جهار پسر مکرک ازیشان علیحه با دشاهی شیده درین جوان شب فرزندان چنگیزخان که نهاده می شود
ازان ایشان بنی شعبه فرزندان ایشان شیده می آید هر یکی در آستان یک شعبه فرزندان و علیحه مفرد خواهد آمد اورادان کوکان جوون سپتانی مغزنجو آشینم
هم الجاشعبه فرزندانش شیده می آید و دختراز دکان جون ایشان پران ایشان پران بنی ایشان نیمی از قومی اندو شعبه آن قوم ذکر ایشان آن شب چشیدن مناسب
نباشد و صور میچنگیزخان وجد دوشعب و برین جیات و شعب و بین هیات است که اثبات می یاب

قسم دوم در تاریخ و حکایات چنگیزخان از ابتدا و ولادت او تا زمان جانیت با دشاهی صورت تخت و خواتین و شهزادگان و امرا در حالت
جلوس بر سریر خانی و نسب امرای او و نوجها کاراه او و در سرو نجها کرده دست او و او و مقداراز زمان با دشاهی او آخر عهد و ذکر وفات او
چون مبنی این کتاب و وضع این تاریخ بر بیان نظارت کشمشعبه فرزندان با دشاهی مترومی و با کرشیم تقریر کنیم الخ در اصل تاریخ و حکایات مشروع نمایم قسم اول این

religions. Hoping to build upon Güyük's open-mind-edness, Pope Innocent wrote two letters to the khan explaining the basics of Christianity and urging him to be baptized. Innocent explained that as Christ's representative on Earth, it was his responsibility "to lead those in error into the way of truth and gain all men for Him." If Güyük were baptized, the odds were good that the rest of the Mongols would convert, too, because history had taught the Catholic Church that once a king entered the Church, his people followed.

In 1245, the year the pope gave him his assignment, Father John was sixty years old—an old man by the standards of the thirteenth century—but he was hardy, with a gift for languages, and experience representing the interests of the Catholic Church and his religious order, the Franciscans, in Europe and North Africa. He traveled with a fellow Franciscan, Benedict the Pole, and together they set out from Poland for the Mongol-occupied territories of the Ukraine and Russia.

In his narrative of their expedition, John records that as they set out on their mission he and Benedict "feared that we might be killed by the Tartars [John's term for the Mongols] or other people, or imprisoned for life, or afflicted with hunger, thirst, cold, heat, injuries and exceeding great trials almost beyond our powers of endurance—all of which with the exception of death and imprisonment for life fell to our lot in various ways in a much greater degree than we had conceived beforehand."

The Mongol commanders whom John and Benedict met in the Ukraine and Russia recognized the importance of their mission and hurried them from one outpost to the next so they would arrive at Karakorum, the Mongol capital, in time to witness Güyük's inauguration as Great Khan. Their Mongol guides forced the two friars to ride at top speed,

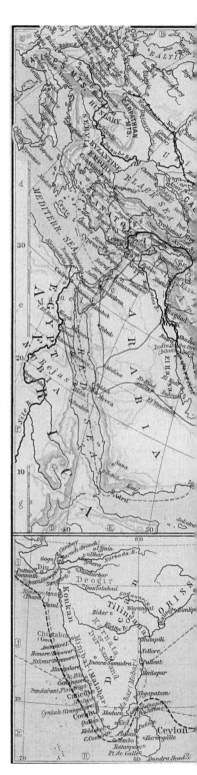

This map shows the route of Father John of Plano Carpini, Pope Innocent IV's emissary to Güyük, grandson of Genghis Khan. It took Father John nearly six months to reach Güyük, after enduring storms of snow, dust, and hail.

Land routes
Sea
Route of John of Pian de Carpine, 1245-1247
" William of Rubruck (Rubruquis), 1253-1255
" Marco Polo, 1271-1295
John of Pian de Carpine began and ended his journey at Lyons.
All routes shown in the map are approximate.
Mediaeval names in hair-line, thus Cambalec.
For further details in western Asia see p. 99.
Scale 1:40 000 000

stopping five or six times per day at way stations where the entire party changed to fresh horses. Father John never became accustomed to the awkward size of Mongol horses—the horse's wide belly stretched his legs uncomfortably, and every jolt as the pony trotted across the steppe sent a spike of pain up his spine.

The five-and-a-half months John spent riding through the mountains and deserts of Central Asia were wretched and often terrifying even for a tough, disciplined man possessed of a sense of mission. He and Benedict were traveling during Lent, when they were forbidden to eat meat or dairy products. Consequently, their diet consisted of millet boiled in water and seasoned with salt. "We were so weak," John recalled, "we could hardly ride."

"NOW YOU SHOULD SAY WITH A SINCERE HEART, 'I WILL SUBMIT AND SERVE YOU.'. . .IF YOU DO NOT OBSERVE GOD'S COMMAND, AND IF YOU IGNORE MY COMMAND, I SHALL KNOW YOU AS MY ENEMY."

—A letter from Güyük Khan, Genghis Khan's grandson, to Pope Innocent IV

Even when at last he reached the safety of the khan's camp, Father John had no comfort: he arrived in the middle of a blinding dust storm. To keep from literally being blown away, Father John and his companions had to lie flat on the ground as great clouds of stinging dust swirled around them. Then, as the Mongols were preparing for the coronation of Güyük, a violent hailstorm struck, leaving deep piles of hailstones throughout the camp. This aberration was followed immediately by a heat wave that melted the hailstones so quickly as to produce a flash flood that washed away tents and drowned 160 men.

"To conclude briefly about this country," John wrote, "it is large, but otherwise—as we saw it with our own eyes during the five and a half months we traveled about it—it is more wretched than I can possibly say."

Many months later, when Father John returned safely to Europe, he brought to the pope a menacing letter from Güyük Khan. In a haughty tone, Güyük dismissed out of hand the idea that he "should become a trembling Nestorian Christian, worship God and be an ascetic." Then the khan turned the tables on the pope. "Now you should say with a sincere heart, 'I will submit and serve you.' Thou thyself, at the head of all the Princes, come at once to serve and wait upon us! At that time I shall recognize your submission. If you do not observe God's command, and if you ignore my command, I shall know you as my enemy."

LIFE ON THE STEPPE

No one knows where the Mongols came from. Their language is said to be part of the Turkic-Manchu family, which suggests the Mongols could be related to the Turks, or to the people of Manchuria, or both. Another theory proposes that they are from the same ethnic group as the Huns who devastated the Roman Empire in the fifth century C.E. Ancient Chinese sources tell of a fierce warrior nation called Hsiung-nu—perhaps these were the Mongols.

The most that can be said with certainty is that, according to the Chinese sources, by 400 B.C.E., there were a people dwelling in the vast grasslands far to the north of China. They were nomads who moved their flocks of sheep and herds of cattle and horses from summer pastures on the open steppe to winter pastures in sheltered valleys. Our Chinese informant adds that these nomads sheltered in round felt tents and had no written language.

Although the term *Mongol* suggests a unified nation, they were not truly united until Genghis Khan made them one. For most of their history, they were a collection of independent tribes and clans who formed temporary, ever-shifting alliances. Loyalty among the Mongols was limited to a small circle of people. There were chiefs with authority over these loose coalitions, but there was no central authority, no king, no emperor, no khan of all the Mongols (although Genghis's great-grandfather had almost achieved that goal).

In most times this spirit of independence was tempered by a necessity for the Mongols to cooperate with each other. The steppe is immense, stretching from Hungary to the west and the mountains of Manchuria to the east, from the forests of Siberia to the north and the sand-and-gravel wasteland of the Gobi Desert to the south. In summer, temperatures can soar to 104° Fahrenheit (40° Celsius)—and there is no shade. In winter, temperatures drop so far below freezing that frostbite can occur in minutes.

But even in fine weather the steppe is unsettling: it is a vast ocean of grassland with few landmarks to assist travelers and no cities or towns to offer security, only the isolated tribes who may or may not consider the traveler an enemy. To travel across the bleak, empty steppe is to feel at all times exposed, isolated, and unprotected.

In spite of hundreds of thousands of square miles of lush grass-land, the steppe is not suitable for farming—the soil is poor, and the growing season is only four months long. The Mongols adapted to this harsh land, becoming nomadic herders, primarily of sheep, who supplied meat, milk, cheese, wool, and felt for the Mongol tents, which are known in the West as *yurts*; the correct term is *ger*, pronounced with a hard *g* and rhyming with "dare."

<hr>

Bow Power

Historian and travel writer John Man tells how in 1794 a member of Turkey's embassy staff in London gave a demonstration of the power of a composite bow. It was received wisdom in England that since the Hundred Years' War of the fourteenth and fifteenth centuries, the English longbow was the deadliest weapon drawn by man. The Turkish archer Mahmoud Effendi, secretary to the Turkish ambassador in London, fired his arrows 415 yards (379 meters) against the wind, 482 yards (441 meters) with it. The English spectators were humbled—an arrow fired from an English long-bow rarely traveled 350 yards (320 meters). Mahmoud refused to accept any praise, however, saying that his master, the sultan in Constantinople, was so strong that his arrows traveled twice as far (a courteous although obvious exaggeration—no archer has ever shot an arrow half a mile).

In the nineteenth century, archaeologists discovered a stone stele in Mongolia dating from the 1220s and bearing an inscription that records an archery competition to which Genghis Khan was a witness. He had just returned from the conquest of what is now Turkistan, and to celebrate his victory Genghis called for a feast with the traditional Mongol games of wrestling, horse racing, and archery.

The inscription reads, "While Genghis Khan was holding an assembly of Mongolian dignitaries . . . Yesunge shot a target at 335 *alds*." Yesunge was Genghis's nephew, and apparently an extremely strong man, because an *ald* measures a little over 5 feet (1.5 meters). In other words, his shot traveled more than 1,675 feet (511 meters). No wonder Genghis erected a memorial to commemorate Yesunge's feat.

To erect a *ger*, Mongol women made a wooden lattice for the walls that they set up in a circle, with long wooden poles mounted on top to form the pointed crown of the tent. When the felt was hung on this frame, the topmost point was kept open so smoke from the interior central fire could escape. Inside, the ground was covered with Persian carpets; there were iron and copper cooking pots, steel swords and daggers, and luxury items such as little chests of tea and perhaps some silk garments. All of these things the Mongol family would have acquired either through trade with passing caravans or by looting the tents of rival Mongol tribes.

The traditional Mongol dwelling is a circular felt tent known as a *ger*, also known as a *yurt*. Persian carpers kept the ground inside the tent warm; the top was left open so smoke from the interior fire could escape. akg-images / VISIOARS

THE HORSE AND THE BOW

In addition to sheep, the Mongols also raised oxen to pull their heavy wooden carts and even some camels, but the steppe's primary gift to the Mongols was a hardy breed of wild horse. Archaeological evidence tells us that 6,000 years ago the inhabitants of the steppe hunted wild horses for meat; 4,000 years ago they had domesticated them.

Compared to the thoroughbreds of the Western world, the Mongol horse is an unattractive animal—short, barely taller than a pony, with a thick neck, a big, distended belly, and a shaggy coat. But these horses are

Although shorter than other breeds, the Mongolian horse is fast and hardy—essential qualities on the steppes. Mongols would frequently change horses, allowing them to cover 80 miles (128 kilometers) or more a day. akg-images

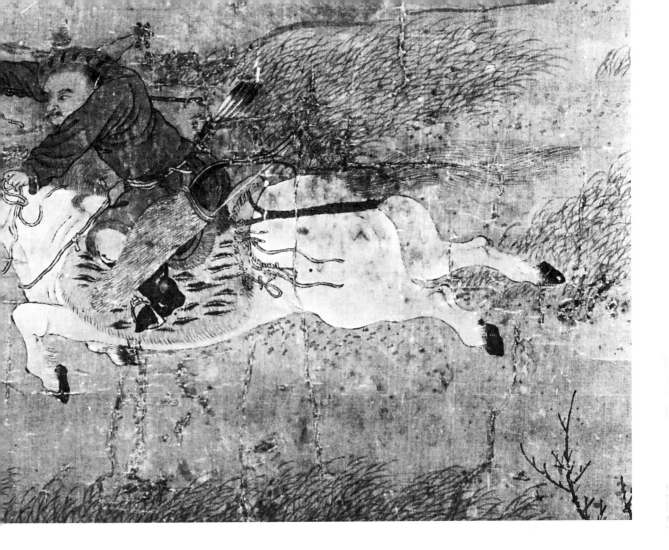

fast, and they can survive winter temperatures that would kill other breeds by digging through the snow with their hooves until they reach the frozen grass beneath. Even today many Mongols own at least one horse, and horse racing remains one of the "three manly skills" by which Mongol males prove themselves (the other two are archery and wrestling).

Because the Mongols did not grow crops of any kind, they had no beer or wine, but from mare's milk the Mongols made *koumiss*, a kind of beer with a high alcohol content. There are many accounts of Mongol warriors and chiefs dying young as a result of heavy drinking.

Most historians and archaeologists believe the stirrup was developed in Central Asia, very likely by the Huns. The stirrup gave a rider stability on horseback while making it easier to maneuver his mount. The stirrup also enabled the Huns, the Mongols, and other mounted nations of Central Asia to fight on horseback.

Their weapon of choice was the bow. The Mongol composite bow was their "secret weapon." Unstrung, it stands three feet high, but its shape is unlike familiar bows such as the English longbow. When a longbow is drawn, it forms a perfect curve; in the center of the Mongol bow, however, is a small piece of composite material a few inches long that bends inward toward the archer. This innovation, combined with the composite materials of the bow, make it very hard to draw—Mongol boys began practicing very early to build the necessary upper body strength to use the bow effectively. By the time a Mongol male was old enough to ride into battle, he could expect his arrow to travel almost 500 yards (457 meters) at a speed of approximately 186 miles (299 kilometers) per hour, which would give it enough force to pierce steel armor.

The composite bow was the product of thousands of years of trial and error. It requires thin strips of deer or cow horn, wood, sinew (an animal's Achilles tendon was preferred), and glue made by boiling down animal tendons or fish bones. The wood forms the inner core of the bow to which the craftsman glued successive layers of sinew and horn.

VOLUNTARY KINSHIP

The basis of Mongol society was the clan, an extended family of blood relatives and relations by marriage. The next largest group was a Mongol tribe, which differed from tribes that defined themselves by descent from a common ancestor or membership in a particular ethnic group. Among the Mongols, a tribe was collection of people who shared a common political interest or ambition. As such, the tribe was fairly open—anyone could join, provided he had foresworn his loyalty to his previous tribe.

There was another system of voluntary kinship in which a man became a sworn brother, known as an *anda*, to the leader of a tribe. *Andas* would cut their fingers or hands and exchange blood to become

"blood brothers." Because this was the highest level of voluntary kinship, the would-be *anda* was required to give up the duty he owed to his family and clan as well as his tribe. An *anda* was considered on par with the chief's biological brother.

During peacetime, an *anda* was free to do as he wished, as long as his actions did not undermine the interests of his chief. During time of war, however, the chief expected his *anda* to give him absolute

The Mongols' main weapon was the composite bow, which they learned to use beginning as children because its materials and notched shape made it so difficult to draw. The Granger Collection, New York

obedience. There is a story of *andas* who disobeyed their chief's express command and delayed going into battle in order to loot their enemy's camp first. The chief punished these disobedient *andas* by confiscating everything they plundered when they should have been fighting.

RELIGIOUSLY INDIFFERENT

Although the Mongols took kinship and loyalty seriously, religion rested lightly on them. Most Mongols were shamanists, but there were Muslim Mongols, Buddhist Mongols, Nestorian Christian Mongols, and eventually even Russian Orthodox Mongols.

Pope Innocent IV had hoped that Father John of Plano Carpini's mission to Güyük Khan would pave the way for a nation of Roman Catholic Mongols. Studying this state of affairs, the eighteenth-century English historian Edward Gibbon asserted, "A singular conformity may be found between the religious laws of Zingis (sic) Khan and Mr. [John] Locke." Gibbon's claim is wildly overstated; on the subject of religion, what a man believed simply did not matter to the Mongols. They were not the forerunners of religious tolerance; they were simply indifferent to religious differences.

Shamanism, the primary Mongol religion, is a difficult religious system to define because it varies from society to society. In general, shamanist societies do not gather together to worship a god or gods; rather, they believe the world is full of invisible spirits that are forces of good and evil. Shamans, an elite group of mystics, are necessary to attract the good spirits and drive out or keep at bay the evil spirits.

The Mongol form of shamanism included ancestor worship, with each family enshrining in their tents images of their ancestors, known as *ongghot*. As long as the family venerated the *ongghot*, they could expect to enjoy good fortune.

Another aspect of Mongol shamanism is a belief in nature gods, the two most important being Tengri, the supreme god who ruled the heavens, and Itügen, the goddess of the earth and of fertility. Given that the two dominant features of the Mongol world were the endless steppe and the enormous blue vault of the sky overhead, the worship of a sky god and an earth goddess makes perfect sense.

As for shamans, they enjoyed high status in Mongol society. The shaman dressed all in white, rode a white horse, and carried the emblems of his office—a staff and a drum. In trances the shaman would exorcize evil spirits that were harming children or causing illness; he could also summon herds of game for hunters. One of the shaman's most highly valued attributes was his ability to foretell the future. He did so by placing the shoulder blade of a sheep in a fire and reading the cracks produced by the heat.

Although the shamanist Mongols had no houses of worship, they considered high places especially sacred. If a Mongol had a particular request to make of Tengri, he would climb to the highest mound he could find and pray directly to the sky god for aid. The ritual required the Mongol to uncover his head when he reached the summit and kneel nine times with his belt draped around his neck as a sign of humility. Genghis Khan performed this ritual at the beginning of his career when he prayed to Tengri to inspire all Mongol warriors to follow him. As history tells us, that prayer was answered.

THE FIRST GREAT KHAN

As harsh as the physical environment of the steppes was, the interaction among the Mongol tribes and their relations with their neighbors could be nearly as bad. Early in the twelfth century the Mongols were at war with the Tartars, a tribe closely related to them, and with the Jin (or Chin) dynasty that ruled in northern China.

AT THE BANQUET THAT FOLLOWED THE CEREMONY, KABUL KHAN GOT DRUNK, LEANED OVER, AND GAVE THE EMPEROR'S BEARD A PLAYFUL TUG. THIS WAS AN UNFORGIVABLE INSULT, BUT XIZONG CONCEALED HIS ANGER.

At the time a Mongol chief, Kabul Khan, built the largest alliance to date to bring an end to bloody squabbles among rival Mongol tribes. The Jin emperor, Xizong, was also eager to see peace in the lands along his northern border, so in 1125, to cement a friendship with Kabul Khan, Xizong invited him to his coronation. At the banquet that followed the ceremony, Kabul Khan got drunk, leaned over, and gave the emperor's beard a playful tug. This was an unforgivable insult, but Xizong concealed his anger. When the day arrived for

Kabul Khan to return home, the emperor sent him away with many gifts. But once the Mongol chief had left the city, the emperor sent a detachment of cavalry to arrest him and bring him back to the Jin capital for punishment.

Kabul Khan escaped his pursuers, and war erupted between the Mongols and the Jin. The fighting dragged on for twenty-two years, until the Jin emperor was ready for peace. It is said that in exchange for a treaty, Kabul Khan demanded an annual tribute of 250,000 head of cattle and 300,000 bales of silk. Xizong accepted the humiliating terms, but watched for an opportunity to strike back at the Mongols.

After the death of Kabul Khan (about the year 1150), the Mongol warriors and chiefs elected his first cousin, Ambakai, to succeed him. Meanwhile, the Jin had been forming an alliance with the Mongols' old enemies, the Tartars. The Tartars ambushed Ambakai while he was taking his daughter to meet her bridegroom; they also captured Kabul Khan's eldest son, Okin-barkak, who had been part of the wedding party. True to their arrangement, the Tartars handed over their prisoners to the Jin, who avenged themselves on Kabul Khan's family by nailing Ambakai and Okin-barkak to large wooden structures built to resemble donkeys.

Ambakai was succeeded by one of Okin-barkak's brothers, Khutula, a "Mongol Hercules." According to the *Collected Chronicles of the Mongols*, a history of the Mongols written by the Persian historian Rashid al-Din in 1308, Khutula's "voice was like thunder, his hands like the paws of a bear; and with these hands he could break the spine of the strongest man."

For all his superhuman qualities, Khutula's campaign to avenge his brother and his uncle failed. The Jin and the Tartars worked together again, crushing Khutula's army in a decisive battle near Lake Buir on the present-day China-Mongolia border.

"MUTUAL SLAUGHTER"

This defeat destroyed Mongol morale and Mongol unity. Blaming Khutula and his family for their losses on the battlefield, the tribes refused to unite under a single khan. Each tribe struck out on its own, or in rare instances allied itself with another tribe. Tribes and clans warred incessantly, killing each other's warriors, carrying off each other's wives, enslaving each other's children.

Years later, a shaman named Teb Tengri recalled for Genghis's sons what those years were like. "Everyone was feuding," he said. "Rather than sleep they robbed each other of their possessions . . . The whole nation was in rebellion. Rather than rest they fought each other. In such a world one did not live as one wished, but rather in constant conflict. There was no respite, only battle. There was no affection, only mutual slaughter."

In their rage Mongols slaughtered their enemies' flocks, stole their horses, and left survivors of the raid to starve on the steppe. To escape such a wretched existence, the best warriors offered themselves as *noker*, or devoted followers, to a chief who was strong enough to protect them. In times of war the *noker* formed an elite fighting force around the chief. In peacetime they guarded him while he slept, and performed humble tasks such as watching the sheep and horses, even serving the chief at meals. Through this arrangement, promising young warriors could enjoy the kind of loyal kinship that had existed among the Mongols when they had been a strong, unified people, when their lives and property had been secure and their enemies had lived in fear of them.

But even with these voluntary bonds of *andas* and *noker*, the Mongols were fragmented, and that made them weak. It would take an exceptional man to unite them.

CHAPTER 2

THE SAVAGE BOYHOOD OF TEMÜJIN

■ ■ ■

ABOUT THE YEAR 1155, YESÜGEI, A CHIEF OF THE MONGOL BORJIGIN CLAN, WAS HUNTING WATERFOWL WITH HIS HAWKS ALONG THE BANKS OF THE ONON RIVER WHEN HE HEARD THE CREAK OF A TWO-WHEELED OX CART. INSIDE BENEATH THE AWNING SAT A YOUNG BRIDE DRESSED IN A RED SILK GOWN, CROWNED WITH A TALL HEADDRESS, AND HER FACE COVERED WITH A HEAVY RED VEIL. RIDING ON HORSEBACK BESIDE THE CART WAS A YOUNG MAN WEARING THE TRADITIONAL WEDDING FINERY OF THE MERKIT TRIBE—A RED SILK ROBE WITH A BROAD GOLD BELT WRAPPED AROUND HIS WAIST. THE BRIDE'S NAME WAS HÖELÜN, AND HER NEW HUSBAND WAS CALLED CILEDÜ.

Hooding his hawks, Yesügei turned his horse and galloped back to his camp, where he urged his elder brother Nekün and his younger brother Dāritai to arm themselves and help him steal a wife.

A short time later, Ciledü saw the three brothers galloping swiftly across the steppe. The ox could never outrun Mongol horses, and if Ciledü took Höelün on his horse, they would still be overtaken. In a frenzy of indecision he whipped his horse forward and rounded a small hill, but there was no place for them to hide. Then he turned back to the cart, uncertain what to do.

According to *The Secret History of the Mongols*, which was written shortly after Genghis Khan's death, Höelün made the decision for

Yesügei, Genghis Khan's father, was hunting with his hawks when he first saw Höelün,
his future wife and the mother of the future leader. He kidnapped her and made her his wife,
common practice at that time. © SuperStock / SuperStock 463-6952-N-P30D

Ciledü. "Did you notice those three men?" Höelün asked. "They look as if they want to take your life . . . If only you are spared, you will always find a girl or a woman like me." Then she tore off her shirt and gave it to Ciledü as a keepsake. With the three brothers bearing down on them, the bridegroom could not waste any more time; whipping his horse, he sped off along the banks of the Onon.

Yesügei and his brothers gave chase briefly, just to make certain that Ciledü was gone. Then they turned back to the ox cart where Höelün sat bewailing the loss of her husband. *The Secret History of the Mongols* tells us, "She went on wailing loudly until her voice stirred the waters of the Onon River, until it resounded throughout wood and valley." With Nekün riding ahead, Yesügei holding the lead rope, and Dāritai walking beside the shaft, the brothers turned the cart and headed home, where Yesügei would be married to Höelün.

As emotional as she was over the loss of her bridegroom, Höelün's response to the kidnapping offers readers a snapshot of her character. Out of a sense of pragmatism, she urged Ciledü to ride away and save himself. Such willingness to face hard facts, and her resourcefulness in dealing with them, would enable her throughout her life to turn bad situations to her advantage.

The Secret History of the Mongols, our source for this story, is the only authentic Mongolian account of the life of Genghis Khan. It is a collection of historical incidents, oral history, family legends, and folklore that was written down a decade or so after Genghis's death in 1227. Although no historian would claim that *The Secret History of the Mongols* is 100 percent factual, it does give us at least a true glimpse of Mongolian life in the late twelfth and early thirteenth centuries. The dialogue recorded in the book may not be verbatim transcripts of what Genghis, his family, his allies, and his enemies actually said, but it does give us the sense of how Mongols spoke more than 800 years ago.

A ROYAL FAMILY

Yesügei belonged to the Borjigin clan, which Mongols regard as a royal family. Contemporary Mongols boast of their Borjigin ancestry the way people in the West boast of being descended from the Hapsburgs or the Romanovs. And the Borjigins have reason to be proud. Yesügei's grandfather was Khabul Khan, the first Mongol chief to attempt to unify his people. His uncle was Khutula, the "Mongol Hercules," whose defeat at the hands of the Jin and Tartars early in the

1160s shattered Mongol power, unity, and morale. And his son was Genghis Khan, one of the most brilliant commanders and conquerors the world has ever known.

There are no Mongol birth records—in the twelfth century they had no written language—so establishing a birth date for the leading characters in the story of Genghis Khan is a matter of estimates and best guesses. When Yesügei and his brothers abducted Höelün, she would have been about sixteen years old, and he about eighteen or twenty years old. Given that the average life span in the twelfth century was thirty-five to forty years, it was typical for boys and girls to marry while they were still in their teens.

YESÜGEI'S GRANDFATHER WAS KHABUL KHAN, THE FIRST MONGOL CHIEF TO ATTEMPT TO UNIFY HIS PEOPLE. HIS UNCLE WAS KHUTULA, THE "MONGOL HERCULES," WHOSE DEFEAT AT THE HANDS OF THE JIN AND TARTARS EARLY IN THE 1160s SHATTERED MONGOL POWER, UNITY, AND MORALE. AND HIS SON WAS GENGHIS KHAN, ONE OF THE MOST BRILLIANT COMMANDERS AND CONQUERORS THE WORLD HAS EVER KNOWN.

The exact circumstances of Yesügei's life are unknown to us, but we can draw a few conclusions from certain elements of his story as recorded in *The Secret History of the Mongols*. It appears that he was not a rich man, because he brought only one horse along to offer as a gift to his son Temüjin's future in-laws. Yet he must have been a well-respected warlord because when his friend Toghril asked for help in reclaiming the leadership of his tribe, the Keraits, Yesügei was able to raise an army of Mongols that gave Toghril the victory.

There are mythical elements in *The Secret History*, but the abduction of Höelün is not one of them. Bride-napping was commonplace among virtually all the nomadic tribes of Central Asia. These were exogamous societies, which means the men looked for wives outside their

own people. Because most nomads lived in small camps of only a few dozen people, exogamy was a practical way to avoid incest and ensure a steady influx of fresh blood into the tribe. Not all marriages began with an abduction—many Mongol marriages were arranged by the fathers of the prospective bride and groom—but carrying off the bride of a man from another tribe was considered acceptable and even admirable in a warrior society.

A NEWBORN HERO

Höelün belonged to the Olkhunut tribe, a people that occupied some of the richest pasturing land on the steppe. Her family would have had herds of horses, sheep, goats, and cows, and she would have enjoyed a protein-rich diet of meat and milk. The home to which Yesügei took her was not nearly as lush. The Borjigins occupied an area on the northern fringe of the steppe, very close to the forest-covered mountains of southern Siberia. Their herds were small, so warriors also had to be skillful hunters. On good days they returned to their families with a string of fresh fish or a brace of ducks, or even a deer from the forest. On days when their luck was poor they brought home a few marmots or even rats.

Six months after her abduction and marriage to Yesügei, Höelün announced that she was pregnant. The day she went into labor, Yesügei was away, raiding the camp of a Tartar chief. The women of the family would have taken Höelün inside the *ger*, hung a bow and arrows over the door to ward off evil spirits, and sent for a female shaman to serve as midwife and read any omen that might accompany the birth. The story goes that the baby boy entered the world clutching in his right hand a blood clot as large as an adult's knuckle. The midwife-shaman declared this was a sign that he would be a man of great strength, a newborn hero for the Mongols.

The same day Höelün gave birth, Yesügei returned home from his raid with several Tartar prisoners, including a chieftain named Temüjin. Following Mongol custom, he named his son after his

A sixteenth-century Indian illustration depicts Yesügei and Höelün inside a handsome palace. In fact, Genghis Khan's parents never dwelt in anything but a felt tent. Ögödei, Genghis's son, was the first Mongol to reside in a palace, much to the scorn of Mongol traditionalists.

akg-images / Werner Forman

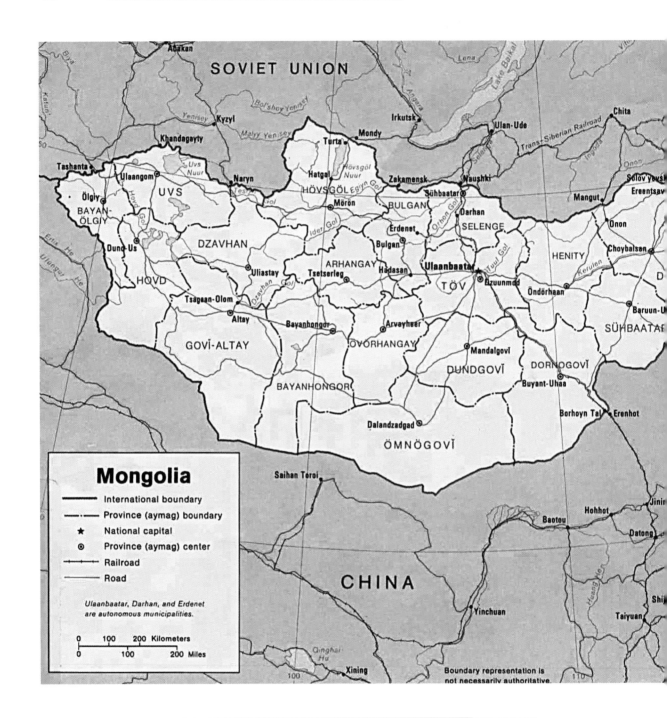

Temüjin was born near the Onon River, seen here in the northeast corner of modern-day Mongolia. No one knows exactly where he was born, as the name of his believed birthplace, Deliün Boldaq, does not exist anymore. Courtesy of the University of Texas Libraries, The University of Texas at Austin

highest-ranking captive. The reason for this custom has been lost to history, although it may have been a form of tribute to his foe, and a way of declaring that Yesügei had appropriated the brave spirit of a worthy rival for his son.

The date of Genghis Khan's birth is in dispute, ranging from 1155 to 1167. The consensus in Mongolia is that he was born in 1162, and in 2002 the country celebrated Genghis's 840th birthday. The place of his birth is also unknown; *The Secret History* says he was born in his father's camp beside the Onon River at a place called Deliün Boldaq. No such place-name exists today, but in 1962, to mark the 800th anniversary of Genghis's birth, the Central Committee of the Communist Party in Mongolia erected a monument to the khan at Dadal Somon, which, because it is also along the Onon, is as good a place as any to commemorate Genghis's birth.

THE FAMILY

Höelün was not Yesügei's only wife, nor Temüjin his only son. The first woman he married, Sučigel, had already born him two sons, Bekter and Belgütei. There is much confusion about the status of Höelün. *The Secret History* suggests that Höelün was Yesügei's senior wife and Temüjin his true heir. Yet the stories of Temüjin's childhood after the death of his father portray Bekter acting as the head of the family. At this distance, it is impossible to sort out the precise status of each member of Yesügei's family.

After Temüjin, Höelün had four more children—three sons, Khasar, Qačiun, and Temüge, and a daughter, Temülün. The boys would have learned to ride and shoot a bow. Temüjin's best friend was Jamuka, and they were so close that they formed an *anda* while they were still children.

The Secret History records two incidents from Temüjin's early childhood. Once, when the clan was packing to move to a new pasture, they left the toddler Temüjin behind. The lost child was discovered on the steppe by another clan leader, Tarqutai, known as the Fat Khan, who took him into his own *ger* and cared for little Temüjin as if he were his own son. How long the child remained in Tarqutai's camp is unknown, but years later, when Temüjin had become the famous Genghis Khan, Tarqutai boasted that he was the first teacher of the great conqueror. At some point, Temüjin reunited with his family, but again we do not know the circumstances.

A BETROTHAL

The second episode from Temüjin's childhood is better known and had long-term consequences. When he was eight years old his father took him on a journey to find his future bride among Höelün's tribe. He would not marry at age eight, but he would be betrothed; then, in his teens he would return to claim his wife (just as unlucky Ciledü had done). Yesügei and Temüjin never reached Höelün's family; en route they met Dei Sečen, a hospitable chief of the Onggirat tribe who lived near Lake Kulun. He invited the travelers to rest and dine in his *ger*, and there Temüjin met Dei Sečen's daughter, Börte, described in *The Secret History* as a nine-year-old girl "who had light in her face, who had fire in her eyes." Temüjin developed a terrible crush on Börte; this was the girl he wanted to marry.

When Yesügei broached the subject of betrothing their children, Dei Sečen, as good manners required, offered every imaginable excuse why such a match was unwise, but then Börte's brother, Alchinoyon, spoke up in favor of the marriage; he was about Temüjin's age and the two boys had struck up a friendship very quickly. So, now adopting the role of the indulgent father, Dei Sečen dropped all his objections and consented to the betrothal.

Yesügei presented the chief with a horse he had brought along as a gift for his future daughter-in-law's family, and he agreed to let Temüjin stay with Dei Sečen for an unspecified period of time. This custom was widespread among the Mongol and the Turkic tribes of Central Asia—it gave the girl's family an opportunity to study the character of the future bridegroom while giving the bridegroom a chance to demonstrate his honorable intentions by watching the herds or hunting or performing any other service his future father-in-law might require.

There was another reason for leaving the young prospective bridegroom with his future parents-in-law: Mongol fathers demanded a high bride-price for their daughters, a price that few Mongol families could meet. The Italian Franciscan who visited the Mongols in the thirteenth century, Father John of Plano Carpini, reported that some fathers insisted upon such an exorbitant bride-price so "that sometimes girls are quite grown up before they marry." The extra horse that Yesügei had brought along was applied to Börte's bride-price, but the balance would be worked off by Temüjin during the year or more he lived with Dei Sečen's family.

For both Yesügei and Temüjin this was a very good match. The Onggirat were one of the most powerful Mongol tribes. Years later,

Temüjin's alliance-by-marriage with the Onggirat would give him a power base that helped him unite the Mongols into a single nation with himself as Great Khan.

A MURDER

Yesügei set out for home alone. Somewhere on the steppe he came across a party of Tartars who had made camp for the night and were cooking their evening meal. Yesügei had raided Tartar camps and held Tartar warriors for ransom. But the people of the steppe followed a strict code of hospitality—in such a dangerous environment, no one, not even an enemy, could be denied food, drink, and a place by the fire. Although this band of Tartars recognized Yesügei—some of them had been his prisoners—they invited him to join them for the night. However, one of the Tartars poisoned a bowl of fermented mare's milk before handing it to Yesügei to drink.

AT THE DEATH OF THEIR CHIEF, YESÜGEI'S MEN LAMENTED, "THE DEEP WATER HAS DRIED UP, THE SHINING STONE IS SHATTERED." BUT THEIR GRIEF DID NOT EXTEND TO SYMPATHY FOR THE WIDOWS HÖELÜN AND SUČIGIL AND THE SEVEN CHILDREN.

Yesügei parted from the Tartars the next morning, and somewhere out on the steppe he began to feel sick. Three days later, when he finally reached home, he could barely cling to his horse. His family helped him down and carried him into their *ger*, but there was nothing that could be done for him. Yesügei was dying. He sent Monglik, one of his most reliable men, to bring Temüjin home from Dei Sečen's camp. The retainer set off immediately, but by the time he and Temüjin returned, Yesügei was dead.

At the death of their chief, Yesügei's men lamented, "The deep water has dried up, the shining stone is shattered." But their grief did not extend to sympathy for the widows Höelün and Sučigil and the seven children. The men Yesügei had trusted—including his own brothers—began to pack up their belongings, dismantle their *gers*, and round up their herds. They were leaving, and they would not permit Yesügei's wives and children to come with them.

We can imagine the older boys standing shocked and disbelieving, the younger children crying, as the people they had known all their lives rode off, leaving them to die on the steppe. Höelün made one final effort to rally her late husband's men to her side; jumping on a horse, she grabbed the tribal standard and rode after them. It was a dramatic gesture that persuaded a handful to come back, but these did not remain long. Without a strong lord to protect them, they were as vulnerable as Yesügei's widows and orphans.

Charakha, an old man who had followed Yesügei for many years, denounced the warriors as they rode away. One of them turned back and drove his spear into Charakha's chest.

A SECOND MURDER

Höelün was in a desperate position. There was not a single man to protect them, and not one sheep or goat left to provide milk. But she did not give up. Every morning she went methodically across the steppe collecting edible berries, roots, and wild vegetables. Temüjin and his brothers fished in the Onon River, set traps for small animals such as rabbits and marmots, and hunted birds with their bows and arrows.

By Mongol custom, fish and game were fairly divided. With the entire family struggling to survive, this principle was especially important, but Sučigil's sons, Bekter and Belgütei, refused to share what they caught, keeping it for themselves and their mother. Once, when Temüjin and Khasar were hunting, they brought down a lark, but Bek-

وسبب اینک آن موضع را بای براق سلجیره می خواند قدیم جهت باذتا هان نا
بردند نام اوبای براق وندان موضع که دسته اندوطی رهوه کده وسلم رهبغز صرا

In 1202, Genghis Khan (center), waged war against the Tartars, a Turkic tribe that eventually became part of his empire. The Tartars were responsible for poisoning Genghis's father, Yesügei, to death.

Ms Pers. 113 f.29 Genghis Khan (c. 1162–1227) Fighting the Tartars, from a book by Rashid-al-Din (1247-1318) (gouache), Persian School, (14th century) / Bibliotheque Nationale, Paris, France / The Bridgeman Art Library International

ter and Belgütei, who were older and stronger, took it from them. A more serious incident occurred when Temüjin and Khasar caught a large dace, a freshwater fish that would have been a welcome addition to the family's diet that night; Bekter and Belgütei took that from them, too. If this continued, soon Höelün and her children would be too weak to hold on to whatever food they had collected; Sučigil and her children would grow strong as Höelün and her children slowly starved to death.

YEARS LATER, AFTER HE HAD TAKEN THE NAME GENGHIS KHAN, TEMÜJIN SAID, "IT IS TO BELGÜTEI'S STRENGTH AND KHASAR'S PROWESS AS AN ARCHER THAT I OWE THE CONQUEST OF THE WORLD EMPIRE.

But Temüjin and Khasar had another reason to worry: according to Mongol custom, a younger brother was entitled to marry his brother's widow, but Yesügei's younger brother had not exercised that right. The next male in the family who had rights over the widow was Höelün's eldest stepson. At that time Bekter was perhaps thirteen years old, but as the eldest stepson he had a clear right to marry Höelün. If he chose not to marry her, he still had the right to sexual relations with her.

The Secret History does not say whether Bekter planned to marry or merely sleep with his stepmother, but Temüjin and Khasar were not willing to wait to find out. They swore they would never permit Bekter to become head of their family.

A day or two after the dace incident, Bekter left the camp and walked out on the steppe. Temüjin and Khasar, armed with bows and arrows, followed him. They found their half-brother sitting on a small mound. Keeping low to the ground, Khasar approached him from the front, while Temüjin crept up from behind. Bekter saw them coming, but did nothing. Perhaps this was an expression of contempt for his half-brothers, or a demonstration of his fearlessness; whatever his reason, he stayed where he was. "Why do you regard me as a lash in the eye," he called to Temüjin and Khasar, "a thorn in the mouth?" Bekter's passivity did not impress the boys; they fired their arrows, striking their eldest half-brother in the chest and the back. They left him in the tall grass, not even bothering to see whether he was dead. Bekter was about thirteen, Temüjin about eleven, and Khasar about nine or ten years old.

When Höelün learned of the murder she berated her sons, comparing them to wild animals. "You who have destroyed life . . . [are] like a panther assailing a cliff," she said, "like a lion uncontrollable in its rage." Höelün was not only rebuking her sons for acting like out-of-control animals, she was also reminding them that in their vulnerable position, they couldn't afford more enemies. Perhaps his mother's rebukes stung, but Temüjin had the satisfaction of knowing that he had made himself the head of the family.

Belgütei made no attempt to avenge his older brother, which has led some historians to conclude that he must have recognized that Bekter had violated the Mongol code and Temüjin was within his rights to pass judgment on his half-brother. After all of Yesügei's sons had grown to manhood, Belgütei became one of Temüjin's best warriors. Years later, after he had taken the name Genghis Khan, Temüjin said, "It is to Belgütei's strength and Khasar's prowess as an archer that I owe the conquest of the World Empire."

CHAPTER 3

A FRIENDLESS BOY'S FIRST ALLIES

■ ■ ■

THE RIDERS WERE STILL FAR OFF WHEN HÖELÜN SPOTTED THEM GALLOPING ACROSS THE STEPPE, STRAIGHT FOR HER FAMILY'S TINY CAMP. AS SHE RAN BACK TO THE TENTS SHE CALLED HER CHILDREN, STEPCHILDREN, AND SUČIGIL, ORDERING THEM TO FLEE INTO A GROVE OF TREES IN A NEARBY RAVINE. WHILE KHASAR READIED HIS BOW AND BELGÜTEI PILED UP HEAVY BRANCHES TO FORM A PALISADE, HÖELÜN AND TEMÜJIN LOOKED FOR A PLACE WHERE THE THREE YOUNGEST CHILDREN COULD HIDE. DEEP IN THE RAVINE THEY FOUND A ROCKY CREVICE, DEEP ENOUGH TO CONCEAL QAČIUN, TEMÜGE, AND TEMÜLÜN. MOTHER AND SON LEFT THE LITTLE ONES THERE, THEN HURRIED BACK TO WHERE KHASAR AND BELGÜTEI WERE TRYING TO HOLD OFF THE RAIDERS.

The Tayičiuts belonged to a tribe that had been friendly to Yesügei while he was alive. A group of them, led by Tarqutai the Fat Khan, had been encamped with Yesügei when he died. When Yesügei's retainers abandoned Höelün and the children, Tarqutai and the Tayičiuts did the same. Why Tarqutai, who prided himself on saving Temüjin's life when he was a toddler, turned against the family is another one of the unsolved mysteries in this story—the sources do not tell us what motivated the Fat Khan.

Back at the wall of tree branches, Höelün and Temüjin found Khasar exchanging arrow fire with the Tayičiuts. It was a hopeless

A sympathetic Tayičiut named Sorqan Šira broke Temüjin out of the cangue, then hid him inside a pile of cotton wool until he could escape the Tayičiut camp. Getty Images

situation—three young boys and their mother could not drive off sea-soned warriors. Then one of Tarqutai's men shouted to the besieged family, "Send out your elder brother Temüjin. We have no need for the rest of you!"

Temüjin was only eleven or twelve. The idea of being taken away as a prisoner of these men frightened him. He leapt on his horse and rode hard toward a small wooded knob, where he hid in the trees. Tar-qutai and his men set off after the boy, leaving Höelün and the rest of the children unharmed. The Tayičiuts surrounded the knob and waited; they knew Temüjin could not escape, and hunger would even-tually drive him out in the open. And they were right. After several days, Temüjin, half-starved, stumbled out of the woods and surren-dered to Tarqutai.

TEMÜJIN THE CRIMINAL

The Secret History, which is the principal source for the story of Temüjin's capture, offers no explanation for Tarqutai's decision to cap-ture Temüjin, but it does provide a few hints. It records that one day Tarqutai's thoughts turned to Höelün, Sučigil, and the children. He said to his men, "The little rascals have shed their down, the snotty ones have grown up."

This suggests that Tarqutai was worried that Höelün's sons would seek revenge on the Tayičiuts for abandoning them to die. Yet once the Tayičiuts had Höelün and the children pinned down in the ravine, they did not make any attempt to break through Belgütei's palisade and massacre the family; instead, they asked only for Temüjin. Some histo-rians believe that a type of kinship or other form of allegiance existed between Tarqutai and Bekter, who had been killed by his half-brothers Temüjin and Khasar. That is an interesting possibility, but if family ties or an oath bound Tarqutai to avenge Bekter, why didn't he demand the surrender of Khasar as well as Temüjin?

Our only clue is what Tarqutai did after Temüjin surrendered: he locked a *cangue* around the boy's neck and wrists. The *cangue*, an instru-ment used to punish criminals, remained in use throughout China and Mongolia until the Communist revolution in 1949. By putting Temüjin in a *cangue*, Tarqutai made known his intentions: he was not holding Temüjin hostage until a ransom was paid, or keeping him as a slave, or training him in warfare so one day Temüjin would become one of the chief's retainers. Tarqutai had come to Höelün's camp to seize her eldest son and punish him, and the only serious crime Temüjin committed was the murder of Bekter.

TARQUTAI'S PRISONER

The *cangue* is a heavy portable wooden stock or pillory that is clamped around the neck and wrists. In this position the prisoner is immobilized and entirely dependent on his captors: he cannot eat unless they put food into his mouth; he cannot drink unless they hold a cup of water to his lips. Most humiliating of all, when he feels the need to relieve himself he must ask his jailers to pull down and then pull up his trousers.

The *cangue* makes it impossible for the wearer to lie down, so he must sleep sitting up. The prisoner gets no relief from the weight of the *cangue*, or the cramps that torture his arms, which are locked in the same position for days on end. Adding to the pain is the rough wood that chafes the neck and the wrists, rubbing them raw, leaving wounds open to infection.

Tending to a prisoner in a *cangue* was tedious, so Tarqutai rotated Temüjin among the many families in his encampment. Only one treated the boy with any kindness—a warrior named Sorqan Šira, his wife, two sons, and daughter took pity on Temüjin; after dark the boys unlocked the *cangue* so Temüjin could lie down and get a decent night's sleep. Unfortunately for Temüjin, he could not live permanently in Sorqan Šira's tent.

THE ESCAPE

When a festival in honor of the full moon came around, Temüjin was living with a family who treated him like an animal. They gave one of their adolescent sons, a weak, scrawny boy, the privilege of leading the prisoner around by a rope. On the day of the festival, Temüjin's "guard" led him into the crowd of hard-drinking revelers, who mocked the prisoner and praised his keeper.

Sometime after midnight, when all the Tayičiuts were passed out in the tents, Temüjin made his move. Summoning all his strength, he swung the *cangue* at the head of the dozing boy who was supposed to be watching him, then dashed out of the tent toward the woods that grew along the Onon River. Behind him he heard the boy crying, "I let the prisoner escape!" This was followed by the frantic sounds of men on foot and on horseback racing for the woods. Wading into the Onon, Temüjin tried to hide in the river, but he hadn't the strength to sub-

merge the heavy wooden *cangue* and keep it under water. In the light of the full moon he was certain someone from the camp would spot his head bobbing above the surface, and someone did—Sorqan Šira. He whispered to Temüjin, "Lie just so; I shall not tell them."

When some Tayičiuts came near the place where Temüjin was trying to hide, Sorqan Šira reported that he'd seen no sign of the boy. He assured them they would find Temüjin after daybreak—no one wearing a *cangue* could get very far.

The Tayičiuts, still drunk and on their way to a hangover, were probably happy to give up the search for the night. Once they were gone, Temüjin did not strike out across the steppe for his mother's camp. Alone, on foot, and locked in the *cangue* it was not likely that he would survive the trek. Instead, watching from the brush along the riverbank, he waited until the searchers were gone, then crept back into Tarqutai's camp and made his way to Sorqan Šira's tent. At the sight of Temüjin, dripping with river water, the family cried out in surprise, but then they got busy. Sorqan Šira and his sons broke open the *cangue* and burned it. The wife helped Temüjin out of his wet clothes, gave him fresh clothes to wear, bandaged the wounds on his neck and wrists, and brought him food. It was still a few hours before dawn, so Temüjin stretched out on the floor to sleep.

In the morning, as the Tayičiuts resumed their search for the runaway, Sorqan Šira hid Temüjin in one of his carts, beneath a heaping pile of wool. Although a couple of the searchers drove their spears into the wool, they missed the boy. When they were gone, Sorqan Šira brought Temüjin back into the tent. That night Sorqan Šira said, "You nearly had me blown to the winds like hearth-ashes. Now go, look for your mother and younger brothers."

He gave Temüjin a black mare with a white mouth; Sorqan Šira's wife packed him cooked lamb and mare's milk. Temüjin rode down to the riverbank and followed the river to his family's camp, but they were not there. It took many days of tracking before he found his mother and brothers and sister near the foothills of Belukha Mountain, close to the

An eighteenth-century French engraving depicts a Chinese criminal imprisoned in a *cangue*, similar to the one imposed upon a young Temüjin by his father's enemy, Tarqutai, khan of the Tayičiut tribe. A prisoner in the 'Cangue' in China, c.1800 (colour engraving), French School, (19th century) / Bibliotheque des Arts Decoratifs, Paris, France / Archives Charmet / The Bridgeman Art Library International

border of present-day Russia and Kazakhstan. Fearful that the Tayičiuts were still hunting for him, Temüjin and Höelün moved the family deeper into the hills. It was hard country, with little game aside from marmots and rodents, but the family felt safe there.

EASY TARGETS

In addition to the black mare Sorqan Šira gave Temüjin, the family owned eight geldings. The horses were essential to their survival: they enabled Höelün and her sons to travel farther in search of food than they would have been able to do on foot. The mare Temüjin brought back from Sorqan Šira was especially welcome because it provided milk, an essential source of protein for the family now that its flocks and herds were gone. The horses made moving to a new camping site faster and less onerous than walking, especially for the small children. Soon Temüjin and his brothers would be old enough to fight in battle, and Mongols always fought on horseback—there was no such thing as Mongol infantry. Furthermore, if hostile raiders ever attacked the camp, the horses were the family's only hope of escape. As a Mongol warlord once put it, "If the horse dies, I die; if it lives, I survive."

Sometime after Temüjin's escape from Tarqutai—it is impossible to establish a precise timeline for the events in Temüjin's life because *The Secret History* rarely mentions the hero's age—horse thieves struck in broad daylight, stealing the family's eight geldings tethered in front of their *ger*. As if Höelün and Temüjin needed any further reminders, the theft underscored their vulnerability: alone on the steppe, with no adult males to protect them, they were easy targets for every passing thief and marauder.

The only horse not run off by the thieves was Temüjin's black mare, because Belgütei had borrowed it to go hunting. When he returned in the evening and learned of the theft, Belgütei volunteered to pursue the thieves. Khasar said that he wanted to go. But Temüjin pulled rank, saying that as the eldest son, recovering their horses was his responsibility.

For three days he tracked the thieves across the steppe, and on the fourth he met a boy about his age who was seated amid a herd of horses, milking the mares. The boy's name was Bo'orču, and he told Temüjin that he had seen men driving eight geldings that morning. "I will show you their trail," Bo'orču said.

After three days of riding, Temüjin's mare needed rest. Bo'orču urged Temüjin to let his mount graze with the other horses and borrow one of the horses from the herd. Then, putting down his leather milking pail, he said, "This kind of trouble might happen to anyone. I'll go with you to get your horses back."

It took another three days for the boys to catch up with the thieves, and when they did it was sundown. Temüjin's eight geldings were grazing beside the thieves' tents, unguarded. In classic Mongol fashion, the boys charged into the camp, rounded up the horses, and drove them off at a run. Hearing the commotion, the thieves rushed out of their tents, fetched their own horses, and went after Temüjin and Bo'orču. By now night was coming on fast, and the horse thieves lost the boys in the darkness.

Bo'orču led Temüjin back to his encampment, where they found his father, Naqu Bayan, in mourning. Bo'orču was an only son, and he had gone off on the horse recovery adventure without telling anyone where he was going. It had been nearly a week since anyone in the camp had seen him. Naqu was convinced his boy was either dead or kidnapped by some rival tribe. When his son entered the family *ger*, Naqu alternately wept for joy and berated Bo'orču for causing his family so much distress. Bo'orču's answer was the type any teenage boy would make, "What is the matter? A good friend came to me in trouble, I became his companion, and went with him. Now I have come back."

After Bo'orču had fetched Temüjin's mare from the herd and packed food for his journey home, Naqu addressed both boys, "You two young men must keep seeing each other, never abandon each other!" Temüjin's circle of friends was still very small, but it was expanding steadily; as he already knew, trying to survive alone on the steppe was virtually impossible.

THE BRIDE

At age fifteen Mongol boys were regarded as men. Soon after his fifteenth birthday Temüjin made a momentous decision: he would find Dei Sečen's encampment and claim his bride, Börte. Seven eventful years had passed since they were together, but Temüjin had had no opportunity to visit his future bride, or even send her messages. After such a long silence, it was not inconceivable that Börte had married another man. Hoping for the best, Temüjin, accompanied by Belgütei, set out to locate the encampment. They found Dei Sečen camped between Mount

Čekčer and Mount Čiqurqu; perhaps the brothers knew this was one of the chief's favorite places, or perhaps they had learned where he was from other Mongols they encountered along the way—*The Secret History* does not say.

"Now at last I see you!" Dei Sečen exclaimed when he saw Temüjin ride into the camp. Börte was still living in her parents' *ger*; she had not married. *The Secret History* does not describe Temüjin and Börte's wedding, no doubt because the audience would have been familiar with the ritual. One of the customs observed in a traditional Mongolian wedding today may also have been part of Temüjin and Börte's wedding celebrations. The bride's attendants ask the groom to prove his strength by snapping the neck bone of a sheep. It's less a test of strength than a well-worn practical joke, because before handing the bone to the groom, the ladies slip a stout stick or a metal rod inside the bone.

A fanciful fifteenth-century French manuscript painting portrays the Ong Khan in the robes of a cardinal of the Catholic Church rather than as a Mongol chief. The nationality of the artist—rather than firsthand knowledge—dictated Mongol appearance in art.

After several days of feasting, the bride and groom set out for Temüjin's home. Börte brought along a gift for her mother-in-law—a magnificent black sable coat. But Temüjin wanted the gift to be given to someone else. Ong Khan had been his father Yesügei's *anda*, or blood brother. "As he and my father have declared themselves sworn friends," Temüjin explained to Börte, "Ong Khan is indeed like a father to me."

This act of generosity was a shrewd decision on Temüjin's part. He was a young man now, and soon would have a family. He had friends and allies such as Bo'orču, his father Naqu Bayan, and Sorqan Šira, but he needed the help of a powerful chief if he was to restore his family's fortunes and become a man of influence himself. Accompanied by all three of his brothers, Temüjin traveled to Ong Khan's camp. The sons of murdered Yesügei stood before Ong as Temüjin presented him with the sable coat. It was a grand gesture likely to prick the conscience of the man who had not acted as a father to his blood brother's fatherless children. And it worked.

Holding the splendid coat, Ong Khan vowed, "In return for the black sable coat, I shall bring together for you your divided people; in return for the sable coat, I shall unite for you your scattered people."

Mission accomplished. Temüjin had restored the bonds of kinship that had once existed between his family and Ong Khan. He had placed the man under obligation, and he had won from the khan an important promise—the rebuilding of his household, which would be the foundation upon which Temüjin could become a khan like his father.

CHAPTER 4

TEMÜJIN'S FIRST BATTLE

WITH A START THE OLD SERVANT WOMAN AWOKE— SHE COULD HEAR HORSEMEN COMING. AS *THE SECRET HISTORY OF THE MONGOLS* TELLS THE STORY, SHE HURRIED TO THE PLACE WHERE HÖELÜN LAY SLEEPING. "MOTHER!" SHE CRIED. "MOTHER! RISE UP QUICKLY! THE EARTH IS SHAKING AND ONE CAN HEAR THE SOUND OF TRAMPLING HOOVES. WILL THEY BE THE DREADFUL TAYIČIUT APPROACHING?"

"Quickly, wake the sons," Höelün commanded.

Within minutes Höelün and her daughter, Temüjin, and all his brothers were mounted and riding off. As the family matriarch, Höelün would have had her own horse, but there were not enough horses for everyone. Those left behind included the old servant woman, Khoakhchin; Belgütai's mother, Sučigil; and Temüjin's wife, Börte.

In the harsh life of the nomads, chivalry was a luxury no man could afford. Temüjin could see as many as 300 riders bearing down on his camp. This was not a raid; this was an attack. They would slaughter him and his brothers, but they would spare the women, taking them back to their tribe to serve as slaves and concubines. If Temüjin escaped now, there was a chance that he would be able to rescue Börte later.

But Khoakhchin was not about to sit down on the ground and wait to be taken captive. She harnessed a speckled bull to an enclosed cart, helped Börte climb inside, and set off. They had gotten only a short distance from the camp when a band of warriors rode up; they were Merkits, the tribe of Höelün's original husband, Ciledü. "Whose people are you?" one of the warriors demanded.

Mongol archers had a distinct advantage in battle because they could turn their saddles and fire arrows at their enemies—with deadly accuracy.

"I belong to Temüjin," Khoakhchin replied. "I came to shear sheep in the big tent and now I am returning to my tent."

"Is Temüjin in his tent?" another warrior asked. "How far is his tent from here?"

"The tent—it is nearby," Khoakhchin said. "But whether Temüjin is there or not I did not notice. I rose and left from the back."

These answers satisfied the Merkits, and they rode off to find Temüjin. Eager to get Börte to some hiding place, Khoakhchin whipped the bull to make him go faster, but as the bull began to trot at a quicker pace the cart bounced over a rock and broke its axle. Khoakhchin was trying to decide what to do next when the Merkits rode up again, this time with Sučigil as their prisoner.

"What are you carrying in this cart?" one of the warriors asked.

"I am carrying wool," Khoakhchin said.

The Merkits were skeptical. Some of the riders dismounted, threw open the door of the cart, and found Börte. With a cry of triumph they dragged her out, forced her to climb on one of their horses, did the same to old Khoakhchin, and with their captives rode for home.

THE FAVORITE OF THE GODS

Yesügei was dead, murdered by his enemies. Ciledü, Höelün's first husband, was also dead. But for the Merkits, Yesügei's abduction of Ciledü's bride about twenty-two years earlier still rankled; it was a stain on the tribe's honor, and they wanted revenge. As word spread among the nomads that Temüjin's fortunes were beginning to improve, the Merkits decided to even the score by punishing Yesügei's heir.

Temüjin was fortunate that his mother's servant had sharp hearing and was a light sleeper: thanks to Khoakhchin he had managed to escape into the forests of Burgan Qaldun, the Mongols' sacred mountain, where he hid with his brothers, sister, and mother. Although a detachment of Merkits had returned to their people with the captive women, the greater part of the 300-man attack force was scouring the mountain for any trace of Temüjin. After several days of fruitless searching, the three Merkit chiefs who had led the attack gave up. They consoled themselves, saying, "We have now seized their women to take our revenge for Höelün! We have had our revenge!"

Temüjin and his family remained in their hiding place for a few days longer, just to make certain that the Merkits had not left behind a band of warriors ready to attack Temüjin once he stepped into the open.

When he did come out, the Merkits were gone. Temüjin attributed his escape to the protection of the sacred mountain. "Every morning I will sacrifice to Burgan Qaldun; every day I will pray to it. The offspring of my offspring shall be mindful of this and do likewise!"

As an animist, Temüjin believed the mountain was a divine spirit that could exercise supernatural power—as it had done in saving his life from the Merkits. Forever after, he and all his descendants would venerate Burgan Qaldun as their special guardian spirit, not unlike a Christian's patron saint.

To express his gratitude, Temüjin made the traditional Mongol offering to a divine spirit by throwing mare's milk into the air and sprinkling it on the ground. Then he unwound his belt and draped it over his neck—a traditional gesture of humility before the gods, because a Mongol's belt was a symbol of his manly vigor. Then removing his hat and striking his chest with his fists—more tokens of respect and humility—he knelt and struck the ground with his forehead nine times in what is known as the *kowtow*.

THIS WAS THE PIVOTAL EVENT IN MARKING TEMÜJIN AS DIVINELY FAVORED. THE MONGOLS BELIEVED A TRULY GREAT LEADER WAS SELECTED BY THE GODS, AND THE GODS ALWAYS GAVE A CLEAR SIGN WHEN THEY HAD CHOSEN ONE MAN ABOVE ALL OTHERS.

This was the pivotal event in marking Temüjin as divinely favored. The Mongols believed a truly great leader was selected by the gods, and the gods always gave a clear sign when they had chosen one man above all others. That Burgan Qaldun had shielded Temüjin when 300 Merkits were searching for him was a clear case of divine intervention. Temüjin was the favorite of the gods and was destined for great things.

Of course, such a belief had a certain self-fulfilling quality: Mongol warriors would want to be associated with the chosen man, which gave him more power and influence, which led to opportunities for him to accomplish great things.

رون وإذ لهم أيدهم إلى اذناب حشه وأخرجهم ونهبوا رحالهم وافاهم
أيدهم على الشوك فرأى الأمير سيف الدولة حرص هؤلاء وطمعهم الكاد
عن آخرهم وعبى عساكره وسوى صفوفه ووقف هو وإخوانه نصر واسمعيل
القية عيانا ولا مر بعضهم بعضا على افعالهم الذميمة وأقدمهم على تلك الاا
المزينة وشعار الملاعبة لكنهم كانوا كثيرين أعدوا العدد وفوا بازاء ومد الفرقان

وامران بقوض الخيام ورحلة الحال فلما رحل نقله ورحله متاوا باشر حسّ
نظنهم انهم قوّون وان حضهم ضعيف فواطيوا بارجلهم اذناب الحيات وق
فى نهب ابتاعه وسلبهم فامر جماعة من عسكره بانهم يحاطون منهم ففعلوا
وعمه بعراجوق في القلب فشاهد خصومهم من اقدام اعلاصه واقبال رايا اه
اللئيمة وندموا ولم تنفعهم الندامة فلاجرم خرجوا من البلد في الثياب الملوّنة والـ

A CHANCE FOR REVENGE

The abduction of Börte presented an opportunity for Temüjin to show he could raise and lead a band of warriors. With only his brothers and a handful of friends to assist him, Temüjin had no chance of rescuing Börte. He would need an army. Accompanied by Khasar and Belgütei, Temüjin rode to the camp of his foster father, Toghril, the Ong Khan. The young men found the khan living in a place *The Secret History* describes as "the Black Forest," beside the Tula River. Entering Toghril's tent, Temüjin came quickly to the point. "The Three Merkit came, taking us by surprise; they seized my wife and carried her off. We have come now to ask you, O Khan my father, to rescue my wife and return her to me." (The Three Merkit Temüjin mentions are the chiefs of the three most important bands of the Merkit tribe.)

Toghril replied, "In return for the black sable coat, even to the complete destruction of the Merkit I shall rescue for you your Lady Börte."

To ensure victory over the Merkits, Toghril told Temüjin to visit his boyhood friend, Jamuka, and ask him to bring his army. While they were still children Jamuka and Temüjin had gone through the *anda* ritual that made them, from the Mongol point of view, as close as biological brothers. Because Jamuka was a few years older than Temüjin, he was better established than his friend, and like Temüjin he had also had had a difficult youth: the Merkits had kept Jamuka as a slave. He would certainly seize upon this opportunity to strike back at the tribe that had humiliated him.

THE RENDEZVOUS

The Secret History reports that the Ong Khan and Jamuka each brought 20,000 mounted warriors to fight the Merkits. This is undoubtedly an exaggeration, but inflating the numerical strength of an army is a literary tradition older than the Bible. It is considered more likely that Toghril and Jamuka each brought about 6,000 men. When they attacked, Temüjin with his handful of followers would take up position in the center, the Ong Khan would be on his right, and Jamuka on his left. The three men agreed to collect their forces and rendezvous in the

Previous page: A thirteenth-century Arabic manuscript shows two rival Mongol tribes charging each other with lances. Although the Persians used lances in battles, the Mongols rarely did. Battle between Mongol tribes, 13th century (manuscript), / Private Collection / The Bridgeman Art Library International

Khenti, a region of soaring mountains and deep valleys that lies in the heart of the Mongol homeland.

Jamuka arrived at the rendezvous site on time, but Toghril and Temüjin were late—three days late. By the time they appeared, Jamuka was fuming. As the historian John Man has observed, all of Jamuka's 6,000 men would have brought along two or three spare horses. That means he had to find pasturage for approximately 15,000 horses. A herd that large could be expected, in a single day, to eat 5,000 acres of grass right down to the ground. Furthermore, at any moment a Merkit scout could spot Jamuka's force and ride back to his chief with a warning.

"Did we not agree that we wouldn't be late at the appointed meeting, even if there be a blizzard?" Jamuka said, making no attempt to control his anger. "Are we not Mongols, for whom a 'yes' is the same as being bound by an oath?"

Although Ong Khan outranked him and Temüjin was his *anda*, both men accepted the tongue-lashing meekly. They had been wrong, and they had jeopardized the success of their mission. But having vented his anger, Jamuka was ready to prepare for the attack on the Merkits.

HER HUSBAND'S VOICE

They found the Merkits about a week later encamped along the Khilok River in eastern Siberia. Hoping to take the camp by surprise, the commanders agreed to cross the river in the middle of the night, but as the first of the warriors clambered ashore, they were spotted by a band of hunters, who raised the alarm. Meanwhile, the first wave of Mongols charged the Merkit camp.

In the darkness, the camp became a place of chaos as screaming women and children fled in every direction while warriors stumbled about trying to find their weapons and horses. Many Merkits did not bother to stand and fight but ran into the night. While the Mongols were cutting down the fugitives and looting their tents, Temüjin rode frantically through the pandemonium, calling Börte's name.

Börte was hiding in a cart with Höelün's servant, Khoakhchin, but when she heard her husband's voice, she leapt out, pausing only a moment to help the old woman climb down. Then together, pushing and shoving against the crowd of panicky Merkits, they moved in the direction of Temüjin's voice. When they found him, each woman seized his bridle. He thought they were Merkits and was about to strike them when the moon came out from behind a cloud and Temüjin could see clearly that it was his wife and his mother's servant who held his horse. Jumping off his horse, Temüjin embraced Börte in the middle of the melee.

CONCUBINES AND SLAVES

With Börte safe and Khoakhchin as well, only Sučigil remained to be found. One of the captured Merkit chiefs told Belgütei where he would find his mother, but when the young man entered the tent through one entrance, his mother, dressed in a shabby sheepskin coat, exited by another. *The Secret History* reports that Sučigil said to someone—whether a Merkit or a Mongol, we do not know—"I am told that my sons have become khans, but here I have been joined with a base man. How can I now look my sons in the face?" With that, she ran into the forest. Belgütei never saw his mother again. In his rage, he began firing arrows randomly at any Merkit who came within range, shouting all the while, "Bring me my mother!"

DURING HER CAPTIVITY BÖRTE HAD BEEN FORCED TO MARRY A MERKIT WARRIOR. WHEN THE CHILD, A BOY, WAS BORN, TEMÜJIN NAMED HIM JÖCHI, WHICH COMES FROM THE MONGOLIAN WORD FOR *VISITOR* OR *GUEST*.

The captured chief identified the 300 warriors who had hunted for Temüjin when he hid in Burgan Qaldun. Temüjin had them rounded up and slaughtered. Then he assembled the dead men's wives and sorted them into two groups, those who would make suitable concubines, and those who were better suited as slaves.

There was one blemish on this rescue mission: Börte was pregnant. She maintained that the child was Temüjin's, and that she had been in the early stage of pregnancy when she was kidnapped, but Temüjin was never certain. During her captivity Börte had been forced to marry a Merkit warrior. When the child, a boy, was born, Temüjin named him Jöchi, which comes from the Mongolian word for *visitor* or *guest*. This has led many historians to believe that Temüjin did not regard the child as his son.

THE MAKINGS OF A KHAN

After the raid on the Merkit camp, the Ong Khan returned to his territory, but Jamuka and Temüjin decided that their households would camp together. They exchanged gifts—each gave the other a horse and a golden belt he had looted from the Merkits. They feasted together. *The Secret History* tells us, "At night they slept together, the two of them alone under their blanket." To contemporary readers that may sound as if Temüjin and Jamuka had become lovers. Such a thing is possible but unlikely. Mongol nomads did not have private bedrooms or even private beds. The entire family, along with close friends and any passing guests, slept together, side by side, in the *ger*. Seen from a twelfth-

The Mongols had few servants. Each warrior was responsible for erecting his own tent and cooking his own meals. Mongol women were eventually freed from the drudgery of housekeeping, however, thanks to the slaves Genghis Khan sent back from the countries he conquered.

century Mongol's perspective, that Temüjin and Jamuka shared a blanket indicated the closeness of their friendship, but not that there was a sexual dimension to their relationship. Furthermore, when Genghis Khan gave the Mongols a code of laws, sodomy was one of the acts that, he decreed, deserved the death penalty.

For a year and a half the two households lived together. Then one day, as the group was riding to a new pasture, Jamuka announced that he and his household would make camp separately. Temüjin, confused by his friend's declaration, didn't reply, but dropped back and waited for the cart bearing his mother and his wife. He repeated Jamuka's news to Höelün, and added, "I couldn't understand these words of his, so I did not give him any answer and decided to come and ask you, mother."

Before Höelün could give her opinion, Börte spoke up. "Sworn friend Jamuka, so they say, grows easily tired of his friends. Now the time has come when he has grown tired of us. . . . Let us not pitch camp, but while we are on the move, let us separate completely from him and move further on, traveling at night."

Within the context of a Mongol's understanding of the *anda* relationship, Börte's suspicion makes perfect sense. *Andas* are companions, and companions remain together. If Jamuka wanted to part from Temüjin and strike out on his own, then he was a potential rival. At that stage it is unlikely that Temüjin dreamed of the day he would be the supreme khan of all the Mongols, but he did have enough pride to imagine that he would be a chief, subservient to no man, Jamuka included. So he took his wife's advice and rode away from the man he had regarded as a brother.

While still a boy, Temüjin had learned that building alliances was essential to survival. Now that he was beginning to acquire power, this experience with Jamuka would teach Temüjin that even an alliance with one's closest friend could be unstable. Börte saw this more clearly than Temüjin, and so she taught him a vital lesson—that a wise leader is one who recognizes early the signs of betrayal and acts quickly to protect himself. And there is another interesting point to this episode—once again, it was a woman in Temüjin's household who gave him crucial advice.

Just as the sun was rising in their new camp, Temüjin and his weary band heard the sound of horses riding swiftly toward them: they were carrying a handful of men from Jamuka's household who had decided to join Temüjin. All morning long more and more riders came, including a few from Jamuka's own extended family.

Why did these men defect to Temüjin? They may have been motivated by principle—by breaking the *anda* relationship, Jamuka had shown himself to be disloyal. Although he was an established chief and warlord, by severing his ties with Temüjin he showed that he could not be trusted. Temüjin, on the other hand, was a rising star among the Mongols who had overcome incredible hardships and obstacles without violating the Mongol code. And because his band was still very small, the men who joined him now had an excellent chance of rising to power, wealth, and influence within Temüjin's emerging tribe.

One of the men who left Jamuka claimed that he had had a supernatural revelation that told him to join Temüjin. He said that in his vision he saw an ox dragging a large tent suitable for a khan. The ox was following the tracks of Temüjin's cart, and as it went along the ox bellowed, "Together Heaven and Earth have agreed: Temüjin shall be lord of the people. I am drawing near carrying the people and bringing them to him."

We needn't take the story of the prophetic ox seriously as the reason for the men's defection; because *The Secret History* was written shortly after Genghis Khan's death, it is probable that this story was included in the narrative to emphasize that Temüjin was destined for greatness. More convincing is the eagerness of Jamuka's followers to give their allegiance to Temüjin. He was only twenty years old at the time, but he had retrieved his wife from her captors, built an alliance with the Ong Khan, and moved adroitly when his alliance with Jamuka showed fissures. Already men could see that he had the makings of a khan.

Next page: This map indicates the homelands of various Asian tribes, before they were conquered and united under Genghis Khan. At its height, the Mongol Empire covered 9 million square miles (24 million square kilometers).

Miles

0	100	200	300	400

0	100	200	300	400	500	600

Kilometres

•Novokuznetsk

U.

•Abakan

S.

•Biysk

Oirats

Yenesei

GORNO ALTAISK RAION

Ulaangom

GREAT

ALTAI

BAYAN-

•Tsengel   •Olgei

OLGEI AYMAG

MONGOLIAN

Bulga

Ke

•Hovd

DESERT

Uliastay•

Naiman

Irtysh

HANGAY MTS.

Karakoru

Altay

Dzag •Galoot

•Erdenzot

•Bayanhongor

MOUNTAINS

M

•Urumqi

O

N

TIEN SHAN

•Hami

UIGHUR

G

O

B

I

D

E

H

•Yumen

C

MONGOLIA

Key

———	Route of Ch'ang Ch'un 1221-24
— — —	Route of John of Plano Carpini 1245-47
—·—·—	Route of William of Rubruck 1253-55
UIGHUR	Empires/Kingdoms
Buryat	Tribes/Peoples
Xanadu•	Historical Cities
┅┅┅	Trans-Siberian Railway
⸬⸬⸬	Areas of Sand
⊔⊓⊔⊓	Great Wall of China

Buryat

S. S. R.

Orianghai

Amur

N

Lake Baikal

tsk

Ulan-Ude

erkid

Khilok

Onon

Kyakhta

khebaatar

Darhan

ga

Orhon

Mongol

▲ Mt. Burkhan Khaldun

HENTEI MTS.

Choybalsan

Arxan

Ulaan Baatar

Kerulen

Tatar

Tamsagbulag

Tuula

Ondorhaan

Jargalant

Baruun Urt

A

G O B I

Mandalgovi

D E S E R T

Saynshand

O L I A

G O B I   D E S E R T

L

alandzadgad

Xanadu

Duolun

Luan

Bayan Obb

Hohhot

Peking

Khanbaliq

RT

ORDOS

Datong

N A

YELLOW
SEA

Huang Ho

NGUT

CHAPTER 5

THE SHOWDOWN THAT MADE TEMÜJIN A KHAN

◼ ◼ ◼

ACCORDING TO A MONGOL LEGEND, TEMÜJIN WAS OUT HUNTING WITH HIS COMPANIONS WHEN HE CAME UPON A SHABBY MONGOL ENCAMPMENT. THERE WERE FEW HORSES AND FEWER CARTS, AND THE PEOPLE WERE UNDERNOURISHED. THESE UNFORTUNATES BELONGED TO THE JEURET TRIBE, ALLIED TO THE TAYIČIUTS, WHO HAD KEPT TEMÜJIN A PRISONER WHEN HE WAS A BOY. MOVED BY PITY, TEMÜJIN INVITED THE JEURETS TO CAMP WITH HIM. WHEN THEY ARRIVED HE SENT THEM CARTS FULL OF FOOD.

The next morning Temüjin ordered his beaters to drive all the wild game they could find toward the Jeurets' camp. The Jeuret men brought out their bows and killed deer, rabbits, and game birds. That night, as the Jeurets sat around their fires, their bellies full for the first time in many months, they marveled over Temüjin's generosity. The Tayičiuts were supposed to be their brothers, yet those false friends had stolen the Jeurets' horses and carts, and even raided their supplies of food. Yet this stranger treated them with abundant kindness.

Then a messenger appeared in the Jeurets' camp: Temüjin invited the entire tribe to join him and become part of his growing coalition. The Jeuret chiefs declined the offer—perhaps they feared angering the Tayičiuts. But two lesser tribal leaders accepted Temüjin's invitation, and brought all the people of their households with them. This band of Jeurets had found a better chief, and Temüjin had more recruits.

A fifteenth-century Persian painting shows Mongols breaking camp, packing their belongings, and lashing them to pack animals. The women were in charge of setting up the tents, while the men took care of the horses.

This incident, which does not appear in *The Secret History of the Mongols*, is part of the body of legends and oral history that grew up around Genghis Khan. It suggests what Temüjin was doing during the period we can date roughly as 1195 to 1205: he was making friends, forming alliances, and generating goodwill among tribes, bands, families, and even individual Mongols. These ties would pay off later when he was ready to seize the ultimate prize—the title of Universal Khan of all the Mongols.

THE GODS SIDE WITH TEMÜJIN

Temüjin's followers had grown to such numbers that he could put 30,000 Mongol riders in the field, according to *The Secret History of the Mongols*. His rising strength was not based on the Mongol clan or tribal system. His own people, the Borjigin, comprised a small percentage of his followers. The people who came to Temüjin were drawn by his personal qualities and the opportunities he offered them. The Jeurets are a good example: they knew firsthand of his generosity. The Tayičiuts, their supposed allies, had robbed and abused them. By pledging their loyalty to Temüjin, these Jeurets were placing themselves under the protection of a much more agreeable master than the Tayičiuts had ever been.

Temüjin did not leave tribal groups that joined him, such as the Jeurets, intact—he dispersed the warriors among many units. His purpose was to replace loyalty to tribal chiefs, which Temüjin perceived as a threat to his own authority, with loyalty to their new commanders and ultimately to Temüjin and the Mongol nation.

It was not just warriors and their families who flocked to Temüjin: Mongols from the lowest level of society, the serfs, had heard that Prince Temüjin showered his people with furs, horses, and other gifts. Increasingly, the serfs ran away from their masters to serve Temüjin, and Temüjin not only accepted their service but also gave them their freedom and let them rise to the rank of warrior—if they had the strength and the necessary skills.

Temüjin and Jamuka continued to jockey for position, each man waiting for the opportunity to strike at the other and become the supreme khan of all the Mongols. In this contest Temüjin had one significant advantage—the shamans favored him. One of the chief Mongol shamans, Teb Tengri, traveled about proclaiming that the Sky God had appeared to him and said, "I have given the whole surface of the Earth to Temüjin and to his sons." With even the gods on his side, Temüjin's ascent seemed certain.

THE BORJIGIN KHAN

Sometime between 1185 and 1190, Temüjin called on all his followers to assemble at Blue Lake near the Black Heart Mountain, a picturesque spot that today has become a popular destination for trekkers. At that point, the Mongol tribes and clans were more or less evenly split between the two chiefs, Temüjin and Jamuka. The primary difference between the two was that established tribes tended to ally themselves with Jamuka while men of a more independent and ambitious frame of mind tended to be attracted to Temüjin.

The meeting at Blue Lake was a *khuriltai*, a tribal assembly to elect a khan. The election was held in an interesting way: the leaders of families and clans who favored the candidate attended the *khuriltai*; those who did not stayed away. To certify the election, attendees memorized a list of all the families and clans who had come to the assembly. (At that time the Mongols had no written language, so memorization and oral history were their only methods of passing information from generation to generation.)

Enough tribal leaders attended Temüjin's *khuriltai* to make him the Borjigin Khan. After the election, in a gesture that was as courteous as it was tactful, Temüjin sent a message assuring Toghril, the Ong Khan, of his loyalty: he was not splitting off from his foster father's household; he was merely attempting to unite scattered bands of Mongols and bring them into the orbit of the Ong Khan. Finally Temüjin asked Toghril to bless him as he took up the responsibilities of khan. As lord of a large, militarily powerful, established tribe, Toghril was not threatened by Temüjin's election. Besides, Temüjin had a reputation for unshakable loyalty. Toghril sent the messenger back to Temüjin with his congratulations and his blessing.

TEMÜJIN'S COURT

The traditional arrangement of a Mongol encampment placed the khan's complex of tents at the center, with the tents of followers scattered around it. Once a khan was elected, he assembled his inner circle, known as an *ordu*, usually comprised almost entirely of his family and relatives. Years later, Genghis Khan would establish *ordus* for each of his sons and give each one his own army. When the Mongols

This Persian painting portrays one of those rare moments when the Mongols fought with swords
on horseback. Mongols usually only drew their swords for hand-to-hand combat. Ms Pers.113 f.49
Genghis Khan (c.1162-1227) in Battle, from a book by Rashid-al-Din (1247-1318) (gouache), Persian
School, (14th century) / Bibliotheque Nationale, Paris, France / The Bridgeman Art Library International

invaded Europe, the Europeans thought the term *ordu*—which became *horde* in English—referred to the immense swarm of mounted fighting men who swept down on their cities and towns.

Temüjin's *ordu* differed from the traditional model. It included his brother Khasar and his half-brother Belgütei, but also his two closest friends, Bo'orču and Jelme. Furthermore, Temüjin expanded his *ordu* to include a carefully selected band of 150 of the best warriors in the camp to serve as his personal bodyguards; 70 were on duty during the day, 80 at night.

In addition to guarding his person and his camp, Temüjin made his *ordu* responsible for functions that might strike contemporary readers as mundane, but were essential in twelfth-century Mongolia. Belgütei, for example, administered the camp's herd of horses, while Bo'orču and Jelme supervised the camp's cooks. Horses, as we have seen, were vital to the Mongols, but having Bo'orču and Jelme oversee the cooks was a personal decision—since the death of his father, Temüjin dreaded the possibility that some enemy would poison him, too.

THE BATTLE BETWEEN TEMÜJIN AND JAMUKA

One year after Temüjin was elected khan, Taichar, a man related to Jamuka, stole horses from Jöchi-darmala, one of Temüjin's followers. Taichar was not a subtle thief—he took the horses while Jöchi-darmala was in plain sight. Jöchi-darmala rode after Taichar and killed him. Typically, this kind of violent give-and-take would have been resolved with Jöchi-darmala paying a fine to Taichar's family, but Jamuka decided to use the death of his relative as a pretext to attack Temüjin.

At first glance it appears that Jamuka at last was making his move to destroy his rival. *The Secret History* records that he rode out against Temüjin at the head of 30,000 warriors (once again, the numbers are almost certainly inflated). Jamuka and his army were well underway before word reached Temüjin of the impending attack. Quickly he gathered his own force—also said to number 30,000 men—and went to meet Jamuka.

SEEING NO OTHER OPTION, TEMÜJIN ORDERED HIS MEN TO RETREAT INTO THE GORGES OF BURGAN QALDUN. IN THIS ROUGH, DIFFICULT TERRAIN, TEMÜJIN AND HIS ARMY LOST THEIR PURSUERS. ONCE AGAIN HE WAS A FUGITIVE, AND ONCE AGAIN THE SACRED MOUNTAIN HAD SAVED HIM.

The Secret History says that because they had assembled in such haste, Temüjin's men and horses were tired by the time they faced Jamuka's army. Jamuka's men and horses, however, had had time to rest, so when the battle began they had the advantage.

Jamuka deployed his men against Temüjin's center and flanks, in an attempt to box him in. Jamuka's archers fired volley after volley into Temüjin's ranks, decimating his troops. They returned fire, but they were exhausted, almost completely surrounded, taking heavy casualties, and unable to break through Jamuka's ranks. Seeing no other option, Temüjin ordered his men to retreat into the gorges of Burgan Qaldun. In this rough, difficult terrain, Temüjin and his army lost their pursuers. Once again he was a fugitive, and once again the sacred mountain had saved him.

JAMUKA'S ATROCITIES

Incredibly, Jamuka called off the hunt for Temüjin; instead, he collected prisoners and began executing them in ways that shocked his fellow Mongols. He took one of Temüjin's officers and beheaded him, then tied the severed head to the tail of his horse. It was a double insult to the dead man and his family: Mongols considered the head the place where the soul dwelled and therefore the most sacred part of the body; to desecrate it by dangling it from a horse's tail polluted the dead man's soul and degraded his clan.

Then Jamuka took 70 young warriors of the Chinos tribe and boiled them alive in huge cauldrons. The Mongols believed that such a dishonorable method of execution destroyed the warriors' souls so they would have no existence in the afterlife.

Jamuka's cruelty to his prisoners and the contempt he displayed for their souls and for their families horrified the Mongols. Mongols who had not yet sided with either of the two contenders now gave their support to Temüjin. He may have been defeated in battle, but he treated all Mongols with respect. In the months and years after this skirmish at the foot of Burgan Qaldun, more Mongols flocked to Temüjin's standard.

PREPARING FOR THE DECISIVE BATTLE

For another decade Temüjin and Jamuka were locked in a stalemate, each gathering strength but neither ready to make a decisive strike against the other. Then, in or about the year 1201, Jamuka called his own *khuriltai*, at which his people elected him Gur-Khan, or Khan of All Khans, or Universal Khan.

The last Gur-Khan had been an uncle of Toghril, the Ong Khan. By assuming this title and claiming authority over all Mongols, Jamuka was defying both Temüjin and Toghril, in effect daring them to take him on. By that time, among Jamuka's allies were the Tayičiuts, the tribe that had nearly brought about the death of Höelün and the children, and who had kept the boy Temüjin locked in the *cangue*.

Temüjin's motives for making war on Jamuka were mounting: avenge himself against his false blood brother, punish him for his disgraceful treatment of prisoners, settle his personal score with the Tayičiuts, and win for himself the title of Gur-Khan. When at last he was ready for war, Temüjin stepped into the background so that his foster father, the Ong Khan, would be in charge of the campaign against Jamuka—it was an act of deference that the Mongols would have appreciated.

The title Gur-Khan held enormous prestige, and the possessor of it would wage war against any other khan who assumed the title. Who would be Gur-Khan of the Mongols was one of the motives for the war between Temüjin and Jamuka.

THE POISON ARROW

So many shamans had flocked to Temüjin that their prebattle rituals were especially impressive, which unsettled many of Jamuka's men. The situation was made worse when a violent thunderstorm broke over the battlefield. As bolts of lightning flashed across the sky, so many of Jamuka's warriors fled in panic that he was forced to retreat.

In the chaos of the flight from the battlefield, Jamuka and most of his fighting men fled in one direction, while the Tayičiuts ran in another. Ong Khan said he would chase down Jamuka, and he ordered Temüjin to pursue the Tayičiuts.

TEMÜJIN HAD JUST CLIMBED ONTO ANOTHER MOUNT WHEN ANOTHER ARROW STRUCK HIM IN THE NECK. AS TEMÜJIN SLUMPED OVER HIS HORSE'S NECK, CLINGING TO ITS MANE, JELME RODE UP AT A GALLOP AND LED HIS KHAN OFF THE BATTLEFIELD.

He caught up with them on a broad, open plain, where, to Temüjin's surprise, the Tayičiuts suddenly halted their headlong flight, turned their horses, and prepared for battle. What followed was a classic Mongol melee, each army charging directly at the other, the men standing in their stirrups as they fired arrows at the enemy. Some of the Mongols carried long wooden poles, like jousting lances, which they used to knock riders from their horses; as the downed warrior struggled to his feet, enemy archers would perforate him with arrows.

The battle raged all day, with neither side gaining the upper hand. Toward sundown an arrow struck Temüjin's horse in the neck, killing it. Temüjin had just climbed onto another mount when another arrow struck him in the neck. As Temüjin slumped over his horse's neck, clinging to its mane, Jelme rode up at a gallop and led his khan off the battlefield. By then night was falling, and both armies retired to opposite ends of the plain to make camp.

By the light of a campfire Jelme examined Temüjin's wound and discovered that the arrowhead was poisoned. Taking a dagger he cut out

The Shamans Prepare for Battle

In Temüjin's camp there were many shamans who had started rallying to him since the spirit of Burgan Qaldun had saved the young hero from the Merkits. Now they performed all the appropriate prewar rituals. They displayed Temüjin's Spirit Banner, a tall, wooden staff surmounted by the chief's emblem from which horses' tails were suspended. The Spirit Banners were a portable shrine that housed a clan or tribe's guardian spirits, including the spirits of their ancestors. Before going to war, chiefs and shamans offered sacrifices to the Spirit Banner, usually a stallion and a mare.

Then the shamans placed the shoulder bones of sheep into a fire until they cracked—the pattern of the cracks foretold the outcome of the battle. If the reading promised victory, the shamans remained, but if the reading foretold defeat, the shamans departed.

On the day of the battle the shamans climbed to a high point where they beat their sacred drums and clapped together their sacred stones to ensure fine weather and invoke the assistance of the spirits. Sometimes this display of supernatural power inspired enemy warriors to desert to the other side.

Mongol shamans beat sacred drums to invoke the blessings of the gods. A Mongol Shaman, 1820 (coloured engraving), Russian School, (19th century) / Bibliotheque des Arts Decoratifs, Paris, France / Archives Charmet / The Bridgeman Art Library International

the arrow, then with his own mouth sucked the poison from Temüjin's wound. Weak, ill, and in pain, Temüjin lapsed in and out of consciousness. There was no food in the camp—when Temüjin pursued the Tayičiuts he had not brought his supply carts with him. Afraid that his khan was dying, Jelme made a bold move—he crept across the battlefield into the Tayičiuts' camp. Keeping to the edge of the campsite, Jelme scrounged for food. By luck he found a bucket of curds that he grabbed and hurried back to Temüjin. The curds, washed down with a little water, restored Temüjin's strength and, he always believed, saved his life.

THE ARCHER

During the night, many Tayičiuts, who had no idea that Temüjin had been wounded, slipped away from their camp; they were not willing to spend another day fighting the Borjigin Khan. By dawn so many Tayičiuts had run off that the Tayičiut Khan found himself unable to put up a decent defense. Following the example of his warriors, he fled the battlefield, too.

THE TWO BLOOD BROTHERS MEET AT LAST; TEMÜJIN, TRUE TO HIS CHARACTER, OFFERS TO BE GENEROUS; JAMUKA, TRUE TO HIS NATURE, ADMITS THAT HE WILL ALWAYS BE JEALOUS, THAT HE COULD NEVER SERVE TEMÜJIN.

As Temüjin's men fanned out across the plain to hunt for the chiefs and other leading men of the Tayičiut, two Tayičiut warriors rode slowly toward Temüjin. One was Sorqan Šira, the man who years earlier had freed Temüjin from the *cangue* and helped him escape from Tarqutai. The man with Sorqan Šira was named Jirko. He had come to confess that he was the one who had wounded Temüjin with the poison arrow.

This was a bold yet calculated move on Jirko's part. Under the protection or perhaps sponsorship of Sorqan Šira he could have offered Temüjin his services and kept quiet about that poisoned arrow. But if at some future date his secret were revealed, he would appear cowardly. "If now I am put to death by the khan," Jirko said to Temüjin, "I shall be left to rot on a piece of earth the size of the palm of a hand. But if I be favored, for the khan I will charge forward so as to rend the deep water, so as to crumble the shining stone." Impressed by Jirko's courage and candor, Temüjin accepted his service, and gave him a new name—Jebe, which means *arrowhead*.

THE DEATH OF JAMUKA

As for Toghril's pursuit of Jamuka, it was a failure. Temüjin's nemesis escaped, and the skirmishing between them lasted for three more years, until 1204, when four of Jamuka's own men betrayed him and handed him over to Temüjin's people. Foolishly, these traitors accompanied the prisoner to Temüjin's camp, expecting a magnificent reward; they had forgotten that loyalty was the quality Temüjin prized above all others. Instead of rewarding the four men, he ordered their immediate execution.

Then Temüjin turned to his blood brother Jamuka. "Let us each remind the other of what he has forgotten, let us each wake up the other who has fallen asleep."

But Jamuka would not reconcile with Temüjin. In fact, he confessed that if his life were spared, he would only try again to overthrow his *anda*. "If you want to show favor to me, let me die swiftly . . . let them kill me without shedding blood," he said. "Now do away with me quickly."

Temüjin granted this last request, sentencing Jamuka to be strangled, a form of execution that the Mongols regarded as dignified because it did not shed blood or mutilate the body.

This final exchange between Temüjin and Jamuka has the feel of a set piece, a semi-tragic, quasi-happy ending. The two blood brothers meet at last; Temüjin, true to his character, offers to be generous; Jamuka, true to his nature, admits that he will always be jealous, that he could never serve Temüjin. All Temüjin can do is execute Jamuka in a way that preserves each man's honor. It is a poignant moment in Temüjin's story, but also a decisive one: now the way is clear for Temüjin to become khan of all the Mongols.

CHAPTER 6

TEMÜJIN BECOMES GENGHIS KHAN AND THE MONGOL NATION IS BORN

B Y THE YEAR 1200, TOGHRIL, THE ONG KHAN, WAS ELDERLY, FREQUENTLY CONFUSED, AND SOMETIMES AFRAID OF THE EVER-INCREASING MILITARY MIGHT OF HIS FOSTER SON, TEMÜJIN. WHEN TEMÜJIN SUGGESTED A MARRIAGE BETWEEN HIS ELDEST SON, JÖCHI, AND ONE OF TOGHRIL'S DAUGHTERS, THE KHAN ADOPTED AN UNCHARACTERISTICALLY HAUGHTY TONE AND REJECTED THE PROPOSAL. BUT THEN TOGHRIL HAD SECOND THOUGHTS—WHAT IF TEMÜJIN TOOK OFFENSE AND ATTACKED HIM? THE ONG KHAN SENT A SECOND MESSAGE TO HIS FOSTER SON SAYING HE HAD RECONSIDERED THE IDEA AND NOW WOULD BE PLEASED TO SEE A MARRIAGE BETWEEN ONE OF HIS DAUGHTERS AND JÖCHI, ACCORDING TO *THE SECRET HISTORY OF THE MONGOLS.*

Temüjin, never suspecting that he was riding into a trap, gathered his family and friends and retainers and set out for the Ong Khan's encampment. Meanwhile, Toghril had expanded his plot—he would wipe out Temüjin and all his family so there would be no one left to avenge the Borjigin Khan.

Genghis Khan, seated in his tent, is attended by two of his sons, Ögödei and Jöchi, on the right. Jöchi's probable illegitimacy would preclude him from becoming Great Khan after Genghis died. Ms.Supp. Pers.1113. fol.44v Temüjin has himself proclaimed Genghis Khan, his sons Ögödei and Jöchi to the right, from a book by Rashid al-Din (ink and gouache on vellum), Persian School, (14th century) / Bibliotheque Nationale, Paris, France / The Bridgeman Art Library International

قوریلتای بزرک چنگیزخان تومی سیدند بابد ضبط فرمود ولقب چنگیزخان رو مقرر
کث وعزیمت اودکك بیروق بازتاه تكمد سه امان دکلنتن برزرق خان مذکور راجون مبارکی و فرخی مارس مل که سال بوزما ئید سه
مار رجب سنه اثین وسنمایه هجری درآمدیم دز اوائل فصله ها چنگیزخان فرمود ما توقی نه بابد سید بابای کردند محمعیی باعظم
قوریلتای نزدک ساخت ودران قوریلتای لقب بزرک چنگیزخان بدوی معزز کردند ومبارکی بکحت بنشت

Temüjin and his party were about a day from Toghril's encampment when an informer arrived with the dreadful news that the Ong Khan was not planning a marriage but a massacre. Deep in the Ong Khan's territory and far from his own army, Temüjin ordered a classic Mongol tactic—everyone was to scatter in different directions, thereby giving themselves a better chance that some would escape their pursuers. Temüjin, with his brother Khasar and several friends, sped off toward Lake Baljuna, and there he devised his next move. He sent out word to his army to join him as he rode westward from Lake Baljuna toward the Ong Khan's camp.

Within a matter of days thousands of warriors had found Temüjin and were riding with him toward the Ong Khan's encampment. As for Toghril, he believed he had sent Temüjin and his followers scampering to the far corners of Central Asia, so he called for a grand feast to celebrate his victory. In the middle of the feast, Temüjin and his army arrived, taking the Ong Khan and his men entirely by surprise.

THE ONG KHAN'S *ORDU*, HIS INNER CIRCLE—INCLUDING HIS SON AND HEIR SENGGUM—DID NOT WAIT FOR THE ELDERLY KHAN'S ORDERS. THEY FLED IN EVERY DIRECTION.

As the Ong Khan's men ran to take up position around the perimeter of the camp, Toghril sat in his tent trying to decide what to do. His *ordu*, his inner circle—including his son and heir Senggum—did not wait for the elderly khan's orders. They fled in every direction. Toghril, suddenly left all alone, scurried out of his tent, mounted a horse, and ran, too. It is strange that Temüjin didn't pursue him; perhaps he was reluctant to chase down and execute the man he had once regarded as his second father.

In the weeks and months afterward, word trickled back to Temüjin that Senggum had died of thirst in the Gobi Desert, but there was no word of Toghril. There was a rumor that he had ridden to the territory of the Naiman tribe, hoping to find refuge there, but was killed by a guard on the frontier who did not recognize the disheveled old man as the once-great Ong Khan. What happened to Toghril remains unknown. He was never seen again.

THE BIRTH OF THE GREAT MONGOL NATION

With Jamuka dead and Toghril presumed dead there was no one obstructing Temüjin's path to the title of Gur-Khan. It had taken many years for him to reach this point—he was now thirty-eight years old. For six more years, by alliances and compromise and warfare, he consolidated his power over the last few potential rival chiefs.

Then, in 1206 he called a *khuriltai* at the foot of the sacred mountain, Burgan Qaldun. Tens of thousands of Mongols arrived at the site, until the collection of tents stretched for miles in every direction from Temüjin's *ger*, erected in the heart of the immense congregation. Everyone who attended—men, women, and children—knew what was about to happen, and so the formal business of the meeting was delayed for several days to accommodate the general mood of exultation. There was feasting on sheep and cattle from their herds and fresh game brought in by hunters, all washed down by *airag*, also known as *koumiss*, which

The Mongols' Only Alcoholic Beverage

Mare's milk drunk straight from the horse acts as a laxative, so the Mongols fermented it. The process was simple. The milk was strained through a cloth into a large leather bag. This was stirred or churned a few times with a wooden masher, and then the bag was hung at the door of the *ger*. By custom, everyone who entered or stepped out of the *ger* gave the milk a few stirs with the masher. The stirring introduces oxygen into the milk, which encourages fermentation.

After two days of hanging and stirring, the milk becomes *airag* in Mongolian, also widely known by its Turkish name, *koumiss*. It has a slight sparkling character that the Mongols find refreshing; consequently, a bowl of *airag* was always offered to visitors, just as a host today in the West would offer a visitor (depending on the time of day) coffee or cocktails.

During the fermentation process the lactose in the mare's milk is converted into carbon dioxide (which accounts for the sparkling flavor), ethanol, and lactic acid. This conversion of lactose into lactic acid is an especially important consideration among Mongols, most of whom are lactose intolerant.

is fermented mare's milk. The young men would have competed to see who excelled in archery, horse racing, and wrestling—the Mongols' favorite sports. And there would have been chanting and drumming from the shamans.

On the day of Temüjin's installation as Khan of All Khans, he stepped onto a carpet that men of his *ordu* lifted above their heads and in this way carried him to the dais, where a throne was waiting for him. Once he had taken his seat, his bearers kowtowed nine times. Then the assembled thousands, led by the shamans, lifted their hands, palms upward, to the Eternal Blue Sky and prayed for their lord.

GENGHIS KHAN ABOLISHED ALL HEREDITARY TITLES. IN HIS REALM, HE WOULD GIVE RANK AND TITLE TO MEN HE BELIEVED WERE WORTHY, REGARDLESS OF THEIR ANCESTRY.

Then Temüjin broke with tradition. Rather than take the title Gur-Khan, he took a new name, Genghis Khan. Genghis was derived from the Mongol word *chin*, which means *strong and fearless*, and is also related to the Mongol word *chino*, meaning *wolf*, an allusion to the Blue Wolf, a mythical creature who was said to have been the originator of Temüjin's family.

Genghis Khan also renamed his people: they were now *Yeke Mongol Ulus*, the Great Mongol Nation. Gone were the jealous tribes and the ever-shifting alliances among the clans; in their place was a single united people under a single all-powerful lord.

AN EQUAL-OPPORTUNITY ARMY

Historian Jack Weatherford estimates that Genghis's realm covered a territory about the size of Western Europe, with about one million inhabitants and livestock numbering perhaps as many as twenty million.

In 1206, Genghis Khan celebrated his victory over the Tayičiuts. The men on the far left remove dust from the outside of the yurt with stones. akg-images / Werner Forman

When he had been an up-and-coming chief, Genghis had welcomed all types of men to his banner and gave them freedom to rise as high as their abilities and ambition led them. It was a practice that had made Temüjin popular. Now, as Genghis Khan, he made that practice official policy. He abolished all hereditary titles. In his realm, he would give rank and title to men he believed were worthy, regardless of their ancestry.

GENGHIS'S REALM COVERED A TERRITORY ABOUT THE SIZE OF WESTERN EUROPE, WITH ABOUT ONE MILLION INHABITANTS.

He had done something similar a few years earlier when he reorganized the Mongol army. Previously, families, clans, and tribes had fought together in their own units, but Temüjin had wanted to foster an even deeper sense of loyalty and commitment among his warriors. He began with the basic unit of ten men who formed a squad and were under orders to treat one another as brothers; family and tribe did not matter, only the unbreakable ties of the squad. Such an organization was a departure from Mongol tradition, so Temüjin introduced a familiar concept—the oldest man in the squad, like the oldest brother in a family, was the leader. There was a loophole, however: if the oldest man proved unsuitable, his squad could elect one of its own to replace him.

Ten squads comprised a company of 100 men who elected their company leader. Ten companies formed a battalion, and ten battalions formed a *Tümen*, a group of 10,000 warriors. The leader of each *Tümen* was appointed by Temüjin alone.

Because every Mongol male aged fifteen to seventy was obliged to give some type of service to the army, Temüjin's military became the great leveler in which a camel boy had as good a chance of becom-

Genghis Khan presides over a council, which may be a *khuriltai*, an assembly of the leading Mongols to plan a military campaign or elect someone to a leadership position. The Art Archive / British Library

ing the leader of a squad or a company or even a *Tümen* as the son of a khan. By forming an equal-opportunity army, Genghis broke down the old distinctions of class and tribe that had divided the Mongols for generations.

GENGHIS THE LAWGIVER

Having reorganized the army, Genghis Khan turned his attention to Mongol law. There was no formal Mongol code, but there were a host of customs and traditions, many of which lay at the root of petty feuds and intertribal wars. Genghis reviewed all the traditions of his people and abolished those that caused dissension and led to bloodshed.

- He outlawed the abduction of women.
- He abolished the practice of buying and selling wives.
- He declared that all children, whether born of a wife or a concubine, were legitimate.
- He outlawed adultery, but provided broad exceptions: a wife could sleep with her husband's male relatives without fear of punishment; likewise, a husband was free to sleep with the wives of any man of his household. Genghis defined adultery as married people of different households who slept together.
- He forbade any Mongol to enslave another Mongol.
- He made the theft of livestock a capital offense.
- He declared that anyone who found money, property, or livestock and did not turn it over to the local official in charge of lost property would be treated as a thief and executed.
- He established hunting regulations, forbidding hunting from March to October when animals were breeding, and limiting the kill to what a hunter needed for food.
- He exempted clergy of all religions from taxation and serving in the army. Later he would extend these exemptions to other professions he considered essential—doctors, lawyers, teachers, scholars, and undertakers.
- There was one time-honored tradition Genghis kept—all khans, he decreed, must be elected at a *khuriltai*.

Clearly, some of Genghis's laws emerged from his own experiences—the abduction of Börte, the theft of his horses, the years when he and his family lived on roots and rodents because large game was so scarce. Although it is likely that the law code of China had some influence on Genghis—as the dominant civilization in the region, it would have been strange if Chinese law had had no impact at all—it appears that most of the innovations originated with Genghis himself. Like the previous code, Genghis's laws were still administered by tribal chiefs and heads of individual clans.

He also overhauled the hostage system. At that time, handing over one's children to a lord as hostages was an ancient and virtually universal practice. The commanders of battalions and *Tümens* were obliged to send their sons and their sons' best friends to Genghis Khan. Instead of treating the boys as hostages who would be killed if their families demonstrated any sign of disloyalty, Genghis trained them to be the future administrators of his Mongol nation, and later, his empire. In this way he created a new and necessary class of bureaucrats who were personally attached to him. In time, they would be attached to Genghis's capital, Karakorum, the first permanent Mongol town, but at that stage the Mongols were still nomads dwelling in their *gers* as they always had.

THE MONGOL PONY EXPRESS

As lord over a vast realm, Genghis needed some method for collecting information as well as sending instructions to the administrators of his kingdom. To achieve this he drew upon the Mongols' most famous skill—their horsemanship.

He recruited the best riders, assembled stables of fast horses, and founded message stations all across Mongolia. Local families occupied the stations, maintaining the horses and keeping supplies of food and other necessities for the riders.

A rider—known as an arrow messenger because of his speed—could expect to find a station every 20 miles (32 kilometers) or so. Here he could grab something to eat, gulp down a bowl of mare's milk, mount a fresh horse, and set off on the next leg of his journey all within a matter of minutes. A virtually identical system, the famous Pony Express, would be established 600 years later to deliver mail in the American West.

Genghis considered his message transmission system so important that he exempted the riders as well as the people who maintained the stations from military service. This message service was still in operation in Mongolia in the eighteenth century, according to historian Jack Weatherford.

A RIFT IN THE FAMILY

Although he had stripped away the power of the old Mongol aristocracy, clans, and tribes, Genghis had overlooked one other source of influence within Mongol society—the shamans. The shamans, led by Teb Tengri, had blessed his reign, approved of all his innovations, and proclaimed over and over to the Mongol nation that Genghis was the favorite son of the Eternal Blue Sky. As a reward for his support, Genghis made Teb Tengri administrator of the property that belonged to Höelün and her youngest son, Temüge. Teb Tengri invited his six brothers to help him run these estates, and together, according to *The Secret History*, they abused their responsibilities, enriching themselves at Höelün and Temüge's expense, exploiting Teb Tengri's supernatural office to build their own power base among the Mongols, and scheming to undermine Genghis's confidence in his own family. Yet, to all of Teb Tengri's machinations, Genghis remained oblivious.

The seven brothers' first move against Genghis was bold—they waylaid Khasar and beat him up. Stunned and outraged by the unprovoked attack, Khasar—bruised and bloody, his clothes torn and dirty from the fight—went directly to Genghis to demand justice. From his seat Genghis regarded his brother coldly. How, he asked, could Khasar, the strongest warrior in the Mongol nation, have been overpowered by a shaman and his brothers? What Genghis implied was, what had Khasar done to arouse the anger of Teb Tengri, one of Genghis's most loyal and trusted supporters? Humiliated by the beating, stung by his brother's mockery, frustrated by the realization that Genghis would do nothing to right this wrong inflicted against a member of his own family, Khasar burst into tears and left the *ger*.

For three days Khasar avoided Genghis completely, but Teb Tengri, seeing that his scheme was beginning to take effect, called on Genghis to report that he had had two dreams. The first dream was familiar—it promised that all the Mongols would be ruled by Genghis Khan. But the second dream was disturbing because it predicted that the lord of all the Mongols would be Khasar. Then the shaman interpreted the second dream for his khan: Khasar would move against Genghis. To

---

Previous page: Khans traveled in huge tents mounted on wagons and drawn by many oxen. Note the wodden latticework of the tents in the background. Poles mounted on top formed a crown.

prevent such a disaster, Genghis must strike down his brother. Genghis reacted immediately, sending a squad of warriors to arrest Khasar and bring him to Genghis for interrogation.

A MOTHER'S WRATH

News of the rift between the two brothers spread rapidly among the Mongols in the khan's encampment, and it was someone from Genghis's camp who carried an account of these unhappy events to Höelün and Temüge, who lived about a day's ride away. It was night when the messenger arrived at Höelün's *ger* with the report that Teb Tengri had prevailed upon Genghis to arrest Khasar.

The Secret History describes the dramatic scene that followed in detail. In spite of the late hour, Höelün left her tent, hitched her white camel to her black cart, and drove through the night to settle this matter between her sons. She drew up her cart before Genghis's *ger*, climbed down, threw back the entrance flap, and strode into the tent. Genghis, sitting on his chair, and Khasar, kneeling, bound, at his brother's feet, were astonished to see their mother. Without saying a word she untied Khasar, then sat down cross-legged in front of Genghis, opened her coat, reached inside, and drew out her breasts.

"Have you seen them," she asked, her voice trembling with rage. "These are the breasts that suckled you!" Then she launched into a tirade against Genghis, upbraiding him for mistreating his own brother and forgetting the love and loyalty and gratitude he owed to his family. In the face of his mother's anger the great khan was a frightened little boy again. He dismissed the charges against Khasar, gave him his freedom, and swore he would take no action against him. Satisfied, Höelün left Genghis's *ger*, climbed into her cart, and drove back to her own encampment.

Once his mother was gone, Genghis recovered his composure. He would fulfill everything he had promised Höelün regarding Khasar, but he still had one way of striking at his brother—he deprived him of his *Tümen*, his 10,000 armed men, reducing his followers to 1,400. It was another public humiliation for Khasar and a clear statement that Genghis Khan had no confidence in his brother. By the time word of this insult reached Höelün, she was in poor health, too sick to go back to Genghis's camp and scold him again for treating his brother unjustly. Soon afterward, Höelün died. Her precise age is unknown, but she was probably in her fifties.

THE WRESTLING MATCH

According to Mongol tradition, Höelün's estate should have passed to her youngest son, Temüge, who had remained at home to care for her. In flagrant violation of this custom, Teb Tengri seized it. When Temüge confronted the shaman, Teb Tengri's six brothers roughed up the young man, forcing him to kneel and beg the shaman not to kill him.

This latest outrage was too much for Börte. Not only were the shaman and his brothers insulting and threatening the khan's immediate family, but they had also exploited Teb Tengri's sacred office to attract a large following of Mongols that someday might be large enough to challenge Genghis.

IT HAD TAKEN TIME FOR HIM TO ACCEPT THAT JAMUKA, TOGHRIL, AND TEB TENGRI WERE THREATS, BUT ONCE HE GRASPED THE SITUATION HE ACTED DECISIVELY.

Years earlier she had been blunt in her assessment of Jamuka. Now Börte used that same candor to expose the threat Teb Tengri and his brothers posed to the khan and his family. By permitting Teb Tengri to abuse his brothers, Börte said, Genghis was putting his own sons at risk. What if he were to die tomorrow? Did he imagine that Teb Tengri would not try to seize power? And to do so, he would have to eliminate the sons of Genghis Khan.

Once again, Börte's plain speaking compelled Genghis to see a situation he would have preferred to ignore. But now that he had been confronted with it and understood that it challenged his authority and threatened the lives of his sons and very likely of Börte, too (why would Teb Tengri leave such an outspoken enemy of his alive?), Genghis acted.

Sometime later, Teb Tengri, his six brothers, and their father visited Genghis in his tent. Temüge was there, and as the shaman took a seat, the khan's youngest brother grabbed Teb Tengri by the collar of his robe. Genghis, feigning annoyance, declared that if the two men wanted to wrestle they should do so outside. Teb Tengri, livid at the insult, rose to go outdoors, but as he lifted the door flap Temüge gave him a shove that knocked the shaman off balance. As he stumbled over the threshold, three men who were waiting for him seized the shaman. One placed his hands on Teb Tengri's shoulders and braced his knee on his backbone. With a sharp backward jerk he snapped the shaman's spine. With a cry of pain, Teb Tengri fell to the ground.

A moment later Genghis stepped outside. Seeing that the shaman was still clinging to life, he ordered that a small tent be erected over him. Then the khan, Temüge, the three killers, and everyone else in the vicinity walked away, leaving Teb Tengri to die alone.

Genghis Khan's judgment of men's character was not infallible, but neither were his decisions intractable. It had taken time for him to accept that Jamuka, Toghril, and Teb Tengri were threats, but once he grasped the situation he acted decisively. By countenancing the murder of Teb Tengri, Genghis's stature actually increased among the Mongols: his triumph over so powerful a shaman proved that the khan possessed considerable spiritual power of his own. In fact, after the murder of Teb Tengri, the Mongols came to the conclusion that Genghis was not only a khan but also a shaman—a belief that remains widespread in Mongolia to this day.

CHAPTER 7

THE NOMADS CONQUER AN EMPIRE

∎ ∎ ∎

SIEGE WARFARE WAS NEW TO THE MONGOLS. FOR GENERATIONS THEY HAD FOUGHT ALL THEIR WARS ON HORSEBACK ON OPEN GROUND. BUT IN AUGUST 1209, THE TANGUTS, THE OBJECT OF GENGHIS KHAN'S FIRST CAMPAIGN OF CONQUEST, HAD TAKEN REFUGE WITH THEIR EMPEROR LI ANQUAN BEHIND THE WALLS OF THEIR CAPITAL CITY, XINGQING (PRESENT-DAY YINCHUAN).

Unlike the Chinese, the Mongols did not have catapults or the immense bows that fired arrows the size of tree trunks, nor were there engineers in the Mongol army to teach them how to build such complex machinery. They were ignorant even of the tactics that could shorten a siege, such as mining the walls. So the Mongols set up their camp outside Xingqing and waited for the Tanguts to starve, or to succumb to an epidemic, or perhaps finally to march out and face them.

Then Genghis Khan had an inspiration. All around Xingqing was a system of irrigation canals fed by the Yellow River, which, Genghis observed, after weeks of heavy autumn rains, had flooded its banks. Genghis ordered his men to find shovels and picks and dam the river so the current could be turned against the gates and walls of the Tangut capital. Never had the Mongols attempted such a large, complicated building project. With no one in their camp with the expertise to show them how to build a dam properly, the Mongols just kept piling up dirt and rocks. And it worked; they did divert the Yellow River from its usual course. For warriors accustomed to nothing more difficult than

Genghis Khan tried, unsuccessfully, to use the seemingly harmless agricultural irrigation canals against the city of Xingqing, diverting the water to flood the city.

The Art Archive / Freer Gallery of Art

決水復沤和
農候生用莊
桔橰取諸井
翻車取諸塘
香嘗多人力曝

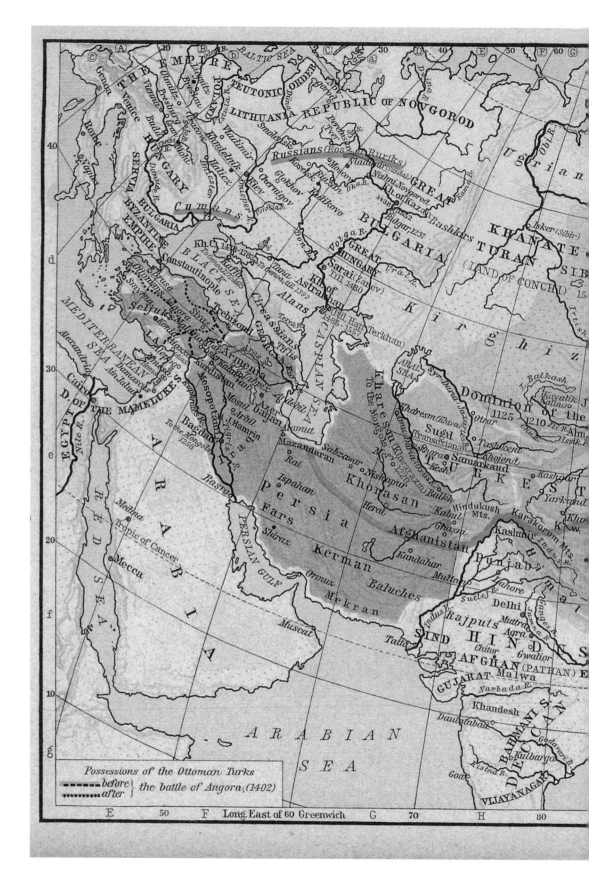

Possessions of the Ottoman Turks
- - - - before } the battle of Angora, (1402)
········· after }

Long. East of 60 Greenwich

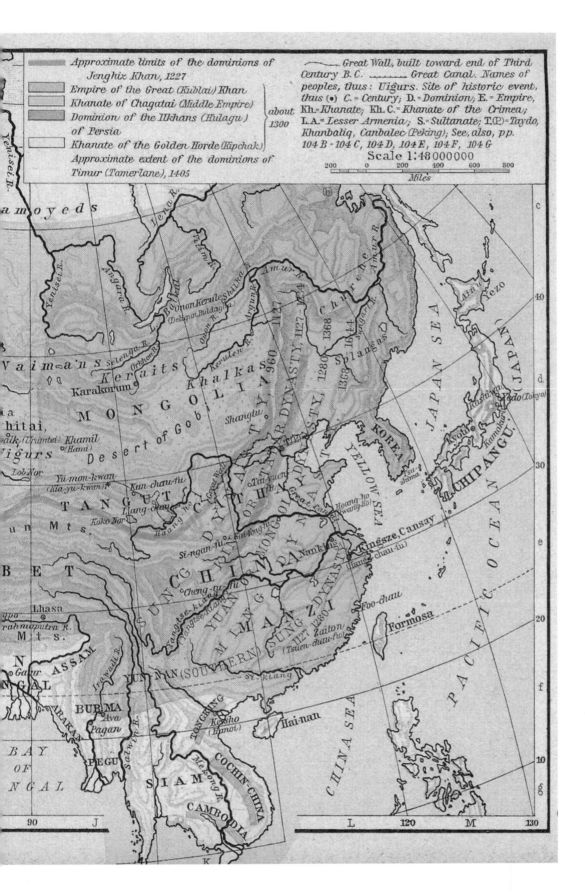

Approximate limits of the dominions of
Jenghiz Khan, 1227
Empire of the Great (Kublai) Khan
Khanate of Chagatai (Middle Empire)
Dominion of the Ilkhans (Hulagu)
of Persia
Khanate of the Golden Horde (Kipchak)
Approximate extent of the dominions of
Timur (Tamerlane), 1405

Great Wall, built toward end of Third
Century B.C. Great Canal. Names of
peoples, thus: Uigurs. Site of historic event,
thus (•) C. = Century; D. = Dominion; E. = Empire,
Kh. = Khanate; Kh. C. = Khanate of the Crimea;
L.A. = Lesser Armenia; S. = Sultanate; T.(P.) = Taydo,
Khanbaliq, Canbalec (Peking); See, also, pp.
104 B - 104 C, 104 D, 104 E, 104 F, 106 G

about
1300

Scale 1:48 000 000

200   0   200   400   600   800

Miles

a wild cavalry charge across the steppes, this monumental excavation project must have been astonishing.

They had barely finished when someone noticed that water was beginning to ooze from the dam's massive earthen wall. The oozing became a trickle, then the trickle a stream. Suddenly, with a tremendous roar, the Yellow River, pent up behind the wall of earth, smashed the dam and rampaged through the Mongol camp, drowning men and horses, overturning tents, and sweeping away weapons and supplies. The fortunate ones, Genghis among them, managed to scramble to high ground. From there, they could look down on a vast muddy swamp, where corpses of men and animals floated amid the wreckage of their camp.

For the Tanguts it must have looked like a miracle wrought for them by the river gods. But for Genghis Khan the disaster outside the walls of Xingqing taught him an important lesson: it took more than fearlessness and great horsemanship to win a war. At that moment, as he surveyed his ruined camp, he knew that none of his people had the skills necessary for this new type of warfare. He would find the men who could teach them, and once they had mastered these new methods, the Mongols would be unstoppable.

TOWNS ON THE STEPPES

The Tanguts were a people of mixed Tibetan and Burmese descent who had settled in the northwestern corner of what is now the Chinese province of Sichuan. Between the seventh and ninth centuries, the Tanguts' ancestral land was the setting for a series of wars between the Tibetans and the Chinese; to escape the destruction and carnage, the Tanguts moved farther north, settling in a region known as the Ordos. This vast country, part steppe, part desert, covered about 83,200 square miles (215,500 square kilometers)—about the size of Idaho—and lay just south of what is now China's Inner Mongolian Autonomous Region.

The Great Bend of the Yellow River forms the border of the Ordos on the west, north, and east. Farther north the Kara-naryn-ula, the Sheiten-ula, and the Yin mountains separate the region from the Gobi

Previous page: On this map the Tangut kingdom is located between the Gobi Desert and Tibet.

The Tanguts were the first nation outside Mongolia that Genghis Khan conquered.

The borders of Genghis Khan's kingdom are outlined in red.

Desert. The Great Wall extended this far, and the soldiers who garrisoned the Wall prevented the Tanguts from settling in the much more fertile lands of China.

The Ordos is not a hospitable country. The soil tends to be a mix of clay and sand, and many of the lakes are filled with saltwater. Most of the steppe is covered with grass and scrub, with small forests growing only along the banks of the Yellow River. The area was filled with wildlife, some of it useful, such as wild horses and asses and two-humped Bactrian camels, others good for hunting, such as gazelles, but also wolves and snow leopards that preyed on the Tanguts' flocks of sheep and goats. Like the Mongols, the Tanguts learned to live on the steppe, but in one significant respect they differed from the Mongols—they built towns.

The Tanguts' evolution from nomads to town-dwellers brought them a sense of permanency and stability that had been absent when they wandered from pasture to pasture. In time it brought them wealth (thanks to the Tangut kingdom's location on the Silk Road) and military might. They acquired new skills (most likely from their Chinese neighbors), including architecture, engineering, and irrigation. But the rising prosperity of the Tanguts also attracted the attention of the Chinese emperors, who were always eager to expand their realm, and of Genghis Khan, who dreamed of using his people's greatest advantage—their near invincibility in battle—to conquer a string of neighboring states that would pay annual tribute to the khan, thereby enhancing his prestige and enriching the Mongols.

THE FIRST KING

In 982, China invaded the Ordos, expecting an easy victory. But a twenty-year-old Tangut named Li Jiqian, a member of the ruling Toba clan, organized the resistance. From his hiding place near Dijingze Lake, Jiqian led a guerrilla war against the Chinese; the Chinese retaliated by murdering Jiqian's wife and mother.

The Sung emperor had vast military reserves that could overwhelm any Tangut army and would eventually track down and destroy the guerrillas; Jiqian's only hope of victory was to ally himself with another major military power. He went to the Khitans, a powerful nation that was on its way to becoming an empire (in the next four decades the Khitans would control eastern Mongolia, most of Manchuria, and a large stretch of land north of the Yellow River). According to some ancient sources, the Khitan emperor Shengzong could field 800,000 men. Eager to extend his influ-

ence into the Ordos, Shengzong agreed to support the Tanguts against the Chinese; to seal the deal Jiqian married a Khitan princess. Then, as a public declaration of his independence from the Sung emperor, Jiqian took the title *Wang*, or King, and according to the custom of the time gave his Tangut kingdom an exalted name: The Great State of White and Lofty. The Chinese referred to it more prosaically as *Xi Xia*, or *Western Xia* (*Xia* being the Chinese name for the Ordos region).

By 997, thanks to Khitan support and the renewed confidence of the Tanguts, Jiqian had an army of 10,000 men. For the next six years Jiqian waged war against the Chinese, battling for control of cities and towns along the White and Lofty frontier. It seemed the war would drag on endlessly, but then an unexpected player entered the scene. In 1004 the Sung emperor Zhenzong received a letter from a Tibetan chieftain named Balaji, who proposed to join Zhenzong in his war against Jiqian. The emperor accepted the offer.

Now Jiqian was fighting on two fronts, against the Chinese to the southeast and the Tibetans to the southwest. Then, after several battles against the Tibetans, Jiqian received a letter from Balaji: he was prepared to surrender. Balaji suggested they meet on the plain outside the Tangut city of Liangzhou to discuss the terms of the Tibetans' capitulation.

At the appointed hour Jiqian rode out of the city with a large escort. Balaji was waiting, his entourage standing around him, and his entire army arrayed in formation behind him. As Jiqian drew near, Balaji suddenly grabbed a bow and shot an arrow that lodged in Jiqian's eye.

The Tibetans attacked Jiqian's escort, but a handful of retainers managed to fight their way out of the ambush and get their wounded king to safety inside Liangzhou. A few hours later Jiqian died; he was forty-two years old.

THE "VIGOROUS AND PERSEVERING LEADER"

Jiqian was succeeded by his son, Li Deming, who brought the years of war to an end by negotiating a treaty with the Sung emperor. He was succeeded in 1032 by his son, Yuanhao, an aggressive, physically robust

---

The Mongols had always fought their battles on the open steppes. During the invasion of the kingdom of the Tanguts they learned the art of siege warfare and how to storm a fortified city.

akg-images / Werner Forman

prince. His skill as a general, combined with an army said to have been 500,000 strong, won him respect even at the court of the Sung emperor, where he was described as "a vigorous and persevering leader versed in military strategy." So the Sung emperor should not have been surprised when an emissary arrived from Yuanhao with news that the "vigorous and persevering leader" had declared himself emperor of Xi Xia, which extended over the present-day Chinese provinces of Ningxia, most of Gansu, and parts of Qinghai, Shanxi, and Inner Mongolia.

THE TANGUTS, ONCE A NATION OF NOMADS, HAD BECOME RICH. THEY MAY NOT HAVE ENJOYED THE FABULOUS WEALTH OF THE CHINESE, BUT THEY WERE RICH ENOUGH TO TEMPT THE MONGOLS.

Over the next two hundred years, Tangut culture flourished thanks to a kind of cross-pollination from China and Tibet. The Tangut emperors brought in Chinese scholars to create something the Tanguts had never had before—a written language (these scholars created a Tangut alphabet of 6,000 characters). From China the Tanguts adopted the art of printing using exquisitely engraved wooden blocks. Tangut artists developed a new style of painting based on Tibetan and Chinese models. Promising young men were educated in state-sponsored schools. As for the Tangut emperors, they imitated the habits and dress of the emperors of China, and even abandoned the religion of their ancestors, Buddhism, to adopt the cult of Confucius, making it the official state religion of Xi Xia in 1146.

The Silk Road, the fabled trade route between China, Central Asia, the Middle East, and Europe, ran through the Tanguts' empire, following what is known today as the Gansu Corridor, a wide belt of fertile, well-watered land where most Tangut farmers and herdsmen had settled. Capitalizing on this easy access to the commerce of East and West, the Tanguts opened markets where they sold camels, carpets, and incense from Persia, Arabia, and other lands far to the west, as well as the much-coveted products of China—silk, tea, lac-

Deception of the Birds

A Tangut king was one thing, but a Tangut who set himself up as an emperor was a claim the Sung emperor would not accept. Once again the Tanguts and the Chinese waged war for control of the Ordos. The Tanguts won, but how they defeated the vast Sung armies is not entirely certain.

One very old story claims that Yuanhao lured a Chinese army into a narrow valley or ravine, where his own army was concealed among the rocks and shrubs. Deep within the valley the Tanguts placed wooden boxes filled with captured birds that made a terrible racket. When the Sung soldiers found the boxes, they opened them to see what was making the commotion. The birds rushed to escape, and the sudden flight of so many birds was the Tanguts' signal to attack.

It is said that the Tanguts slaughtered 20,000 Chinese troops in the valley; in the aftermath of such a defeat, the Sung emperor sued for peace and promised Yuanhao and his successors an annual gift of 135,000 bolts of silk, 2.4 tons (2,177 kilograms) of silver, and 14.3 tons (12,973 kilograms) of tea.

querware, porcelain, carved jade, and medicine. The Tanguts, once a nation of nomads, had become rich. They may not have enjoyed the fabulous wealth of the Chinese, but they were rich enough to tempt the Mongols.

FIRST CONTACT

Genghis's unification of the nomadic tribes into a Mongol nation was unique in the history of his people, but the unification of the Mongols was tenuous; at any moment rival chiefs might break away to regain their old independence. If he hoped to keep his people united and to safeguard his new authority as khan he could not sit quietly upon the steppes. In the past, the way a khan kept the loyalty of his army was to lead them to victory in battle and let them return home with plunder (although, during the days when most Mongol wars were fought among rival clans, the pickings had been lean).

Genghis listened as his scouts described the riches of the cities of Xi Xia, riches unlike anything any Mongol army had ever seen before. If Genghis succeeded in making Xi Xia a vassal state, the Tangut emperor would be compelled to keep a steady stream of silver, silk, and other luxuries flowing into Mongolia.

A wall painting depicts the life of farmers at work during the Northern Sung Dynasty (960–1279). The painting is from the Gansu Province of China, where Tangut farmers had settled before Genghis Khan invaded in the thirteenth century. Farmers at Work, Northern Song Dynasty, 960-1279 (wall painting), / Mogao Caves, Dunhuang, Gansu Province, NW China / The Bridgeman Art Library International

In April 1209 Genghis led his army of approximately 120,000 Mongol horsemen along the Tula (also known as the Tuul) River into the Gurvan Saikhan Mountains, then eastward into the land of the Tanguts. It was a march of approximately 650 miles (1,040 kilometers), the last 200 miles (320 kilometers) across a desert wasteland where there was no grazing for the horses: man and beast would have to survive on what food, water, and fodder they carried with them. Once they reached the Xia Empire they found themselves in a landscape very much like home—vast grasslands crisscrossed by rivers and streams. Genghis sent out raiding parties to bring in sheep and grain from nearby farms and villages while the bulk of the Mongol army set up camp near the Tangut town of Wu-la-hai in the northern region of the Xia Empire.

When the Xia emperor, Li Anquan, learned that the Mongols had entered his lands, he gave his nephew, Li-Tsun-hsiang, and a general, Kao Liang-hui, an army of 50,000 men to destroy the invaders. The expedition ended in disaster: as the Tanguts formed ranks, Genghis ordered a classic Mongol cavalry charge. The Mongols bore down on the Tanguts, releasing a deadly fire of arrows. Some of the horsemen smashed into the Tangut ranks, while others whirled sharply left and right to attack the Tanguts' flanks. It was a massacre, and although Prince

Li-Tsun-hsiang escaped, the general, Kao Liang-hui, was captured. To Kao Liang-hui, Genghis Khan was still a scruffy nomad; when his captors brought him into their khan's presence, the general refused to bow. Genghis ordered his immediate execution.

A FAVORITE TACTIC

After the victory at Wu-la-hai, Genghis and his army set out for Xingqing, the Tangut capital. The only access to the city ran through a single mountain pass that was guarded by an immense fortress. Anquan had sent an army, supposedly of 70,000 men, to garrison the fort; now he sent another 50,000 men as reinforcements. (The stronghold must have been immense indeed if it could house 120,000 men; it is more likely that the historians of the time inflated the numbers.)

Genghis arrived at the pass to find himself in a seemingly impossible situation. His army could not get past the fortress; their horses would never be able to climb the steep slopes of the pass; and there was no way around the mountains. For two months the Mongols waited outside the fortress, looking for some weakness. In the end, they fell back on one of their favorite tactics.

One morning sentinels on the walls shouted the news that the Mongols were packing up their camp and leaving. Burdened with all their equipment, the Mongols would be easy prey, and the commander of the garrison could not resist the chance to punish the invaders. He mustered his troops and led them through the fortress gates in an all-out charge on the Mongol rear.

At the sight of the Tangut army, the Mongols fled. And the Tanguts followed them—straight into the foothills, where the rest of the Mongol army lay concealed among the rocks. Leaping out of their hiding places, the Mongols fired a lethal rain of arrows down on the Tangut garrison. Then they drew their steel swords and swept down on the terrified Tanguts, slaughtering almost all of them. After the massacre, Genghis reformed his warriors and led them through the pass to Xingqing.

THE EMPEROR WEIGHS HIS OPTIONS

From the battlements of Xingqing, the Tanguts had witnessed the Yellow River's destruction of the Mongol camp, and they must have felt relief as well as exhilaration—now the barbarians would leave. But the Mongols who survived the deluge did not pack up and go. They disposed of the bodies of their dead, cleaned up the muddy mess, and reinstated the siege.

In his palace, Emperor Anquan weighed his options. The slaughter of the garrison at the mountain pass fortress proved that the Mongols were resourceful fighters. Their refusal to withdraw from Xingqing even after the river destroyed their camp told the emperor that Genghis Khan was determined to capture his capital. As for the city itself, the supplies would not last forever, and once the defenders were weakened by starvation and sickness, the Mongols would storm the walls and massacre the entire population. The only alternative was to buy off Genghis Khan.

The offer Anquan made was a good one: in exchange for the Mongol withdrawal from Tangut territory, he promised Genghis herds of camels, flocks of hunting falcons, and carts filled to overflowing with silk. In addition, Anquan would give one of his daughters, a young woman named Chaka, as Genghis' wife. It was everything and more that the Mongol khan had wanted when he planned the invasion of Xi Xia. Genghis accepted.

Genghis Khan's first foray beyond the borders of the Mongol homeland had been a success. He had enriched his army, he had won a princess as his bride, and he had acquired his first vassal—an emperor who would send him tribute every year. On the 650-mile (1,040-kilometer) ride back to Mongolia, Genghis had time to plan his next move.

CHAPTER 8

NORTHERN CHINA
FALLS TO THE MONGOLS

■ ■ ■

IN 1210, AFTER GENGHIS KHAN'S RECENT VICTORY OVER THE TANGUTS, A DELEGATION ARRIVED IN GENGHIS'S CAMP FROM THE JIN EMPIRE IN NORTHERN CHINA. EMPEROR WEISHAOWANG, WHO HAD JUST COME TO THE THRONE, SENT THE ENVOYS TO ANNOUNCE HIS ACCESSION AND RECEIVE THE FEALTY OF HIS MONGOL VASSAL.

Some Mongol khans had acknowledged the authority of the Jin emperor to secure his protection from their enemies—it appears certain the Ong Khan was one of the Jin's vassals—but Genghis had never submitted to the Jin. Three years earlier the Jin, recognizing that Genghis had become the most prominent khan among the Mongols, sent their crown prince (the current new emperor) to demand a payment of tribute. Genghis spurned the prince, telling him he would receive no more tribute from the Mongols. Now this prince was emperor and he wanted more than tribute from Genghis Khan.

If everything had gone according to plan, Genghis would have knelt facing the direction of the imperial palace (located in modern-day Beijing), then bowed low, striking his forehead on the ground. This is the famous kowtow, and Genghis made it whenever he worshipped Tengri on the sacred mountain, Burgan Qaldun. To humble himself before the power of almighty Tengri was one thing, but he was not about to abase himself before any man. So Genghis rose from his chair, faced the direction of the Jin palace, and spat.

Then turning to the shocked, speechless envoys, Genghis said, "I thought that the emperor in Beijing was appointed by Heaven. So how

Although this Persian painting shows the Mongols attacking a Chinese city with a cannon, Genghis Khan never had artillery. He did learn siege warfare from captured Chinese, which enable him to breach walled cities such as this one. akg-images / Werner Forman

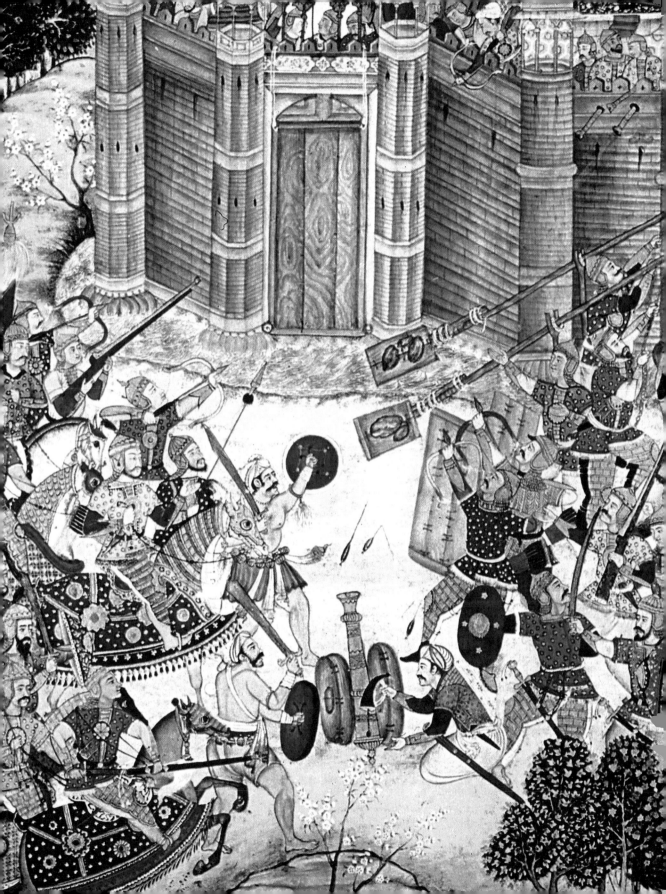

can it be that such a weak and stupid man as the prince of Wei has been appointed to this honorable position?" Without waiting for an answer, he mounted his horse and galloped away. Genghis had just declared war on the Jin dynasty.

THE GOLDEN EMPIRE

The Jin had been known as the *Jurchen* (also known as the *Jurched*); they were bands of tribes who lived in the forests of Manchuria. The Jurchen were a semi-nomadic people who relied heavily on hunting and fishing, and planted a few crops to supplement their high-protein diet. Like the Mongols, the Jurchen were warlike and skilled horsemen.

Sometime after the year 1100, they launched major attacks on their neighbors the Khitan, whose homeland lay along the Yellow Sea in southern Manchuria; next the Jurchen attacked the Chinese kingdom of the northern Sung dynasty. In 1126 the Jurchen captured the Sung capital, Kaifeng, taking the emperor and his court captive. By 1130 the Jurchen ruled their native Manchuria as well as most of Inner Mongolia and northern China. They moved into the Chinese cities they had conquered, proclaimed Shang-ching, near modern-day Harbin, their capital, and established their own Chinese-style dynasty known as the *Jin*, from the Chinese word for gold.

The Jin found themselves ideally located between the peoples of the steppe, such as the Mongols, and the workshops of China. The weapons, armor, cloth, and luxury items such as tea and silk produced by Chinese craftsmen had to pass through Jin territory to reach their steppe-dwelling consumers. Because the nomads expected their khans not only to bring them victory in battle but also to keep a steady stream of Chinese trade goods flowing into their camps, the khans, of necessity, would have to maintain friendly relations with the Jin, which accounts for the submission of Ong Khan and other Mongol chieftains. But Genghis was a khan unlike any other with whom the Jin had had dealings.

In spring 1211 Genghis called a *khuriltai* along the Kherlen River below the peak of Burgan Qaldun; the issue to be discussed was whether the Mongols should attack the Jin Empire. By custom, the number of Mongols who attended the *khuriltai* would decide the question: a high turnout meant the people supported a war against the Jin; a low turnout meant they were opposed.

A large number of Mongols did attend Genghis's *khuriltai*, as well as representatives from their allies, the Uighurs, and their vassals, the Tanguts. Including them in the *khuriltai* was diplomatically shrewd, implying as it did that the Uighurs and Tanguts were more allies than vassals, and respected members of a Mongol-led coalition. But Genghis did not declare war at once; instead, he invited leaders of the clans and tribes to discuss the question with him, and then go and hold further discussions with their own people. In this way Genghis created the impression among the Mongols that he was a chief who valued the opinions of his people.

Then Genghis introduced one further delay: he called upon everyone at the *khuriltai*—men, women, and children—to join him in three days of prayer and fasting while he went alone up Burgan Qaldun to beg for the blessing of Tengri. At dawn on the fourth day Genghis came down the mountain and proclaimed Tengri's message to the Mongols, "The Eternal Blue Sky has promised us victory and vengeance."

Backed by the consensus of the people and their chiefs, and reassured by the blessing of Heaven, Genghis prepared his army for war. As he marched south a courier brought a message from Emperor Weishaowang—now it was his turn to be disdainful. "Our empire is like the sea," he wrote, "yours is but a handful of sand. How can we fear you?"

A FRESH WAVE OF BARBARIANS FROM THE NORTH

Weishaowang's confidence was well founded. For centuries there had been a string of territories between northern China and southern Mongolia populated by former nomads whose ancestors had first raided the country, then occupied it, before finally settling down on farms and in towns. From time to time a fresh wave of tribes or ethnic groups would charge down from the north and seize one or another of these territories for themselves. From the perspective of the Jin emperor, Genghis was just another northern barbarian ready to ignite another petty war in the buffer zone between civilized China and the barbarous steppes.

No one in the Jin Empire could have foreseen the calamity that was about to overtake them. For that matter, as Genghis rode south with his army, he had no grand design for world conquest; his aim was to eliminate an arrogant emperor who obstructed the free flow of trade goods from Sung China. The Mongols' victory over the Jin would spark a war of conquest that would make them masters of an empire reaching from India to Hungary, from the Pacific Ocean to the Mediterranean Sea.

As historian Jack Weatherford put it, "In a flash, only thirty years, the Mongol warriors would defeat every army, capture every fort, and bring down the walls of every city they encountered. Christians, Muslims, Buddhists, and Hindus would soon kneel before the dusty boots of illiterate young Mongol horsemen."

NO ONE IN THE JIN EMPIRE COULD HAVE FORESEEN THE CALAMITY THAT WAS ABOUT TO OVERTAKE THEM. FOR THAT MATTER, AS GENGHIS RODE SOUTH WITH HIS ARMY, HE HAD NO GRAND DESIGN FOR WORLD CONQUEST; HIS AIM WAS TO ELIMINATE AN ARROGANT EMPEROR WHO OBSTRUCTED THE FREE FLOW OF TRADE GOODS FROM SUNG CHINA.

It was a 400-mile (640-kilometer) trek across the Gobi Desert to Jin China. Genghis set out in early spring when the melted snow from the mountains filled the streams and watered the grasslands of the Gobi for a few weeks before the summer heat scorched everything dry. Historians estimate that Genghis traveled with an army that numbered between 100,000 and 120,000 men, plus an immense baggage train and enormous herd of horses (each Mongol horseman brought two or three fresh mounts).

They did not all travel together. First came the scouts, followed by the logistics officers, and then the advance guard. To preserve the element of surprise for as long as possible, the scouts took prisoner or executed on the spot any wayfarer who crossed their path. The logistics officers watched for suitable locations where the army could camp. Behind them rode the advance guard, 30,000 horsemen led by Jebe and Mukhali, both of whom had joined Temüjin about the year 1200 when he was building his coalition of Mongol tribes. The entire advance guard was under the supreme command of Subotai, who since boyhood had been one of Genghis's closest friends.

THE BLACKSMITH'S SON
Subotai and his older brother Jelme came from a tribe known as *forest Mongols*, distinct from steppe-dwelling Mongols such as Genghis and

his family. Subotai's people were not nomads, they were settled in villages amid the forest on the western edge of Lake Baikal. While the steppe Mongols lived in felt tents, the forest Mongols built log houses for themselves. They supported themselves by tending herds of reindeer and hunting, fishing, and trapping. The forest Mongols had a reputation for being skilled metalworkers—Subotai's father was a blacksmith. During the summer months it was common for the blacksmiths to leave their homes in the forests and make the rounds of Mongol camps on the steppe, offering their services to repair weapons and metal cooking pots.

Because the terrain of the dense forests was not suited to horses, the forest Mongols were not as accomplished riders as their steppe-dwelling cousins. But the forest people had their own set of skills: during the winter they lashed wooden skis or skates made of animal bones to the soles of their boots so they could hunt game on the snow and ice.

Around the year 1190, when Subotai was about fourteen, he left his home in the forest to join Temüjin's band of warriors. His older brother Jelme, about twenty-two years old, had been serving with Temüjin for four years; if he made occasional visits home, Jelme probably told stories of Temüjin's heroism in battle and his generosity to his followers; perhaps Jelme bragged a bit about being a member of Temüjin's inner circle. These stories would have been enough to attract an energetic teenager such as Subotai.

At age fourteen Subotai had no military skills, and his horsemanship at that stage was certainly amateurish compared to steppe-born Mongol boys his age. Because he was Jelme's brother, Temüjin consented to see this young recruit and, living up to his reputation for generosity, Temüjin appointed Subotai doorkeeper of his tent. With the humble responsibility for keeping the felt flap securely shut against the wind came the tremendous privilege of listening in on the military and political discussions among Temüjin, his commanders, and his advisors.

Furthermore, Subotai was assigned to an experienced Mongol officer who taught the boy how to ride, shoot a bow, and master the maneuvers of the Mongol cavalry. The training Subotai received was standard for all Mongol boys, but he received his true military education sitting at the door of Temüjin's tent, soaking up the discussions of strategy and tactics. By the time he was twenty-three, Subotai was taking part in these discussions himself.

His first recorded experience as a tactician took place about 1197, when Temüjin was at war with the Merkit tribe. Temüjin offered Subotai 100 of his finest warriors to attack a Merkit camp, but Subotai had a better idea: he rode into the enemy camp, where he announced that he had deserted Temüjin and was offering his services to the Merkit chief. The chief accepted the offer. As he questioned Subotai about the location of Temüjin and his army, the "deserter" convinced the Merkit that he had nothing to fear because the Mongols were far off. Consequently, when Temüjin attacked the camp the Merkits were taken by surprise.

THE FOREST PEOPLE HAD THEIR OWN SET OF SKILLS: DURING THE WINTER THEY LASHED WOODEN SKIS OR SKATES MADE OF ANIMAL BONES TO THE SOLES OF THEIR BOOTS SO THEY COULD HUNT GAME ON THE SNOW AND ICE.

This incident set the pattern Subotai would use with great success time and again—lead the enemy into believing he was about to do one thing, then turn around and do the opposite. The element of surprise is any commander's greatest weapon, and Subotai became a master of it. Historian Richard Gabriel places Subotai on par with Julius Caesar and Napoleon as a military strategist and commander.

BREECHING THE GREAT WALL OF CHINA

The Great Wall of China we see today with its broad stone battlements and massive watchtowers did not exist in 1211. The wall the Mongols would confront was constructed only partially of stone. Most of the materials were timber and hard-packed earth. It had been started in the third century B.C.E. by China's first emperor, Qin Shi Huang, specifically to keep out the Mongol nomads. Now it was manned by thousands of guards along its entire length. (Exactly how long the Wall stretched in the thirteenth century is unknown, but it was certainly less that than the 4,000 miles [6,400 kilometers] it reached by the end of the Ming dynasty in 1644.)

Jin scouts who had eluded the Mongol scouts reported back to the emperor that an army of about 30,000 Mongols under the command of Subotai was making straight for the eastern end of the Great Wall, the part closest to the imperial capital. Weishaowang's generals sent a large army to reinforce the garrison at the capital, then sent more men to strengthen the Great Wall's garrison as well as the secondary defenses behind it. Then the Jin waited for the Mongols to attack.

But the attack never came. Instead, the Jin generals received terrible news that the vast Mongol army led by Genghis Khan himself had crossed the Great Wall at the western end. The invaders had not fired a single arrow, nor lost a single man: the guards at the western section of the wall were Onguts, a tribe the Jin had subdued years earlier, and the Onguts were related to the Mongols. As they saw Genghis's immense army approaching the Great Wall, the Ongut guards had two choices—fight and die for the Jin Empire that had conquered them, or save their lives by going over to the Mongols. Choosing life over loyalty, the Onguts threw open the gates of the Great Wall and the Mongols surged into China.

THE FIRST BATTLE

The Jin generals scrambled to revise their battle plan and intercept the Mongols before they attacked the capital. They pulled

Subotai rose from the boy who guarded Genghis Khan's tent flap to become his greatest general. His mastery of the element of surprise proved to be his greatest weapon against the enemy.

Souboutai, famous general in the service of Genghis Khan (c.1162-1227) illustration from 'Grandeur and Supremacy of Peking', by Alphonse Hubrecht, 1928 (engraving), French School, (20th century) / Private Collection / The Bridgeman Art Library International

their forces away from the fortresses at the eastern end of the Great Wall and began, very slowly, to move west to meet the Mongols. The generals acted cautiously, holding back their cavalry so that it moved at the same pace as the infantry, and sending out scouts to find the Mongol force.

Genghis and his Mongols, meanwhile, moved swiftly and, informed by his own scouts of the snail's pace of the Chinese advance, Genghis took the initiative and selected the place for his first battle against the Jin. The northern passes through the mountains in what is now the Shanxi province were the gateway to the Jin capital, opening onto a broad, flat plain, and here Genghis waited for the enemy.

The Jin army emerged from the mountains, saw the Mongols, and immediately went into formation—infantry in the center, cavalry on the right and left wings. Members of the Jin nobility comprised the cavalry. They rode large warhorses that were strong but lacked the speed and maneuverability of the Mongol horses. The core of the infantry consisted of professional troops, but they were outnumbered by raw peasant conscripts who lacked training and discipline.

The Mongols attacked first, with wave after wave of swift cavalrymen firing volley after volley of armor-piercing arrows into the tight ranks of the Jin infantry. With their shields the professional Jin troops would have been able to deflect some of the Mongol arrows, but the unprotected conscripts who lacked shields and armor fell by the hundreds. Then Genghis sent in a second wave of horsemen to attack the Jin cavalry. The Jin nobles tried to give battle, but on their heavy mounts they made no headway against the Mongols' ability to make fast, deadly strikes. Yet in spite of the Mongols' withering fire, the Jin army held its ground.

The battle raged all morning. Then, at noon, Subotai appeared leading the 30,000 men of the advance guard. No surviving document explains his sudden arrival on the battlefield, but he must have been trailing the Chinese, careful to keep out of sight. With his fresh troops he fell upon the Jin's flanks and their rear. Under such pressure, resistance among the Jin cavalry collapsed; the panicked horses reared, trampling the infantry, and the entire Jin military degenerated into bloody chaos.

Again and again the Jin troops sought some means of escape, but the Mongols had them hemmed in, cut off from all hope of retreat back into the mountain passes. Completely surrounded, the Jin army was annihilated. Tens of thousands died that day. Nine years later a Taoist monk, Ch'ang-Ch'un, crossed the site of the battle and reported that the field was still littered with human bones.

CONFUSION AND TERROR

For all their prowess on the battlefield, the Mongols suffered significant disadvantages in the Jin Empire: they were unaccustomed to the hot, humid summer climate with its swarms of mosquitoes and flies; they had to find some way to control the hundreds of thousands of peasants in the countryside; and then there were the Jin's walled towns and cities—the Mongols had learned a few things about siege warfare in their war against the Tanguts, but they were not yet masters of it.

Genghis compensated for these deficiencies in several ways. First, he cultivated a new ally in the heart of the Jin Empire. A century earlier the Jin had conquered the Khitan tribe, reducing them to a vassal state. Genghis declared that he had come into China to liberate the Khitan, who were, after all, related to the Mongols and spoke the same language. Khitan men of fighting age, nobles as well as commoners, flocked to Genghis's side. The nobles were especially useful in explaining Chinese culture to the Mongols.

Yelü Chucai, a Khitan nobleman, proved to be particularly valuable to Genghis; although only in his twenties, Chucai had experience as a government administrator, and he advised Genghis how to govern a huge foreign population. It was Chucai who told Genghis that he must become more than a conqueror. "You can conquer China on horseback," he said, "but you must dismount to rule her."

As for the local population, Genghis implemented a policy of confusion and terror. His Mongols rampaged across the country, slaughtering countless peasants, carrying off their harvests and livestock, then torching their villages and farms. On other occasions they destroyed the villages, but let the peasants live—thereby creating a huge population of homeless, starving people that strained the imperial government's resources (assuming that the emperor would take responsibility for their care). The massacres and displacements had the desired effect; when the Mongols began to round up the peasants for forced labor, the frightened villagers and farmers did not resist.

Each Mongol warrior became the foreman of a work crew of 10 peasant men. They hauled water for the army and the horses, cooked food, and cared for the other livestock. When the Mongols besieged a town, the peasants carried rocks and baskets of earth to fill in the moat.

The more intelligent peasants taught the Mongols how to assemble and operate siege engines such as catapults or the towers on wheels that would be rolled up to the town's walls. Such machinery was still new to the Mongols, so when they captured a town or city they separated engineers from the rest of their prisoners and put them to work constructing more siege engines.

Sometimes, to terrify the garrisons and inhabitants of towns, the Mongols would drive their peasant captives before their army. If the Chinese soldiers stationed along the battlements fired, this vast, wailing crowd of Chinese men, women, and children would be the first casualties. But the mass of weeping peasants did more than serve as human shields—the Mongols forced them into the moats and defensive ditches that surrounded towns. Once the trenches had been filled up, the Mongols, carrying scaling ladders, charged across the mass of living bodies and stormed the town walls.

THE PLUNDER OF AN EMPIRE

For three years Genghis waged war in Jin China, destroying armies and ravaging the countryside. During one six-month period the Mongols leveled ninety towns and fortresses. Fear of the enemy led several Jin generals to renounce their allegiance to the emperor and offer their services to Genghis Khan. Some of these generals brought their armies with them; in fact, by 1214, forty-six Chinese divisions were fighting for the Mongols.

The war brought incredible hardships upon the people of the Jin Empire. When food ran out in besieged cities and towns the inhabitants turned to cannibalism. In the countryside, tens of thousands of displaced peasants sought food and shelter—usually in vain. In their desperation, they rioted against local government authorities, which brought the wrath of the emperor down upon these helpless, desperate people. At one point the army that Emperor Weishaowang sent in to put down an especially large peasant revolt ended with the slaughter of 30,000 rebels. While Jin China descended into chaos, the Mongols showed no signs of withdrawing, and Weishaowang refused to discuss a truce with Genghis Khan. The only respite the Jin Chinese enjoyed was during the summer, when the Mongols retired north to Dolon Nor, or the Seven Lakes, to escape the heat and humidity they found intolerable.

In late summer 1213, a palace coup led by one of the emperor's generals, Heshi Liezhizhong, murdered Weishaowang. A general named Xuanzong, one of Weishaowang's relatives, became emperor. Within a few months the new emperor found himself besieged by Genghis Khan. Almost immediately, Xuanzong sent a courier to Genghis suggesting they negotiate a peaceful settlement. The emperor swore to be Genghis's vassal and gave the Mongol khan a Jin princess to be his wife. As the first installment of tribute he presented Genghis with an enormous amount of gold, silver, and silk, as well as 500 young men, 500 young women, and 3,000 horses.

The Mongols had never known such luxury. They received so much silk they used it to wrap and pack the booty they had taken in the war: chests full of black tea, caskets full of jewels, casks of perfume, trunks of sandalwood and other aromatics, jars of wine, crates of porcelain and carved jade. Captive teenage Chinese boys loaded the carts with the treasures of their homeland, and when the caravan was ready to set off, captive Chinese musicians and singers entertained the convoy.

The Mongol Warriors' Diet

A Mongol warrior ate large quantities of meat, milk, and yogurt. Thanks to this high-protein diet, they were robust men with healthy teeth and strong bones.

According to Marco Polo, the Venetian merchant and traveler, each Mongol warrior traveled with a supply of dried meat and dried curd that made lighting a cooking fire unnecessary—he could eat these rations while riding. In addition, every warrior had 10 pounds (4.5 kilograms) of milk dried down to a paste. By mixing a handful with water he had a high-protein meal that could sustain him all day. Polo also tells us that if a Mongol were lucky enough to get fresh meat but had no opportunity to cook it, he placed it under his saddle to tenderize it for eating later. This is said to be the origin of steak Tartar (*Tartar* being a name the Europeans used interchangeably for the Mongols).

The peasant conscripts who fought for the Jin, on the other hand, lived almost entirely on a carbohydrate diet of various types of grains usually boiled down to a soupy gruel. The lack of protein in the peasants' diet stunted their growth, weakened their bones, rotted their teeth, sapped their energy, and made them susceptible to illness.

An adult metabolism burns through carbohydrates quickly, and an army of infantry on the move even more so. If a Chinese infantryman had to go without rations, within a day or two he would be weak from hunger. The protein-fed Mongol, on the other hand, could fast for a day or two with his strength barely diminished. If necessary, he would renew his strength by making a small incision in his horse's neck and drinking the blood.

Traveling with this great hoard were hundreds of engineers, physicians, astrologers, technicians who could make gunpowder, goldsmiths, even chefs—all men Genghis Khan valued because they possessed skills the Mongols lacked. Genghis was bringing them home to elevate the life of his people to heights they had never imagined. The floor of every *ger* would be thick with carpets, every Mongol woman and child would be wrapped in silk and draped with gold and silver. The plunder of an empire was coming to the barren steppes of Mongolia.

THE FALL OF BEIJING

The Mongols got no farther than Dolon Nor when they were obliged to stop and make camp. It was summer, and there would be no water or grass in the Gobi Desert for such an enormous column of men and animals. They would have to wait for cooler weather.

Meanwhile, Emperor Xuanzong and most of his court had moved farther south to the city of Kaifeng, leaving his son the crown prince and several generals behind to administer the capital. It is thought that Xuanzong felt too exposed in Beijing should the Mongols ever decide to return. Kaifeng was far enough away to seem beyond Genghis's reach. This may have been the emperor's rationale for abandoning his capital, but the khan read his actions differently: he was reneging on the truce by moving his base of power to Kaifeng in preparation for reclaiming the Jin Empire. Genghis called up his army, now fresh from weeks of rest among the Seven Lakes, and led them back to Beijing.

As word spread that Genghis Khan was coming, whole regiments of Jin troops, with their officers, deserted to the Mongols. The Jin crown prince and his generals fled the city.

If the Chinese troops had remained loyal, and if the crown prince and the generals had resolved to defend their capital, it is possible that they could have driven off the Mongols. Beijing in 1215 was enclosed within 26 miles (42 kilometers) of battlements with ninety defensive towers. Inside, the city was divided into four distinct quadrants, each essentially a separate heavily fortified town. For three months Genghis's troops besieged the Jin capital, breaking down its defenses

---

Previous page: To escape Genghis Khan, the emperor of the Jin dynasty in northern China fled to the city of Kaifeng, pictured here, far to the south and beyond the reach of the Mongols.

akg-images / Werner Forman

with siege engines built for them by their captive Chinese engineers and mechanics. Trebuchets, which could hurl heavier objects a farther distance than ordinary catapults could, pulverized the city walls. Catapults sent clay pots of fiery liquid crashing into the city, where they caused whatever they struck to explode into flames.

In May, the Mongols breached the walls of the doomed city. Rampaging through the streets, they cut down anyone, civilian or soldier, as they rushed toward the imperial palace. Once inside they raped the ladies of the palace, slaughtered the eunuchs who served the imperial household, and then stripped the palace of its treasures.

In the town there was no mercy for the citizens of Beijing. To escape being gang-raped by the Mongols, many young girls ran to the walls, climbed up onto the battlements, and threw themselves off. A few weeks later, when ambassadors from the Khwarazm Shah arrived in Beijing, they found human corpses rotting in heaps amid mile upon mile of burned-out houses.

In his war against the Tanguts, Genghis Khan had only wanted a vassal. In his war against the Jin, he wanted independence and plunder. But once the Jin emperor and the crown prince essentially abandoned their empire, administration of Jin China fell to Genghis. He was, whether he had intended to be or not, lord of an empire. Having enjoyed this tremendous victory, he began to dream of other conquests. Genghis Khan's victory over the Jin was the true beginning of the Mongol Empire.

CHAPTER 9

GENGHIS KHAN INVADES THE MUSLIM WORLD

I N LATE WINTER 1220, ALA AD-DIN MUHAMMAD II, EMPEROR OF KHWARAZM, TRANSOXIANA, AND KHURASAN, RODE WITH A HANDFUL OF FOLLOWERS INTO THE VILLAGE OF ASTARA ON THE WESTERN SHORE OF THE CASPIAN SEA, NEAR THE BORDER BETWEEN MODERN-DAY IRAN AND AZERBAIJAN. ONLY WEEKS EARLIER, THE SHAH HAD BEEN ONE OF THE WEALTHIEST AND MIGHTIEST RULERS IN THIS PART OF THE WORLD, WITH AN IMMENSE ARMY AND A MAGNIFICENT PALACE IN HIS CAPITAL, SAMARKAND. ON THIS DAY HE LOOKED NO DIFFERENT THAN ANY OTHER DUST-COVERED, ROAD-WEARY STRANGER DRESSED IN DRAB TRAVELING CLOTHES.

The shah and his men hurried to the waterfront, where they hired a fishing boat and pushed off for Abeskum Island. The travelers had gotten a good distance from the shore when they saw a mass of horsemen charging through the village, riding straight into the sea, and firing volley after volley of arrows—all of which fell far short of the boat. By a matter of minutes the shah's Mongol pursuers had missed capturing him.

THE MARVELS OF SAMARKAND

Ala ad-Din Muhammad's empire embraced modern-day Iran, Turkmenistan, Uzbekistan, Tajikistan, and Afghanistan, as well as parts of Kazakhstan, Pakistan, Iraq, and Azerbaijan. The vast desert of Kyzyl Kum protected the shah's northern border from invaders. The Hindu

The 1220 fall of Samarkand, an enormously wealthy city of 500,000 inhabitants, was one of the greatest triumphs of Genghis Khan's career. akg-images

kingdoms of India and the Buddhist kingdom of Kara-Khitai along the shah's eastern border served as a buffer between him and the Mongols.

But to be on the safe side, Muhammad kept a standing army said to number 400,000 men. It was a tremendous drain on the imperial treasury, but the shah was extremely wealthy. Several important trade routes, including the fabled Silk Road, passed through his realm, bringing to his markets the riches of China, India, Europe, Africa, and Arabia. He chose as his capital the loveliest and most opulent of the trade route cities, Samarkand. At a time when no more than 40,000 people lived in London and the population of Paris hovered somewhere between 50,000 and 80,000, Samarkand boasted half a million citizens who dwelled inside the city walls or in the pleasant suburbs.

Samarkand was a city of great opulence and great marvels. In its factories were woven gold and silver lamé. Chinese craftsmen produced rag paper, an innovation in great demand throughout the Middle East. To reach a broader market, farmers packed their melons and eggplants in snow inside lead chests—the first attempt at refrigeration so fruit and vegetables would arrive at far-off markets perfectly fresh.

Members of the shah's court built their own splendid palaces in Samarkand and furnished them with rare treasures gathered from across the known world. It was said that when Muhammad and his entourage went hunting, the men wore cloth of gold and brought along their tame cheetahs. To finance this grand style, the shah burdened his subjects with heavy taxes. If any town or district refused to pay, Muhammad sent in his Turkish troops to kill and plunder.

By 1216 some of the shah's Persian subjects were plotting with Nasir, the caliph of Baghdad, to overthrow Muhammad. It was a foolish scheme. By this time the caliph's military muscle had atrophied, his realm was limited to Mesopotamia (modern-day Iraq), and Muslim rulers paid little more than lip service to his spiritual authority (the caliphs of Baghdad traced their line back to the uncle of the Prophet Muhammad). The shah summoned his army and marched on Baghdad

A present-day map indicates the locations of Genghis Khan's invasion of the Middle East, including modern-day Afghanistan, northern Iran, Turkmenistan, and Azerbaijan. Courtesy of the University of Texas Libraries, The University of Texas at Austin

MIDDLE EAST

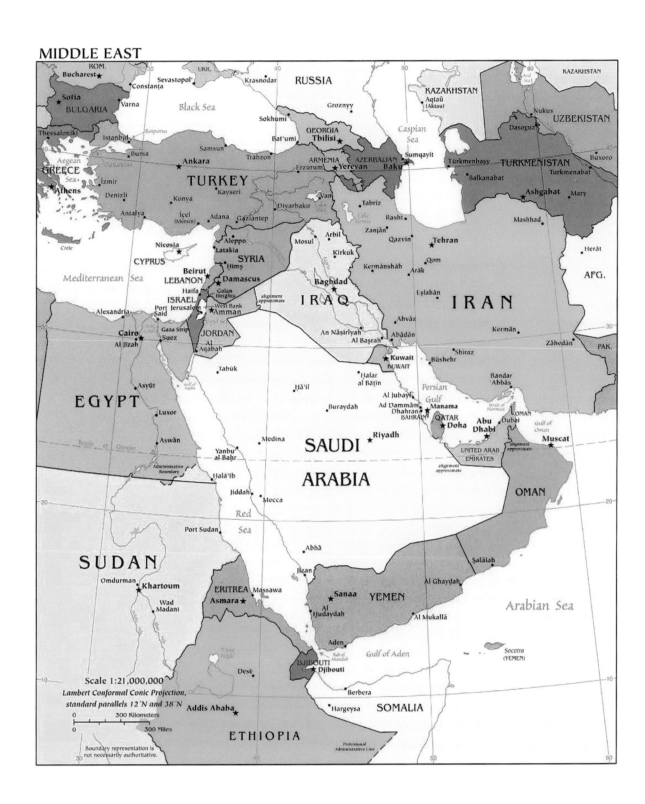

Scale 1:21,000,000
Lambert Conformal Conic Projection,
standard parallels 12°N and 38°N

0   300 Kilometers
0   300 Miles

Boundary representation is
not necessarily authoritative.

to depose Nasir and replace him with a figurehead who would answer to the emperor of Khwarazm.

But while crossing the mountains that guard present-day Iraq's eastern border, a howling blizzard swept down on the army. Blinded by the snow, many bands of soldiers became separated from their units. Most of these stragglers died of the cold; the rest were killed by Kurdish bandits. With the strength of his army weakened and his surviving men demoralized, Muhammad ordered a retreat back to Samarkand.

THE AMBASSADORS

When the shah reached Bukhara, he was informed that three envoys had been waiting for him. They brought magnificent gifts, including carved jade and ivory, cloaks spun from the wool of white camels, and a huge nugget of gold. Furthermore, the ambassadors delivered into the shah's hand a letter from their lord, Genghis Khan. "My country is an anthill of soldiers and a mine of silver," the Mongol khan wrote, "and I have no need of other lands. Therefore I believe that we have an equal interest in encouraging trade between our subjects." There was no signature—Genghis could not write—but there was a seal, and beneath it a line that read, "The seal of the Emperor of Mankind." Genghis was making a bold claim, but it did not impress Muhammad, who styled himself, "The Chosen Prince of Allah, the Shadow of Allah on Earth, the Second Alexander."

Genghis was approaching the shah because the Muslim world had things the Mongols wanted: steel helmets, shields, and scimitars, chain mail that made the wearer invulnerable to arrows, not to mention luxury items such as exquisite glassware and the fabled carpets of Bukhara. As for Muhammad, he had had no contact with the Mongols, but he had heard of their conquests far to the east. If Genghis were now master over the trade routes to China, it was in Muhammad's interest to sign a commercial treaty with him, and that is exactly what he did.

Soon after the treaty was signed the first Mongol caravan arrived in the city of Otrar in what is now Kazakhstan on the Syr Darya River (known in ancient times as the Jaxartes). The goods the Mongol merchants brought were breathtaking—500 camels weighted down with sable furs from the steppes, silk from China, and masses of gold and silver. Inalchuq, the governor of the city, dazzled by so much treasure, sent a letter to the shah claiming that the merchants and the Mongol ambassador who accompanied them were all spies. Muhammad replied that if the governor's suspicions could be proved, the Mongols should all die. Inalchuq did not bother with an investigation; he executed the ambassador, the merchants, even the camel drivers, then confiscated the trade goods. One slave escaped, and it was he who brought to Genghis the news of Inalchuq's treachery.

Genghis's response to this gross insult was calm and diplomatic. He sent another ambassador, Ibn Kafraj Boghra, a Mongol who was a Muslim, with an escort of only two Mongol warriors, to Samarkand to ask the shah to punish the troublesome governor. In reply, Muhammad had Boghra beheaded, and burned the beards off the Mongols' faces—a contemptuous act that not only symbolically unmanned the warriors, but also scarred them so they could never grow a beard again. Then the warriors were given Boghra's severed head and sent back to Genghis. When he saw his disgraced and mutilated envoys, Genghis cried, "May Heaven show me the grace of finding energy for revenge!"

The sources do not offer an explanation for Muhammad's unforgivable treatment of the Mongol envoys. Historian James Chambers has suggested that perhaps Muhammad regretted his decision to make a treaty with a barbarian infidel, or perhaps he had such faith in his army that he felt he could treat Genghis with contempt. Whatever his reasons, the shah had brought war down upon his head.

THE FIRST CLASH

In winter of 1219, as Genghis Khan assembled his horsemen, Muhammad drew up his vast army all along the Syr Darya River on his eastern border. The line of troops stretched 500 miles (800 kilometers), and there were lines of communication that linked the front line with the great cities of the shah's empire. Muhammad had brought out his 400,000 Persian and Turkish professionals, as well as thousands of armed slaves. The professional troops looked magnificent in their steel helmets, bearing before them highly polished steel shields, and wearing steel swords at their belts. Muhammad had complete confidence in this splendid army, but his son Jalal ad-Din did not share his father's confidence.

Jalal possessed a better sense of military strategy than his father did. He protested that it was madness to attempt to defend a 500-mile-long (800-kilometer) front. The army was spread too thin, and anywhere the Mongols chose to attack the men of Khwarazm would have insufficient numbers to repel them, and it would take many hours before reinforcements from Samarkand or any other city could reach the front. Jalal urged his father to exploit the element of surprise and attack the Mongols now. Muhammad dismissed his son's apprehensions. Genghis was bringing 200,000 men—the army of Khwarazm outnumbered the Mongols two to one. Furthermore, even if the Mongols broke through, the people of Khwarazm had little to fear—the Mongols were barbarians, incapable of conducting a siege or breaching the walls of a fortified city.

The shah was mistaken. In the Mongol baggage train were yaks and camels that carried the dismantled pieces of mangonels and other types of catapults and siege engines. Traveling with the army were Chinese engineers who were expert at building bridges, constructing earthworks, and even diverting the course of rivers to flood the enemy's positions.

When news reached the shah and the prince that a Mongol force, 30,000 strong led by Jebe, was entering the Fergana Valley, Muhammad gave his son permission to ride out with 50,000 men and crush the invaders.

It had been a brutal crossing through passes of the Tian Shan Mountains. The Mongols slogged through snowdrifts five or six feet deep. At the highest altitudes—13,000 feet (3,962 meters) —men and horses died of exposure, in spite of the horses' legs being wrapped in yak hide and the men in double layers of sheepskin. They lost some of their supplies in blizzards, and jettisoned more in order to move quickly and unencumbered through the mountains. When at last they descended into the

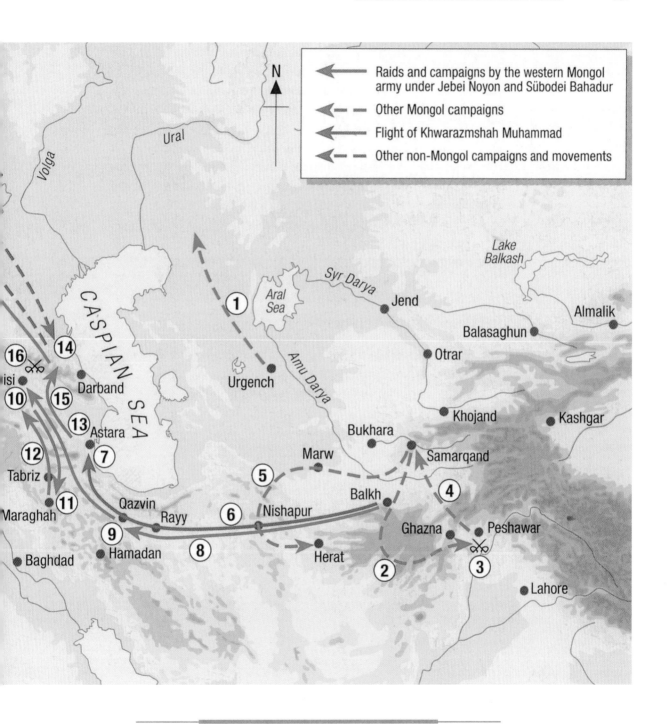

N

Raids and campaigns by the western Mongol army under Jebei Noyon and Sübodei Bahadur
Other Mongol campaigns
Flight of Khwarazmshah Muhammad
Other non-Mongol campaigns and movements

This map spotlights Mongol campaigns in the Muslim world, as well as Georgia, Russia, and the Ukraine. It also shows the flight path of Muhammad Shah—hunted by Subotai and Jebe—to the Caspian Sea, where he died on a small island.

Fergana Valley, they entered a paradise. It was spring, and the wheat fields and vineyards were green with new growth. Jebe sent out foraging parties to requisition grain and cattle from the farmers. The first consignment was just returning to Jebe's camp when Jalal and his 50,000 men arrived.

The men of Khwarazm looked splendid mounted on thoroughbreds, their steel helmets and shields glinting in the sun. As for the Mongols, they had probably never looked worse. Both men and horses were clearly exhausted, undernourished, and in no condition to fight a major engagement. Still, Jebe would not back down.

AS THE MONGOLS SURGED INTO THE CITY, THEY BROKE WITH THEIR USUAL POLICY OF RESERVING THE MOST USEFUL INHABITANTS—INSTEAD, THEY MASSACRED ALMOST THE ENTIRE POPULATION.

As Jalal gave the order to advance, the Mongols fell back. This was an old Mongol ploy to convince the enemy that they had the upper hand; usually it caused the enemy to break ranks and charge, at which point the Mongols would turn and attack the disorderly, disorganized troops. The men of Khwarazm did follow, but at a distance, and Jalal kept them in order. Seeing that the Khwarazm army was not taking the bait, Jebe ordered his men to turn and charge. With trumpets blaring and cymbals crashing, Jalal led his men in a charge, too, and the two armies clashed in the foothills above the Fergana Valley.

The Mongols' physical condition worked against them, and the heavy armor of the Khwarazm army gave them an advantage. Nonetheless, the Mongol method of fighting—wheeling around their enemy, firing lethal volleys of arrows into their ranks, then riding off to regroup and attack again—was still effective even in the Mongols' weakened condition. By the end of the day each side had lost about 15,000 men, but ultimately it was the Mongols who retreated back into the mountains. Jalal had a victory.

A LONGING FOR PRECIOUS THINGS

At his main camp, Karakorum, on the Orkhon River just north of the Gobi Desert, Genghis planned his invasion of the Khwarazm Empire. He divided the main force of his army into four divisions of 50,000 warriors each. Genghis and Subotai commanded one division, and Genghis's sons, Jöchi, Ögödei, and Chagatai, commanded the other three. When Jebe returned to Karakorum with the survivors of his battle against Jalal, he was assigned to Jöchi's division.

The Mongols rode directly toward Otrar, a well-fortified city defended by 80,000 men, to avenge their dishonored and murdered ambassadors and merchants. The Persian historian Ala-ad-Din Ata-Malik Juvaini said that as the Mongols advanced, the people of Otrar "beheld the surrounding countryside choked with horsemen and the air black as night with the dust of cavalry." The khan's three sons and Jebe surrounded Otrar, but Genghis and Subotai were nowhere to be seen.

Even with their siege engines and the experience and ingenuity of the Chinese engineers, it took the Mongols five months to breach the city walls. As the Mongols surged into the city, they broke with their usual policy of reserving the most useful inhabitants—instead, they massacred almost the entire population. But the battle was not over. The survivors of the garrison, along with the governor, Inalchuq, had barricaded themselves inside the citadel. From the battlements they witnessed the rape and slaughter of their families and friends, but they were powerless to help them.

Once all the inhabitants of Otrar had been killed or enslaved, the Mongols began a second siege, this time of the citadel. Those inside the citadel put up a desperate defense, but after two months the Chinese war machines battered down a portion of the wall, and the Mongols entered to massacre the last survivors. The garrison had run out of arrows, so the fighting inside the citadel was hand to hand. The governor had climbed onto the roof of his house, where he pried up the tiles and hurled them down on the Mongols. Any Mongol sharpshooter could have picked the frightened man off the roof, but Genghis Khan had given orders that Inalchuq must be taken alive, so the Mongols undermined the foundations of the house, and when it collapsed, hauled out the bruised but still living governor. They dragged Inalchuq to Genghis's headquarters many miles to the north where the great khan delivered his sentence: because the governor had such a longing for precious things, let molten silver be poured into his eyes and ears until he was dead.

Rationalizing Terror

The campaign in China had taught the Mongols how to be more efficient in plundering a town and disposing of its inhabitants. Before marching into the Khwarazm Empire, Genghis banned the Mongols' wild smash-and-grab style of looting, replacing it with a method that was more orderly and much more fruitful. After a town was conquered, the Mongols herded everyone outside the walls; once the town was empty, Genghis sent detachments in to go street by street, house by house, shop by shop, and load into carts everything of value.

Meanwhile, in the fields outside the city, the Mongols executed all the survivors of the city garrison whom they regarded as the greatest threat. Chinese clerks divided the civilians into groups: the most desirable from the Mongol point of view were scientists, artisans, and physicians, but they also prized individuals who spoke several languages or could manage camels and other domesticated animals. The second group they spared were strong young men who could do heavy physical labor such as assemble siege engines or build defensive earthworks. Healthy men and women would be sent to Mongolia as slaves, and others might be marched to far-off slave markets and sold. The sick, the disabled, the elderly, and the children comprised the final group—all these the Mongols killed.

In Europe and in Arab lands it was customary to spare aristocratic prisoners whose families or whose king would pay a high ransom to get them back. Because most of the noblemen who could be captured were also high-ranking officers in his enemy's army, Genghis considered it madness to ransom an experienced commander so he could fight the Mongols again at some future date.

As Genghis saw it, the best thing to do with captive noblemen was execute them. As for noblewomen, as long as they were healthy their lives could be spared, but they would spend the rest of their days in slavery.

When the Mongols captured the city of Urgench, they found Ala ad-Din Muhammad's mother. The Mongols killed all the members of her court, as well as two dozen members of her family. Then they sent the miserable woman with other captives to be sold as slaves in Mongolia. No one knows what became of the Empress Mother of Khwarazm. No doubt she spent the rest of her life sweeping out her master's *ger*, cooking his food, and tending his livestock.

Genghis even found a use for refugees. Experience had taught him that fear could be a very effective weapon in a military campaign; consequently, every time he destroyed a city he spared the lives of a few of the inhabitants—they would spread the news of Mongol cruelty and invincibility, which would persuade other cities to surrender and live rather than resist and be destroyed.

A NATURAL TARGET

After the fall of Otrar, the sons of Genghis traveled through the Syr Darya region, picking off the many towns and fortresses that guarded the Khwarazm Empire's eastern frontier. As for Genghis Khan, he still had not set foot in the land of the shah.

Then, unexpectedly, early in 1220, he appeared west of Bukhara, at the rear of the shah's forces. It was incomprehensible: Genghis, accompanied by Subotai, had led his 50,000 men north to a distant ford of the Syr Darya and marched into the Kyzyl Kum Desert, a wasteland the people of Khwarazm had always regarded as impassable. Yet Genghis and his Mongols had made the 400-mile (640-kilometer) trek and taken Muhammad's army completely by surprise.

> THE GENERALS PERSUADED ONE ANOTHER THAT IF THEY ESCAPED BUKHARA WITH THEIR TROOPS AND GATHERED REINFORCEMENTS, THEN THEY COULD ENGAGE THE MONGOLS ON THEIR OWN TERMS AND DRIVE THEM FROM THE SHAH'S EMPIRE. BUKHARA WOULD HAVE TO BE SACRIFICED.

Genghis's goal was Bukhara, one of the great cities of the Muslim world. For centuries it had been a cradle of poets, artists, historians, mathematicians, and Islamic scholars. The city's schools trained students in all the sciences, in law, and in music. And of course, Bukhara was famous for its workshops where the famous Bukhara carpets were woven. After Samarkand, it was the second-most important city in Muhammad's empire. For all these reasons Bukhara was a natural target for Genghis Khan.

A garrison of 20,000 Turkish troops manned the battlements, but their generals believed that number was insufficient to defeat the Mongols. The generals persuaded one another that if they escaped Bukhara with their troops and gathered reinforcements, then they could engage the Mongols on their own terms and drive them from the Shah's empire. Bukhara would have to be sacrificed.

On the appointed night a flotilla of boats and ships of every size filled the Zeravshan River almost from shore to shore. As quietly as they were able, the 20,000 Turkish troops clambered aboard the boats, eager to sail down the river before dawn, before the Mongols who had besieged the city could see them. But their desertion did not go undetected—Mongol scouts reported the garrison's movements to Genghis, who sent a large detachment to follow the Turks and prepare an ambush. A few miles from Bukhara, when the garrison waded ashore, the Mongols fell on them, killing almost every man.

Back in Bukhara, the senior civilian officials as well as the chief imams resolved to surrender to Genghis, hoping he would spare them because they had not so much as fired a single arrow at his men. Genghis granted the city clemency, but his mercy did not extend to the city's governor and his guard, who had locked themselves inside Bukhara's citadel—Genghis would deal with them later.

THE WRATH OF GOD

When Genghis rode into Bukhara to inspect the city, he was astonished by the beauty and size of the buildings. Stopping outside one particularly impressive structure, he asked if it was the palace of the shah. No, a man replied, it was the Friday Mosque, the house of Allah. Genghis dismounted and entered. Seeing the *mimber*, or pulpit, he climbed up and addressed the crowd that had followed him inside. "In the countryside there is neither fodder nor meat," he told the crowd. "My horses are hungry, my men want food. Open your storehouses."

The keepers of the storehouses hurried away to do the khan's bidding, but the Mongols had not waited, and had already broken down the storehouse doors.

Genghis made the mosque his headquarters. He commanded the noblemen and imams to groom and feed his horses inside the sanctuary. He called for musicians and dancers to come and entertain him. Because there were no mangers in the mosque, the khan's men opened

Speaking from the *mimber*, or pulpit, of the Friday Mosque in Bukhara, Genghis Khan demanded food for his men and fodder for his horses. Genghis made the mosque his headquarters during his siege in 1220. Or 2780 fol.61 Genghis Khan addressing a congregation at the mosque in Bukhara, from a Shahinshanama, c.1397-98 (vellum), Persian School, (14th century) / British Library, London, UK / The Bridgeman Art Library International

the exquisitely wrought containers that held copies of the Koran, dumped out the holy books, and filled the empty chests with fodder. They lit cooking fires on the marble floors, and spent the rest of the night in a wild celebratory banquet. Bukhara's Chief Imam, Mevlana, who was forced to tend a Mongol warrior's horse, looked on while his magnificent mosque was profaned and lamented, "The wrath of God has overtaken us!"

The next day the Mongols herded all the citizens of the town into the fields beyond the walls, and then began stripping Bukhara of its treasures. Once the city had been picked clean, the Mongols turned their attention to the governor and his men. Archers fired flaming arrows into the citadel, and soon the fortress was engulfed in flames from which no one escaped.

Suddenly, to the grief of the citizens, the fire leapt over the citadel walls to a few neighboring buildings. Although the palaces and mosques and madrassas, or Islamic schools, were constructed of stone, the rest of Bukhara was built of wood. As the fire roared through the streets and alleys, the Mongols made no effort to fight it—after all, there was nothing of value left in the city. When the fire had subsided and Bukhara was a vast smoking ruin, the Mongols forced the inhabitants to tear down the city walls and the stone structures and dump the debris into the moat. Aside from low piles of rubble, nothing remained of Bukhara.

True to his word, Genghis spared the citizens of Bukhara, permitting them to go and find shelter where they could. But he made one exception—strong young men were taken from their families and sent under guard as forced labor at the siege of Samarkand.

A MISCALCULATION

Now Genghis turned his army toward Samarkand, Muhammad Shah's capital, about 167 miles (268 kilometers) from Bukhara. With its double ring of defensive walls, twelve iron gates, twenty-four defensive towers, a population of half a million, and a garrison that numbered 100,000, Samarkand was the strongest city in Muhammad Shah's realm.

Genghis hoped to find his nemesis there, but at the first warning that the Mongols were marching on the city, Muhammad had mounted his fastest horse and ridden away, leaving lesser officers to defend his capital. As the Mongols approached the city, about 50,000

The Fate of Nishapur

One city that surrendered was Nishapur, the home of the renowned Persian poet Omar Khayyam. After accepting the city's submission, Genghis Khan left a few Mongol administrators behind and moved on to the next town. The people of Nishapur, thinking they had found a chink in the Mongol armor, rose up and killed the khan's administrators, and took control again of their city. When word of the uprising reached Genghis, he marched his army back to Nishapur and prepared to storm the town.

During the battle a Persian arrow struck and killed the khan's son-in-law, Tokuchar. To console his daughter, Genghis asked her to decide Nishapur's fate: the grieving widow demanded the death of every man, woman, and child in the town.

And she wanted one thing more—the Mongol warriors were to decapitate the corpses and arrange the heads in three separate piles—for men, women, and children.

Of course, the Mongols did not have a monopoly on atrocities. On one occasion Jalal al-Din captured 400 Mongol warriors. He had the prisoners tied behind horses and forced to run to the city of Isfahan, where all were taken into the main square and publicly tortured to death. On another occasion, a Khwarazm commander executed his Mongol prisoners by hammering nails into their skulls—a method of execution that was intended to outrage the Mongols, who believed the head was sacred because it was the dwelling place of the soul.

Persian infantry marched onto the plain outside the city walls, and braced themselves for the famous Mongol charge. But instead the Mongols feigned a retreat. Believing they had the upper hand, the Persian infantry pursued the enemy. They were far from the safety of the city walls when the Mongols sprung their trap: the retreating horsemen suddenly turned and charged, while more Mongols came out of their hiding places, first to attack the Samarkand infantry's right and left flanks, then to circle behind and cut off any possibility of retreat. The Persian chroniclers say that none of those troops survived the Mongol ambush.

The defeat demoralized the rest of the garrison and the people of Samarkand. Five days later the Kankali Turkish troops, allies of the Persians, collected their families and their belongings and deserted to the Mongol side. It is said that the Turks numbered 30,000. With their garrison so severely depleted, the people of Samarkand gave up the fight.

The Kankali Turks congratulated themselves on their foresight, but they had miscalculated; Genghis Khan despised traitors. He sent his men among the Kankalis to kill them all.

As for the inhabitants of Samarkand, they were driven onto the plain. Genghis appointed a sheikh governor of the district and spared 50,000 men, women, and children. As usual, men with useful skills were separated from the crowd, along with sturdy young men for the work crews. The rest of the people of Samarkand, perhaps as many as 400,000, were slaughtered.

THE FLIGHT OF THE SHAH

The fall of Bukhara and Samarkand, along with the destruction of his armies and the capture of his mother, unnerved Muhammad Shah. He no longer thought of driving out the Mongols, only of saving his skin. First he rode south toward the Afghan border. In a Muslim country he might find allies and fresh troops to help him reclaim his empire, and in those wild mountains it would be nearly impossible for the Mongols to track him, unless some Afghan tribesman betrayed him. So the shah fled to the province of Kharasan on what is now Iran's eastern border. He stopped for a time in the Shi'ite shrine city of Qazvin, but there was no place where Muhammad felt safe. "I will rout him out," Genghis had sworn. "I will devastate any country that gives him refuge."

To make good on his oath, Genghis sent 20,000 men under Subotai and Jebe to hunt down the shah. Thanks to good intelligence, the two generals picked up the shah's trail quickly, and by ordering their horsemen to change mounts often, the Mongols covered 80 miles (128 kilometers) or more per day.

The shah's situation was desperate. His son, Jalal al-Din, was pinned down fighting the Mongols in the north; Muhammad's great army was destroyed; his immense wealth was reduced to what he had with him; and his retinue was a few hundred men, many of questionable loyalty. Afraid that some in his entourage might murder him in his sleep, Muhammad began slipping out of his pavilion after dark to spend the night in a nondescript tent such as a common soldier used. One morning he returned to his pavilion and found it riddled with Persian arrows.

The lords of Persia's rural provinces had offered many thousands of troops to their shah, but battle was no longer on Muhammad's mind. He rejected the offer and rode hard toward Baghdad, where he hoped the caliph's army could drive off any Mongol attack. Outside the town of Hamadan, some Mongols caught up with the shah and skirmished with his followers, but they did not recognize Muhammad among the fighters. In an effort to throw off Subotai and Jebe, the shah turned away from Baghdad and galloped with a small entourage to the Caspian Sea. The ruse worked, and he reached the sea before the Mongols realized their mistake.

From the town of Astara the shah escaped with his followers by boat to a tiny island in the Caspian Sea. Sick, weak, and exhausted, Muhammad Shah died there, completely destitute. There was not even a clean piece of cloth to use for the shah's shroud, so one of Muhammad's attendants stripped off his shirt and the body was wrapped in that. The shah's few companions buried the body in an unmarked grave, then scattered before the Mongols came. Subotai and Jebe found the island where Muhammad Shah had died, but they never discovered the grave. It did not matter—the shah was gone and Genghis Khan was now lord of the Khwarazm Empire.

CHAPTER 10

THE MONGOL STYLE
OF WARFARE

T HE MONGOLS ARE FAMOUS AS SUPERB HORSEMEN, AMONG THE BEST THE WORLD HAS EVER KNOWN. IT WAS A SKILL, OF COURSE, BUT IT WAS ALSO A NECESSITY: GIVEN THE IMMENSE SIZE OF THE STEPPE, HORSEBACK WAS THE ONLY WAY A MONGOL COULD COVER A GREAT DISTANCE SWIFTLY AND IN COMFORT.

Once they left the steppe, however, they found that their traditional well-honed cavalry tactics were useless against walled towns and fortresses. It is part of Genghis Khan's genius that he learned to adapt to these new circumstances and triumph over his enemies.

The relationship between a Mongol warrior and his officers and commanders was not just hierarchical; it was also personal. An officer who abandoned a wounded Mongol warrior on the battlefield was executed on the spot. The lives of his warriors were precious to Genghis Khan, who avoided hand-to-hand combat whenever possible because it increased casualties among his men. On an open battlefield, he avoided a direct, all-out charge into the enemy's ranks, preferring a variety of cavalry and archery maneuvers that kept the Mongols at a safe distance of 200 to 300 yards (183 to 274 meters) from an enemy's front ranks.

The Mongols' favorite tactic, feigning a retreat to draw out the enemy, has already been discussed. But they had other ways to mislead and intimidate their enemies. One night in 1204, when Genghis was at war with the Naiman tribe, he ordered each of his men to light five campfires, each some distance apart, to create the impression that the Mongol force was five times larger than its actual size. Also, if the Mongols knew they were outnumbered, they sent a few warriors to the

Mongols wore fur caps with earflaps, heavy wool pants, thick-soled riding boots, and a *deel*, a heavy, ankle-length wool robe. They wore no armor into battle.

rear, had them tie tree branches to their horses' trails, and ride back toward the main army. The branches dragging on the ground stirred up a great cloud of dust that led the enemy to believe that Mongol reinforcements had arrived.

SELF-SUFFICIENCY ON THE BACK OF A HORSE

Mobility was key to the Mongols' success in battle. They were an all-cavalry army, at a time when every other army was dominated by infantry. Furthermore, each Mongol warrior brought three or four horses with him; when one horse was tired, he switched to a fresh mount. By rotating through his private "herd," the Mongol ensured that each horse received three or four days of rest before it was mounted again. When speed was a factor, the Mongols would change mounts several times during a single day, a system that enabled them to cover up to 80 miles (128 kilometers) between dawn and dusk—an astonishing achievement at a time when most commanders were pleased if their army traveled 15 miles (24 kilometers) in a day.

Each Mongol warrior carried his equipment in a single skin bag, yet what he did carry made him self-sufficient. To make fires he carried flints; to sharpen his iron or steel-tipped arrows he brought a file; he had a lasso for rounding up livestock or pulling enemy riders from their horses. He had a small cooking pot and a fishing line. He had two canteens, one for water, another for dried curds of mare's milk. And he brought along rations of dried meat. The bag in which the Mongol carried his equipment was not only waterproof but also was so tightly sewn that it could be inflated and used as a flotation device when fording a river.

A Mongol's clothing consisted of heavy wool pants, a fur cap with earflaps, thick-soled riding boots, and a *deel*, a heavy ankle-length wool robe. Some men wore into battle a jerkin or tunic made of laquered, interwoven strips of leather. This, along with a thick raw silk undershirt, was often their only form of armor. One man in ten carried a tent for himself and the other nine men in his squad.

Each Mongol was armed with a dagger, a hatchet, a sword, perhaps two or three javelins, and a light shield made of leather pulled tightly over a wicker frame. Some Mongols had a mace, a battle-ax, or a twelve-foot-long lance from which a hook protruded—the hook could be used to snag an enemy rider and wrench him off his horse.

But the most important weapon in every Mongol's arsenal was the bow. Typically, each warrior carried two bows, and they were always made the same way: thin layers of horn and animal sinew were glued to a wooden frame and then lacquered to make it waterproof. The double curve of a Mongol bow (as opposed to the single curve of an English longbow) made an arrow travel faster, farther, and with more power. (For more information about the Mongol bow, see chapter 1.)

CHINESE MEDICS

The Mongols brought their herds of sheep and cattle with them, milking and slaughtering them along the way. For variety and to save their own supplies, they looted stores of food from enemy farms and towns. Sometimes, if they were not pressed for time, they hunted wild game.

A Mongol camp was organized according to an unchanging pattern. No matter how late a division or a detachment might arrive at camp, it knew its assigned position exactly. The commanders and officers' tents stood in the center, surrounded by guards, and then by the general mass of soldiers.

For each 1,000 men there was a medical team. After Genghis's conquest of Jin China, the medical units were staffed by skilled Chinese physicians. These Chinese medical men also introduced an innovation to Mongol battle gear: because Mongol warriors lacked chain mail, the Chinese doctors suggested they wear a shirt of thick, tightly woven raw silk next to their skin. Any arrow that struck a Mongol would be impeded by the shirt, making a much less serious wound. Mongol warriors knew from experience that arrow wounds were difficult to tend. The barbs of some arrowheads made them onerous to extract—they either had to be cut out or pushed through and out the other side of the torso or limb, a process that was agonizingly painful, created even more damage than the original wound, and increased the likelihood of infection.

The Chinese surgeons explained that the silk fabric would prevent the arrow from burying itself deep in a warrior's flesh. To remove the arrow, the surgeon pulled the silk gently, forcing the arrowhead to pop out of the wound, thereby causing less damage to the surrounding tissue. Although the Chinese medics convinced the Mongols to wear silk undershirts, they had no success in persuading the Mongols to bathe or wash their clothes. Consequently, the risk of infected wounds remained a problem.

FOUR-FOOTED VETERANS

It comes as no surprise that Mongol warriors valued their horses above all their other possessions. It would not be going too far to say that the Mongols regarded them more like companions than equipment. A horse that had been ridden in battle was treated like a veteran soldier. When a horse was too old, ill, or lame for fighting, it was not killed but was put out to pasture for the rest of its life. There was one exception: at the death of a Mongol warrior, his favorite horse was killed so man and horse could be buried together and their spirits ride through all eternity in the afterlife. At Genghis's funeral, forty of his horses were sacrificed and buried with the great khan.

It was common for Mongols to deck out their horses with elaborate harnesses and saddles decorated with copper or silver. Mongols who rode the warhorses of the heavy cavalry protected their mounts with armor that covered the head, shoulders, and chest.

In the thirteenth century, when Genghis Khan conquered northern China and Kublai Khan conquered southern China, there was a minor industry among Chinese sculptors, painters, and porcelain makers to turn out lovely images of horses, because that was the one subject that was certain to appeal to China's Mongol overlords. (For more information on Mongol horses, see chapter 1.)

ORGANIZING THE HORDES

Genghis was the supreme commander of his army. He consulted with his generals and his inner circle of trusted advisors, but the ultimate formulation of a plan or strategy belonged to him. Once he had delivered his plan to his generals, however, they were free to execute it as seemed best to them, taking into consideration terrain, the strengths and weaknesses of the enemy, the condition of their own troops, and a host of other factors that could determine victory or defeat. And Genghis wanted victories. If his generals had to tinker with his strategy to achieve it, he did not object.

Because the Mongols had no written language, conveying orders accurately along the line during a march or in the middle of battle was a problem. To make it easier to memorize a message, officers composed their orders in simple rhymes set to well-known tunes. This was extremely effective because the Mongols, like other nonliterate societies, had excellent memorization skills.

As Genghis's sons reached adulthood he made them commanders over various armies, also known as *ordus*, from which is derived the English word *horde*. Originally, an *ordu* was a collection of *gers* in which dwelt the household of a Mongol chief—not unlike the royal court of a king. When Genghis assigned armies to his sons, the term *ordu* came to be applied to the household or court each son gathered around himself, as well as to the prince's thousands of fighting men.

When Genghis named his sons commanders the title was, by and large, honorary because the actual military decisions for each of the armies was made by Genghis's generals. As the princes mastered the art of war, they were given more authority over their hordes. From the time he first became a chieftain, Genghis had always emphasized skill and merit over birth and rank, and he applied that principle even to his own sons.

BECAUSE THE MONGOLS HAD NO WRITTEN LANGUAGE, CONVEYING ORDERS ACCURATELY ALONG THE LINE DURING A MARCH OR IN THE MIDDLE OF BATTLE WAS A PROBLEM. TO MAKE IT EASIER TO MEMORIZE A MESSAGE, OFFICERS COMPOSED THEIR ORDERS IN SIMPLE RHYMES SET TO WELL-KNOWN TUNES.

The elite division in Genghis's army was the Kashik, or Imperial Guard, a body of 1,000 of the finest, most experienced warriors, men he trusted absolutely. They guarded the khan around the clock, and during battle they surrounded him completely so no enemy warrior could come near him. To distinguish the Kashik from the rest of his army, Genghis dressed his guard in black *kalats*, or tunics, gave them black armor, and mounted them on black horses. In time of war they were careful of their khan's safety; in time of peace they trained every day, all day long. Because they were occupied continuously, the Kashik had slaves who did all the things other Mongol warriors did for themselves—raised their tents, cooked their food, cleaned their clothes and equipment, and groomed their horses.

THE GREAT HUNT

Mongols began training for war when they were still young boys, when their fathers gave them their lessons in riding and shooting a bow. Constant practice at horsemanship and archery throughout childhood and adolescence produced in every generation an army of young men who were accomplished riders and skilled marksmen. But Genghis Khan wanted more from his Mongols—they had to learn to act as a cohesive unit. To achieve this, he introduced the Great Hunt.

At the beginning of each winter (assuming the Mongols were not occupied by war), every warrior assembled at a specified location for a three-month-long hunt. The Mongols were stretched across the steppe along a line 80 miles (128 kilometers) long. Riding deliberately they flushed out all manner of wild game, and drove the animals before them. On a certain day the right and left wings of the column would pivot forward, driving the game toward the center. The final maneuver completely encircled the animals, forming what historian James Chambers has described as "a huge human amphitheater with thousands of terrified animals crowded into its arena."

During the drive no animal could be killed and no animal was permitted to escape; a man who let even a rabbit find its way through the Mongol line was punished—and so was his commanding officer. The purpose of this regulation was to test the warriors' watchfulness and agility. In the case of truly dangerous animals—wolves, tigers, and boar—it was a test of a warrior's courage and resourcefulness to prevent them from escaping without wounding or killing the animals.

On the final day of the hunt Genghis rode into the center of the circle to kill whatever animals he wished. Then he withdrew to high ground to observe the rest of the hunt. Wild game such as deer were shot down with arrows, but many warriors, their adrenaline pumping for three months with no release, embraced the hunt as an opportunity to display their courage. There are stories of men dismounting and entering the circle with a sword to fight packs of wolves or wild boar.

A Mongol chief holds an arrow, the most important weapon in every Mongol's arsenal. An arrow shot from a Mongol bow could travel 350 yards (320 meters), 100 yards (91 meters) farther than an arrow shot from a standard longbow. A Turkoman or Mongol Chief holding an Arrow, from the Large Clive Album, 1591-92 (paint on cotton), Persian School, (16th century) / Victoria & Albert Museum, London, UK / The Stapleton Collection / The Bridgeman Art Library International

SONG
EMPIRE

Yangtze

There are also accounts of Mongols, crazed with a kind of battle frenzy, who fought tigers with their bare hands (and, of course, were killed).

The Great Hunt was never permitted to become a massacre. By tradition, a delegation of elderly men and young princes would approach Genghis and beg for clemency for the animals. The khan would grant it, and the circle would break up so the surviving beasts could escape to their natural habitats.

Throughout the three months of the hunt the divisions and detachments of warriors received orders that required them to maneuver as one or some of the animals would escape. The hunt, then, was a massive drill that accustomed the entire Mongol army to executing complicated maneuvers on the battlefield without giving any advantage to the enemy force.

PILOTS ON HORSEBACK

Typically, the Mongol army went into battle arrayed in five ranks, two of heavy cavalry and three of light cavalry (the men and horses of the heavy cavalry wore heavy metal armor, while the light cavalry wore leather and silk armor or no armor at all). The light cavalry dashed back and forth in front of the enemy lines, peppering them with arrows. If the enemy advanced, the Mongol light cavalry retreated, but turned in their saddles, continuing to fire arrows behind them. They could perform this maneuver because they had stirrups, an innovation that many historians have come to believe were invented by the Huns, another nation of Central Asian nomads who may have been related to the Mongols.

Although archaeologists have never found stirrups in any Hun's grave, that is not entirely unexpected—the Huns were not metalworkers, and their stirrups were probably made of leather or perhaps leather and wood, material that would decompose in a grave. The ancient Romans and other European peoples did not have stirrups, but after the Huns' invasion of the Roman Empire in the fifth century C.E., stirrups began to appear in Europe. This circumstance has led some historians to conclude that the Huns introduced the stirrup to Western Europe.

The stirrups gave a rider stability; they served as a kind of mini fighting platform from which the rider could swing a sword or fire a

Previous page: The Great Hunt was a three-month-long drill that schooled the Mongol army in acting as a huge but cohesive unit, executing complicated maneuvers they could then use on the battlefield.

bow without fear of losing his balance and falling off his horse. The early twentieth-century military historian Basil H. Liddell Hart wrote that with their withering firepower and remarkable mobility, mounted Mongol warriors were the forerunner of pilots of fighter aircraft.

BURNING TAR BARRELS AND GUNPOWDER BOMBS

A favorite Mongol tactic was the *mangudai*, a kind of suicide charge in which the light cavalry attacked the enemy head on, only to break up and scatter before striking the front lines. The Mongols hoped the seeming confusion of the *mangudai* charge would lure the enemy into charging after the retreating light cavalry, at which point the heavy cavalry would attack, and Mongol archers would leap out of their hiding places to mow down the disorganized enemy troops, thereby causing even more havoc.

Typically, the Mongol light cavalry bore the brunt of the fighting. Only after they had weakened and confused the enemy were the heavy cavalry brought out to finish the job. To the pounding of a huge kettledrum known as a *naccara*, the heavy cavalry rode at a trot, bearing down on the enemy in complete silence. Finally, screaming their war cry, the heavy cavalry lowered their lances and hurtled themselves into the ranks of their demoralized foes.

THE EARLY TWENTIETH-CENTURY MILITARY HISTORIAN BASIL H. LIDDELL HART WROTE THAT WITH THEIR WITHERING FIREPOWER AND REMARKABLE MOBILITY, MOUNTED MONGOL WARRIORS WERE THE FORERUNNER OF PILOTS OF FIGHTER AIRCRAFT.

Held in reserve at the rear were the Mongols' catapults. A light model could throw a 2-pound (1-kilogram) missile more than 100 yards (91 meters), while the heavy catapult could throw a 25-pound (11-kilogram) missile more than 150 yards (137 meters). Mongols used their catapults to hurl burning containers of tar at the enemy front lines,

which gave them the cover of a smoke screen. Their Chinese engineers made incendiary bombs and grenades that caused panic when they landed amid men and horses. Toward the end of the thirteenth century, the Chinese invented gunpowder bombs for their Mongol masters, which caused even more damage on the battlefield.

The catapults and other siege weapons both fascinated and delighted the Mongols. First, the men firing the machines were well outside the range of enemy fire and virtually free from any risk of the hand-to-hand fighting the Mongols abhorred. Second, the catapults' missiles resulted in so much more damage, death, and chaos than even the most accurate Mongol archers could inflict on the enemy.

The curved Mongol bow is depicted in this fourteenth-century Persian manuscript illustration. The double curve of a Mongol bow made an arrow travel faster, farther, and with more power than the standard English longbow. © SuperStock / SuperStock 463-7369-I-P30D

WINNING WAS THE ONLY THING

The Mongols took pride in winning. Commanders of other nations who tried to buck up their defeated troops by praising them for fighting well (although not successfully) would have mystified the Mongols. A fight that did not end in victory was a source of disgrace. Furthermore, the Mongols had a second requirement for victory—the complete annihilation of the enemy army. That is why, after capturing a city, Genghis Khan always had his men massacre the garrison.

At the Battle of the Sajo River in Hungary in 1241, the Mongols had the army of the king of Hungary completely surrounded, when suddenly they backed away, creating an opening through which the Hungarian troops could escape back to Budapest. The Hungarians stripped off their armor, threw down their weapons, and ran—which made them easier targets than when they were surrounded but still armed. The Mongols took their time giving chase, slaughtering the panicky, defenseless men along the road and hunting them down in hiding places in the woods and villages along the way. By the time the Mongols were finished—and they pursued the Hungarians all the way to the gates of Budapest—between 50,000 and 70,000 Hungarian fighting men lay dead. It did not matter to the Mongols that they had won by playing a cruel trick on their enemy; all that mattered was that they had won, and they were poised for their next victory.

CHAPTER 11

THE PASSING OF GENGHIS KHAN

■ ■ ■

BY SUMMER 1222, THE LAST HOLDOUT OF THE KHWARAZM EMPIRE, THE CITY OF MULTAN IN MODERN-DAY PAKISTAN, HAD FALLEN TO GENGHIS KHAN. IT WAS SAID THAT ALEXANDER THE GREAT HAD PASSED THROUGH MULTAN EN ROUTE TO HIS INVASION OF INDIA. PERHAPS INSPIRED BY THE EXPLOITS OF THE YOUNG CONQUEROR, GENGHIS, NOW ABOUT SIXTY YEARS OLD, DID THE SAME. HE LED HIS ARMY OUT OF THE MOUNTAINS OF THE PUNJAB AND ONTO THE PLAINS OF THE INDUS RIVER. THERE HE WOULD SUFFER HIS FIRST GREAT DEFEAT.

The Mongols were acclimated to the biting cold of the steppe and dry heat of the deserts, but they were entirely unprepared for the stifling humidity of India during the monsoon months, June through November. Both men and horses fell sick and began to die. Even the Mongols' bows were affected by the muggy atmosphere: they warped, making them useless in battle.

Nonetheless, Genghis would not retreat. He captured a few northern Indian cities and towns, slaughtered a few garrisons and local populations, and rounded up thousands of potentially useful prisoners. But his army could not operate properly in India. Finally, in February 1223, Genghis ordered his men to prepare to return to Mongolia. But once again the seasons worked against him, for he tried to cross the Himalayas in winter. The Mongols forced their thousands of captives to clear the passes of snow, yet they made slow progress, and

Genghis Khan's third son, Ögödei, was the compromise candidate for ruler of the Mongol empire after a violent quarrel broke out between the two eldest sons, Jöchi and Chagatai, following Genghis's death.

no one knows how many prisoners and Mongols died trying to cross the mountains.

When at last Genghis and his men reached home, he called for a *naadam*, a raucous victory celebration of feasting, music, dancing, and the traditional Mongol games—horse races, wrestling matches, and archery competitions. It was the most luxurious *naadam* in Mongol history. For almost twenty years, as Genghis subdued Xi Xia, northern China, and then the Muslim lands of the Khwarazm Empire, a seemingly endless string of caravans had been bringing countless slaves, captives with rare talents, and a flood of luxury goods to the Mongol camps. For this *naadam*, Chinese and Persian chefs cooked, slaves from many nations served, while the Mongols, dressed in silk robes, lounged on soft Bukhara carpets, propped up on silk and velvet cushions looted from countless palaces. They drank *airag* from gold or silver bowls and cut their meat with knives made of Damascene steel while musicians and dancers from China and the Muslim world entertained them. And their mothers, wives, and daughters feasted with the men: the slaves Genghis sent back to Mongolia had freed Mongol women from the drudgery of housekeeping.

THE LAST CAMPAIGN

For three years Genghis Khan rested at home in Karakorum. Although he was master of an immense empire, he still lived in a *ger*, just as he had since childhood. But now he possessed so much wealth that it seemed prudent to have a complex of buildings where his loot could be kept safe. The buildings were designed by captive architects and erected by slaves under the supervision of captive engineers. In addition to storehouses, Genghis also constructed an audience hall. Christian envoys who visited him were struck by how closely the khan's audience hall resembled a church: it was a long, narrow building with a high roof. Visitors approached up a long aisle, at the end of which sat Genghis Khan, surrounded by his sons and his generals. Very likely it was here that Genghis planned his last campaign.

It had been more than a decade since Genghis had forced the emperor of the Tanguts to acknowledge him as his overlord and agree to send annual tribute to the great khan. Recently, however, Burkhan, the Tangut emperor, had lost the servility that Genghis expected of his client kings. When Genghis began his invasion of the Khwarazm Empire, he demanded a Tangut army to reinforce his own; Burkhan replied that if Genghis did not believe he could win this war he should not begin it. At the time, occupied as he was with conquering Muhammad Shah, Genghis could not afford the distraction of punishing the Tangut emperor. But he had not forgotten that act of defiance, and in 1226 he was ready to punish the Tanguts.

During the winter of 1226 to 1227, when he was sixty-two, Genghis retraced his route to Xi Xia across the Gobi Desert. At one point he stopped to round up some wild horses. When a pack of them charged the khan, his own horse took fright and threw Genghis to the ground. The fall may have caused an undiagnosed internal injury, because soon he was running a fever. He had brought along one of his wives, Yesui, who pleaded with Genghis to return to Karakorum where he could rest and Chinese physicians would take care of him. But Genghis refused.

Although he was ill and in pain, he kept up the campaign against the Tanguts for six months, until the summer of 1227, when he could no longer get out of bed. No surviving document gives an account of the final hours of Genghis Khan, nor is there an oral tradition regarding the date of his death, but we do possess a description of his funeral.

Yesui supervised all the arrangements. Genghis's body was washed; dressed in a white robe, boots, and a hat; then wrapped in a white felt blanket. Tucked amid the folds were pieces of aromatic sandalwood that would keep insects away from the corpse. The felt blanket was bound around the body by three golden straps. Three days after his death, Genghis's body was laid inside a cart and a procession was formed to escort him home. Behind the cart a warrior carried the khan's Spirit Banner. This was followed by a female shaman who led Genghis's favorite horse. Behind them came the mourners, including armed warriors, who, according to the traditional account of Genghis's funeral procession, killed every animal and human they encountered along the way, supposedly to keep the location of the great khan's grave a secret.

In 2006 archaeologists working in the Arjai Grotto in Inner Mongolia discovered a fresco, 20 inches long by 14 inches high (51 by 35 centimeters), that depicts an elaborate Mongolian funeral. The scene shows a woman weeping in a palace and a well-dressed nobleman standing near the grave. Suspended over the open grave from the beaks of four white cranes is an ornate coffin in which lies the body of the deceased. The style of dress of the mourners, who stand amid traditional Mongol *gers*, suggests that the fresco depicts the funeral of an important man, whom some historians believe is Genghis Khan.

While on campaign against the Tanguts, Genghis Khan was thrown from his horse and suffered a serious internal injury. In 1227, he died as he had lived, in a felt tent, as shown in this fanciful eighteenth century artwork. He is surrounded by his four sons on his deathbed. Getty Images

There is a theory among scholars that the Mongols did not have a tomb culture, and the bodies of the dead were placed outdoors at some distance from the camp to be devoured by animals and returned to the elements. If this theory is correct, then the elaborate funeral and burial rites that attended Genghis's death is another example of how his life and career often broke with Mongol traditions.

The traditional account of Genghis's burial contradicts the painting. According to the oldest sources, a party of warriors and slaves escorted the body to an undisclosed location. After the slaves had buried Genghis, the warriors killed them, then rode their horses over the khan's grave to erase any trace that the ground had been dug up. Their final act of camouflage was to plant a copse of trees over the grave. According to another version of the burial story, a river was diverted to flow over the grave site. As for the warriors who escorted the body to its grave, once they returned to camp they were killed by their comrades. If the story sounds like a myth, at least one part of it is true—to this day no one knows where Genghis Khan lies buried.

Since the 1990s several archaeological teams have traveled to Mongolia in search of the grave. None has succeeded in finding it. Furthermore, they antagonized the majority of Mongolians who believe that disturbing Genghis's grave would be a gross sacrilege because the great khan's spirit resides there. Nonetheless, there are rumors about the fate of the body. One story tells how in 1937, Soviet troops found Genghis's body in a Buddhist monastery in Mongolia and carried it away to their own secret location. There is also a story about two unnamed French archaeologists who discovered the grave and soon thereafter died, the victims of a curse, much like the curse that guarded the tomb of the boy pharaoh, Tutankhamen.

Between 1954 and 1956 the People's Republic of China built a memorial to Genghis Khan at the town of Xinjie in Inner Mongolia. Inspired by the round Mongol *gers*, the memorial held artifacts believed to have belonged to Genghis Khan. During the Cultural Revolution of the 1960s, Red Guards destroyed the artifacts and tore down the memorial. It has been rebuilt, and replicas of the original relics are enshrined inside. Because the location of the khan's grave is unknown, the memorial has become the site for all ceremonies and celebrations of Genghis Khan's memory.

A FAMILY QUARREL

Genghis Khan had intended his eldest son, Jöchi, to succeed him. He made the announcement in a ceremonial way during a family meeting that he called specifically to settle the question of succession. It was a point of contention among Genghis's sons because they believed, as did most of the Mongols, and even Genghis himself, that Jöchi was the son of the Merkit who had kidnapped Börte forty years earlier. These suspicions were based on sound arithmetic: after Genghis had rescued her, Börte gave birth to Jöchi; for the child to have been fathered by Genghis, Börte's gestation period would have lasted at least twelve months. Nonetheless, Genghis always accepted Jöchi as his son and treated him as such.

According to *The Secret History of the Mongols*, at the family meeting Genghis invited Jöchi to speak first, as was the right of an eldest son on such an occasion. By acknowledging Jöchi as the firstborn, Genghis was stating that he recognized Jöchi as his legitimate heir. If the khan's younger sons sat quietly and listened to what Jöchi had to say, they would be acknowledging that he had seniority and authority over them. So Chagatai, Genghis and Börte's second-born, interrupted, demanding to know whether his father truly intended Jöchi to be the next khan. Before Genghis could answer Chagatai reminded everyone in the tent that Jöchi was illegitimate, the bastard son of a Merkit.

Enraged by the insult, Jöchi pounced on his brother, and the two men rolled about the floor, pummeling each other, while their father pleaded with them to stop. Finally, the brothers had to be pulled off one another, and the meeting broke up.

If Genghis insisted upon Jöchi as his successor, civil war—led by his own sons—might break out after his death, and that would be the end of the united Mongol nation and probably of the great Mongol Empire. So Genghis and his sons worked out a compromise—neither Jöchi nor Chagatai would become khan; instead, Genghis would be succeeded by his third-born son, Ögödei. As a testament of their good faith, Genghis had a scribe put the agreement in writing.

The compromise settled the succession, but it did nothing to repair the breach within the family. After their fight in their father's tent, Jöchi and Chagatai remained jealous and suspicious of each other. Jöchi's bitterness extended to his father, too—he refused to return home to celebrate Genghis's victory over Muhammad Shah, but remained in the Khwarazm lands. Jöchi and Genghis never saw each other again. In 1227 Jöchi died suddenly; no surviving document records the cause of death.

THE NEW KHAN

After his father had been buried, Ögödei, now about forty-three years old, celebrated his succession with a riot of feasting, drinking, and lavish gift-giving. He invited the generals, the nobles, the chief warriors, and his father's most trusted friends, as well as his own inner circle, and countless ordinary Mongols besides, to join him at Avarga, one of the places where Genghis had stored his plunder. Ögödei gave his guests pearls by the handful and bolts of silk. There was so much silk that the guests agreed to wear silk garments of the same color one day, and garments of a different color the next.

Merrymaking was Ögödei's favorite activity, and the Persian historian Juvaini claims that the new khan was ever "treading the path of excess in constant appreciation of wine and the company of beautiful women." The death of Genghis and Ögödei's reputation as a tippler emboldened some of the khan's vassals to stop sending their tribute. In 1230, Ögödei responded by sending 30,000 men to punish rebels in northern China and Central Asia. Ögödei did not accompany the army—he was not a warlord like his father. But he was an innovator, as the Mongol nation was about to learn.

Karakorum on the Orkhon River had been Genghis Khan's favorite campsite and essentially his capital. Although he had built permanent buildings at Karakorum to store his treasures, he continued to live in a felt *ger*. Ögödei was about to change that. He commanded his Chinese architects to build him a palace of stone and timber—the first permanent dwelling in Mongol history. It was a splendid residence: two wings, each about 350 yards (320 meters) long, connected by a

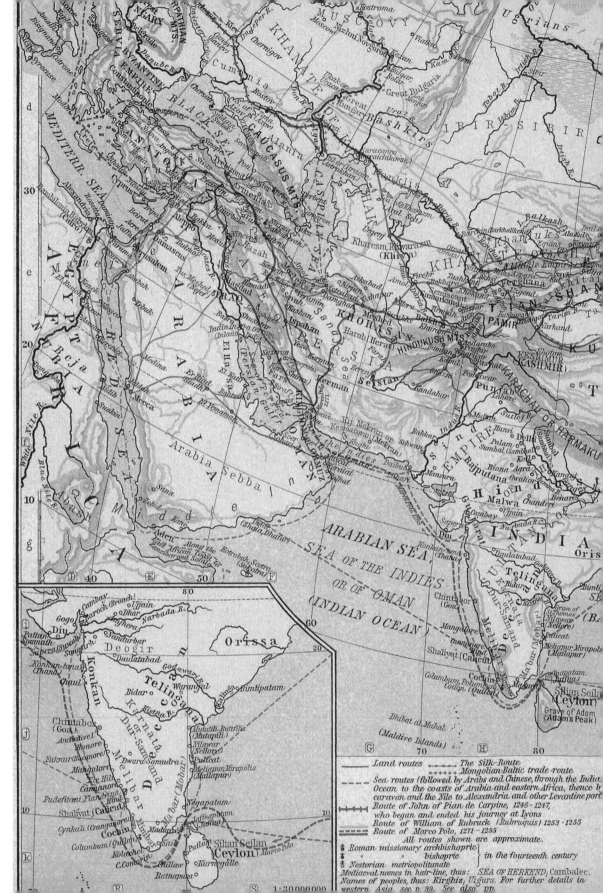

164

MUSCOVY
Nostroma
Ugrians
Nizhni Novgorod
Moscou

SERVIA
HUNGARY
BYZANTINE EMPIRE
Constantinople

KHANATE OF THE
Cumenia
Bashkirs
SIBIR
SIBIRO

BLACK SEA
CAUCASUS MTS.
Alania
Great Bulgaria

MEDITERR. SEA
ANTOLA
Armenia
Caspian Sea
KHAREZM (Khiva)
KHANATE OF
TIAN SHAN

Cyprus
ARMENIA
Hazah
KHORASAN
PAMIR
KASHMIR

EGYPT
(Cairo)
Jerusalem
Damascus
Aleppo
Mosul
IRAQ
Bagdad
Hamadan
Ispahan
PERSIA
Meshed
Herat
HINDUKUSH MTS.
KESHMIR
(KASHMIR)
KARACHAL OR HARMAKU

ARABIA
Medina
Mecca
Fars
Kerman
Seistan
Kandahar
PUNJAB
Lahore
SIND
EMPIRE
Rajputana
Delhi
INDIA

RED SEA
Arabia Sebba
Persian Gulf
GULF OF OMAN
the Indies
Mekran or Sewan
Kesnacoran (Mekran)
Sind
Rajputana
Malwa
Orissa

NUBIA
Beja
Aden
Abash
Sana
Zebid
Melind
(Zfgia, Dhafar)

ARABIAN SEA,
SEA OF THE INDIES
OR OF OMAN
INDIAN OCEAN
Konkan-tana
Thana
Chintabor
(Goa)
Telingana
Bidar
Mangalore
Melibar
Shaliyat (Calicut)
Cochin
Silan Seilan
(Ceylon)
Grave of Adam
(Adam's Peak)

Along the African coast to Zanzibar and Sofala
(Socotra)
Dhabat al Mahal
(Maldive Islands)

White Nile R.
Blue Nile R.

D 40   E 50   F   G 70   H 80

Orissa
80   60   20

Cambay
Baroch (Broach)
Ujjain
Dhar
Narbada R.
Gogo
Diu
Pattan
Somnath
Supera (Suvali)
Songirh
Nandurbar
Deogir
Daulatabad
Godaveri R.
Konkan-tana
Thana
Chaul
Telingana
Bidar
Warangal
Kistna R.
Kalinga
Bimlipatam
Konkan
Karnata
Dur-Samand
Chintabor
(Goa)
Andekive I.
Honore
Fakrur Bacanore
Mangalore
Ely Hill
Camanore
Pudefitani Flandrina
Hind
Shaliyat (Calicut)
Melibar
Mahatili Butfilie
(Mutapili)
Nilawar
(Nellore)
Iwara Samudra
Pulicat
Meliapur, Mirapolis
(Mailapur)
Negapatam
Cynkali (Cranganore)
Cochin
Columbum (Quilon)
Kolochel
C. Comari
Killaw
Ratnapura
Madura
Sadiuputtam
Putlan
Mabar Mobar
Silan Seilan
Ceylon
Marco Polo
Karmeyalle

Land routes ————— The Silk-Route
Mongolian-Baltic trade-route
— — — Sea routes (followed by Arabs and Chinese, through the Indian
Ocean to the coasts of Arabia and eastern Africa, thence by
caravan and the Nile to Alexandria and other Levantine ports
Route of John of Pian de Carpine, 1245–1247,
who began and ended his journey at Lyons
Route of William of Rubruck (Rubruquis) 1253–1255
Route of Marco Polo, 1271–1295
All routes shown are approximate.
Roman missionary archbishopric
„ „ bishopric } in the fourteenth century
Nestorian metropolitanate
Mediaeval names in hair-line, thus: SEA OF HERKEND, Cambalec.
Names of peoples, thus: Kirghiz, Uigurs. For further details in
western Asia, see p. 33. See also pp.

1:30 000 000

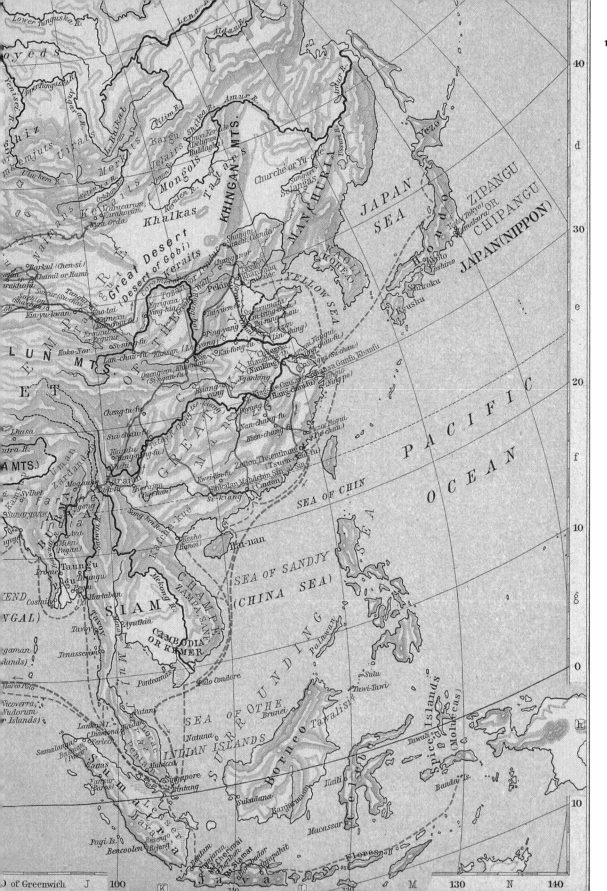

soaring central pavilion. Chinese artists adorned the interior walls and columns with murals and decorative abstract patterns.

The palace had a large garden, and in the center Ögödei's builders constructed an extravagant square gazebo with four large doors aligned according to the cardinal points of the compass. Inside stood a throne on a raised platform. Ögödei sat on the throne, his wives and concubines occupied the level below him, and on the level below the ladies stood the cupbearers, ready at all times to serve the khan more wine, which had become his favorite beverage.

Ögödei had slaves dig a series of artificial lakes that he could view from his garden throne. The lakes attracted flocks of waterfowl, and the khan enjoyed observing the birds, and watching his men hunt them.

TRADITION AT ODDS WITH INNOVATION

In addition to his grand palace, Ögödei built Buddhist and Taoist temples, a mosque, and a church, each staffed by monks, imams, and priests to serve the religious requirements of the members of the khan's court. Although Ögödei continued to practice the traditional Mongol religion, Genghis Khan's wars of conquest had brought the Mongols into closer contact with the various religions of Asia, and some Mongols had converted. At Ögödei's court, the Nestorian sect of Christians was especially prominent, not least because the khan and his three brothers each had a Christian wife. In fact, Ögödei's favorite grandson was a Christian named Shiremun, the Mongol form of Solomon. Historian Jack Weatherford believes that part of Christianity's appeal among Mongols was the name of *Jesus—Yesu* in Mongolian. Yesu means *nine*, the Mongols' sacred number. It also echoed the name of Genghis Khan's father, *Yesügei*.

Like his father, Ögödei was eager to attract merchants to Mongolia. He enacted a series of new regulations to make life easier for merchants, including standardized weights and measures throughout his empire, and he adopted that Chinese innovation, paper money, which was less cumbersome to carry on long treks than gold and silver. He established garrisons along the trade routes to protect merchants from robbers, and

Previous page: Like his father, Ögödei kept the trade routes between Europe and Asia open and secure, as shown in this map, reproduced on pp. 14–15 .

he even planted trees beside the roads that crossed the steppes to shade travelers in summer.

In one respect, however, Ögödei was not at all innovative. Everything the inhabitants of Karakorum needed—even food and water—had to be brought from great distances. The Mongols still had not settled down on farms, and aside from their herds of livestock, all grain, fruit, and vegetables had to be sent across the steppe in carts. Ögödei had founded his city far enough from the Orkhon River that human waste would not contaminate the water, but the wisdom of his decision did not make it any less tiresome for the slaves who were obliged to travel to the river to draw enough water to meet all the needs of the inhabitants. The city's dependence on outside sources for all the necessities of life made it vulnerable. If an enemy army ever laid siege to Karakorum, the city would be starved out in less than two weeks.

THE BANKRUPT KHAN

In spite of the flood of tribute that poured into Mongolia from the subject kingdoms of the empire and the wealth generated by merchants from every part of the known world, by 1235 Ögödei's treasuries were woefully depleted. It was not simply the expense of constructing a city from scratch that put the khan in danger of bankruptcy, but also his profligacy. A khan was expected to be generous to his people—certainly Genghis had been so. But Ögödei was careless about money; he showered the treasures of his empire on his family, generals, friends, and advisors, and on the Mongols in general. To revive his finances, he turned to the method Mongols had always employed when they were in dire circumstances—conquest.

He called a meeting of his generals and advisors to discuss the matter. Some believed Ögödei should invade India; the climate might be unhealthy, but it was a vast, rich country nonetheless. Others argued in favor of an invasion of southern China where the Sung dynasty reigned.

Subotai, Genghis's greatest commander, offered a fresh solution: an invasion of Europe. No one at the meeting had mentioned Europe, because none of them had ever been there. In 1220, during Genghis's conquest of the Khwarazm Empire, Subotai had made a reconnaissance foray into Georgia, a Christian kingdom between the Black and Caspian seas. As Subotai and Jebe were leading their army around the Caspian Sea in pursuit of the fugitive Muhammad Shah, the commanders decided to investigate Georgia and learn what they could about its military—intelligence that would be very useful if Genghis ever decided to invade Europe.

Centuries of defending their borders against Muslim armies had honed the Georgians' fighting skills. By the thirteenth century they possessed one of the finest armies in Eastern Europe, including an elite cavalry of 30,000 knights. When King George IV learned that a Mongol army of about 50,000 men was riding toward his southern border, he called out his cavalry, as well as 40,000 more mounted troops to meet the invaders. On the Kura Plain at the foot of the Caucasus Mountains, George and his army waited. Once the Mongols had formed up at the opposite end of the battlefield, the king gave the order and his cavalry thundered across the plain in an all-out charge. Subotai ordered his light cavalry to strafe the Georgians with armor-piercing arrows. In spite of heavy casualties, the Georgians pressed forward, and as they did so, the Mongols employed their classic tactic, the feigned retreat.

As the Mongols fled across the plain, the Georgian warhorses, burdened with their own armor and the armored knights who rode them, began to tire. As the Georgian cavalry became more and more dispersed across the field with their exhausted warhorses moving more slowly, the Mongols changed to fresh mounts, made an about-face, and attacked, killing thousands of knights. King George and his retinue fled to Tiflis, the capital, and waited for an attack, but the Mongols never came. Subotai had learned everything he needed to know about the Georgians, and resumed his pursuit of Muhammad Shah.

Addressing the meeting in Ögödei's palace, Subotai declared that if a mighty, experienced cavalry such as the army of Georgia could be tricked by a Mongol tactic, the rest of the Europeans were probably no wiser. Subotai predicted easy victories that would bring a fresh supply of plunder, slaves, and tribute to Karakorum.

Ögödei Khan and his advisors were persuaded. The Mongol's next target would be Europe.

THE MONGOLS' FIRST CONTACT WITH THE RUSSIANS

In 1221, Subotai and Jebe were mopping up their conquest of the Khwarazm Empire when they decided to make a foray into southern Russia. Princes from Kiev, Suzdal, Kursk, and other Russian and Ukrainian city-states rode out to meet the invaders, and the Mongol commanders observed something valuable: this was not one army under a single commander, but many small armies each commanded by its own prince who acted independently of his fellow princes.

Curious to learn more, Subotai and Jebe sent ten ambassadors to Khortitsa, an island in the Dnieper River, where the princes of Kiev and Chernigov—both of whom were named Mystislav—had made their headquarters. The ambassadors assured the princes that the Mongols had not come to wage war on the Russians, but on the Kipchak (also known as Cuman) tribe. The two Mystislavs read this clarification as a sign of the Mongols' weakness and fear of the Russian armies. Emboldened by this thought, the princes showed their contempt by executing the ambassadors. It was a clear declaration of war.

As Russians and Mongols prepared for battle, Subotai and Jebe stationed a rearguard of 1,000 men along the Dnieper River. The prince of Galicia, Mystislav the Daring, led 10,000 men across the river in a frontal attack on the Mongol rearguard. Mongol archers cut down hundreds of Russians as they scrambled out of their boats to reach the shore, but the Mongol rearguard was outnumbered ten to one. The Russians killed them all.

The other Russian princes hurried after the men of Galicia. Subotai and Jebe ordered the tactic that had worked in their favor so often— a slow retreat. For nine days the Russians pursued the Mongols across the country north of the Sea of Azov. On May 31, 1223, the Mongols reached the western bank of the Kalymus, or Kalka, River. Here, 18,000 strong, they waited for the Russian force that numbered about 50,000.

Mystislav the Daring led the charge, followed by the princes of Kursk and Volynia. The Mongols lit pots of pitch that covered the battlefield in dense, stinking, black smoke. Their light cavalry rode out of the smoke to mow down hundreds of Russians before disappearing into the black cloud. Unnerved by the smoke and the lightning movements of the Mongols, a division of Kipchaks allied with the Russians fled to the rear, running directly into the advancing army of the prince of Chernigov. By the time the prince had restored order, the Mongols had him surrounded—he and all his men were massacred. Three days later, Mystislav of Kiev agreed to surrender. But Mongol warriors swarmed into the camp and took him and two other princes prisoner. They were brought to the Mongol camp and crammed into a large box covered with a cloth. Subotai and Jebe took seats beside the coffin-turned-dining-table, savoring their dinner as their prisoners suffocated.

CHAPTER 12

"THE DEVIL'S HORSEMEN" INVADE EUROPE

THE VETERAN COMMANDER SUBOTAI HAD BEEN RIGHT THAT RUSSIA WAS AN EASY TARGET FOR A NATION OF CONQUERORS SUCH AS THE MONGOLS. IN 1237, EVERY CITY HAD ITS OWN PRINCE WHO QUARRELED WITH, WAS JEALOUS OF, OR DISTRUSTED ALL THE PRINCES WHO WERE HIS NEIGHBORS.

More than three hundred years earlier, Igor, prince of Kiev, and then his grandson, Vladimir, had labored to unite the many tribes of what is now Russia and the Ukraine into a single realm, thereby making them less susceptible to invasions from enemies such as the Swedes or the Poles. Vladimir died in 1015, and less than forty years after his death his kingdom began to be torn apart by civil wars. According to military historians Richard A. Gabriel and Donald W. Boose Jr., between 1054 and 1224 civil war erupted among Russia's many princes and nobles an astonishing eighty-three times.

Yet when their land was threatened by a new enemy more fearsome than any the country had ever seen before, the Russian princes still would not stand together. Pride was a factor, but so was the hope cherished by each of the princes that the Mongols would wipe out his rivals while he would survive.

A DELAYED INVASION

Thanks to his reconnaissance of Russia a few years earlier, Subotai was aware of the country's weakness. He planned swift attacks against

The inhabitants of Kozelsk put up an especially determined resistance to the Mongols in 1238. In retaliation, Batu Khan had every living creature inside the city killed. The Mongols resemble European invaders in this artwork. *The Siege of Kozelsk in 1238, by Batu Khan, grandson of Genghis Khan, from a series of illustrated chronicles written during the reign of Ivan the Terrible, mid 16th century, / RIA Novosti / The Bridgeman Art Library International*

Batu Khan, Genghis Khan's grandson, led the invasion of Russia, the Ukraine, and Eastern Europe. The invasion was successful in part because of infighting among the region's many nobles, who failed to create a unified resistance. akg-images

each city, picking them off one by one before the Russians had time to come to their senses and unite against the Mongols.

Subotai served as commander for Batu Khan, son of the unhappy Jöchi. Despite his questionable background, Batu, like Genghis Khan's other sons and grandsons, had his own *ordu*, or horde, of 120,000 men. It became known among Mongols as the Golden Horde, supposedly because when on campaign Batu lived in a tent of gold cloth.

Before he invaded Russia, Batu sent envoys to all the princes in the land offering a peaceful transition of power if they agreed to his terms: recognition that he was their overlord; the payment of 10 percent of their property as tribute; and the yielding up of 10 percent of their people to serve as slaves or, in the case of strong young men, to be trained for service in the Mongol army. Every Russian prince rejected Batu's offer, and some went so far as to murder the envoys.

Still, the invasion did not come immediately. Subotai urged Batu to begin by subjugating the Kipchaks and the Circassians, who were members of Turkic tribes, and the Alans, a Persian tribe, all of whom lived in the Carpathian Mountains and the Volga steppes; some were Christians, some were Muslims, and some still worshipped the gods of their ancestors. Subotai's rationale was to ensure that these tribes would not harry the Mongols' flanks and rear while they were advancing into Russia.

In the summer and fall of 1237, Subotai and Batu rolled through the territory of these tribes, crushing resistance in a series of quick, bloody battles. Some Kipchaks fled west to Hungary, where they allied themselves with the king, but the majority of Kipchaks, Circassians, and Alans acknowledged the Mongols as their lords. Because many of these people were skillful horsemen, Subotai and Batu ordered that these conscripts be trained to ride and fight in the Mongol way. Finally, in winter 1237, the Golden Horde rode into Russia.

THE DESTRUCTION OF RYAZAN

In the thirteenth century, Russia was a country with virtually no roads. During winter it became a frozen wasteland where no traveler would venture far from his home. In spring the snow and ice melted, transforming the steppes into an immense bog. The handful of Russian roads and tracks that did exist were dry in summer, but the spring runoff invariably left wide gashes and deep potholes. For this reason, Subotai and Batu decided to invade in winter. They led their army, now numbering nearly 200,000 strong, onto the ice of the country's

At Ryazan, the Mongols encircled the city with a wooden stockade, just as the Romans had done at Alesia in Gaul, above, 1,300 years earlier. akg-images / Peter Connolly

frozen rivers and streams and into the heart of Russia. Their first target was Ryazan.

Ryazan was one of four small, fortified towns located approximately two or three days' ride from each other in an area southeast of Moscow. The four towns were ruled by four cousins, who served at the pleasure of the prince of Vladimir-Suzdal, the leading nobleman in the region. Before the battle began, Batu Khan sent a small embassy led by a female shaman. The shaman demanded submission, hostages, tribute, and slaves; the Russians shouted from the battlements that when they were dead, the Mongols were welcome to take everything.

As their main army laid siege to Ryazan, Subotai and Batu sent divisions to destroy two of the princely cousins' towns, Isteslawetz and Pronsk.

At Ryazan the Mongols tried something new: they built a wooden stockade that completely encircled the town. This was a device Julius Caesar had employed in 52 B.C.E. against the Gauls at Alesia, and it is possible that the Mongols learned of it from Arab or European visitors to Karakorum. It took only nine days for the tens of thousands of Mongols to erect the barrier. Like the Gauls at Alesia, the Russians inside Ryazan found themselves hemmed in with no hope of escape. As for the Mongols, they enjoyed perfect safety on the other side of the stockade as their catapults hurled stones and clay pots filled with flammable liquid at the city, and their archers picked off the soldiers on the city walls.

On December 21, the constant pounding from the catapults had its effect—a portion of Ryazan's walls crumbled. The Mongols poured over their stockade and through the breach into the city. As the people of Ryazan scattered, searching in vain for escape or at least a hiding place, the Mongols made a game of hunting them down. Men were impaled or flayed alive. Women were raped or murdered outright. Priests and monks were slaughtered inside their churches. As for Yuri, the prince of Ryazan, he, his wife, his children, and all his courtiers were massacred.

The Mongols spent days slaying everyone in Ryazan, as well as everyone in the outlying farms, villages, and monasteries. When the killing and burning ceased at last, Ryazan and the land around it was desolate, filled with charred corpses amid fire-blackened ruins. In the end, the Mongols set a few of their captives free to spread the word of the terror that was coming.

THE FALL OF MOSCOW

The prince of Vladimir-Suzdal, also named Yuri, had ignored Ryazan's appeals for help, but now he tried to save Kolomna, the Mongols' next target. He sent his son Vsevolod with an army to reinforce the city. And then, thinking ahead, he sent another army to reinforce Moscow. In the thirteenth century, Moscow was not a great city, but it was an important citadel, strategically located on a bluff above the confluence of two rivers, the Moskva and the Neglinnaya. Nominally, the reinforcements were under the command of Yuri's young son Vladimir, but because

The Mongols invaded Russia and the Ukraine from the south and then turned west
into Poland and Hungary.

The Principality of Moscow about 1300
The Grand Principality of Moscow or Muscovy
(Great Russia) in 1462
Boundary of the dominions of the Golden Horde
(Khanate of Kipchak) till 1480
Routes of Tatar raids
Acquisitions under Ivan III. (1462–1505)
" " Vasili III. (1505–1533)
" " Ivan IV. (1533–1584. Tsar, 1547)
" " Feodor und Boris Godunov (1584–1605)
" " Michael Romanov (1613–1645)
" " Alexis (1645–1676)
" " Peter the Great (1682–1725)
" " Anna (1730–1740)
" " Elizabeth (1741–1762)
" " Catherine II. (1762–1796)

Partitions of Poland
First partition, 1772.
To Russia
" Prussia
" Austria
Second partition, 1793.
To Russia
" Prussia
Third partition, 1795.
To Russia
" Prussia
" Austria

Scale 1:15,000,000

the boy was in his teens and inexperienced, Yuri had sent along his *voivoda*, or senior military commander, to conduct the defense.

Like Ryazan, Kolomna fell easily to the Mongols, and the army Yuri had sent was killed to the last man. Only Vsevolod escaped the carnage, riding hard until he reached the safety of the city of Vladimir about 100 miles (160 kilometers) away. There he found his mother, Princess Agatha, and his younger brothers and sisters—they had all been sent there by Prince Yuri, who hoped the Mongols would be defeated before they could reach Vladimir.

Meanwhile, word that the Mongols were approaching threw the Moscow garrison into a panic. The anonymous author of *The Novgorod Chronicle*, written about 1275, tells us, "The men of Moscow ran away having seen nothing." It is true that many soldiers fled even before the Mongols were in sight, but many more remained to fight, including young Vladimir, the *voivoda*, and their army. But such courage proved useless. Early in January 1238 the Mongols overwhelmed Moscow's defenses. Ordinary soldiers were killed quickly, but officers and noblemen—including the *voivoda*—were crucified, burned, or flayed. Young Vladimir the Mongols kept as a prize prisoner. The Mongols also spared the strongest young men and women of Moscow—they needed more slave labor.

On February 3, the Mongols appeared outside the city of Vladimir. Subotai and Batu Khan sent a delegation to the city's Golden Gate to ask whether Prince Yuri was inside—very likely they were ready to offer terms for surrender. In reply, some men on the battlements fired arrows at the Mongol envoys.

The delegation scattered, but soon afterward the garrison saw another group of Mongol riders approaching the walls, and with them they brought a bedraggled prisoner. It was the prince's son, Vladimir. As the young man's two eldest brothers, Vsevolod and Mystislav, rushed to the parapet over the Golden Gate, the Mongols called to the Russians, "Do you know him?" Then they made their offer—in exchange for the surrender of the city, they would spare Vladimir's life. Agony though it must have been for them, Vsevolod and Mystislav rejected the Mongols' terms, and watched as the Mongols killed their brother.

For six days the Russians watched from their battlements as the Mongols directed their gangs of slaves to assemble catapults and battering rams. The battle began with Mongol catapults hurling heavy stones against the walls and throwing flaming missiles into the city, while teams of slaves swung the massive timber rams and battered all four gates of Vladimir simultaneously.

For five days the Vladimir garrison held off the Mongol assault, until, toward evening on February 14, the Mongols stormed a portion of the city walls and the defenders retreated to the citadel. The Mongols spent that night camped on the battlements. The next morning, they swept down and attacked. Some from the garrison, including Prince Yuri's sons Vsevolod and Mystislav, met the Mongols in the streets— they were all killed without mercy. By noon the Mongols were climbing over the citadel walls. The noblemen and their families and retainers barricaded themselves inside the Cathedral of the Holy Mother of God. As the Mongols pounded on the heavy church doors, all the men inside the church crowded around the bishops and abbots who had taken refuge with them, demanding that the churchmen accept their vows as monks. These rough, violent men believed that if they died as monks— and for them, death was only moments away—then God would forgive their many sins and welcome their souls into the kingdom of Heaven.

To the sickening sound of splintering wood, the door of the church gave way at last and a howling mob of Mongols charged into the church. *The Novgorod Chronicle* tells us that as the Mongols began their slaughter of all the newly made monks as well as the women and children, Archbishop Mitrofan gathered Princess Agatha and her children and shepherded them into the sacristy, the chamber where the rich vestments and precious sacred vessels of the church were kept for safety. The sacristy door was also very heavy, and rather than waste time breaking it down, the Mongols piled wood and brush against the door and elsewhere inside the church, set it ablaze, then ran outside to watch the conflagration. The princess and her family, the archbishop, and anyone who had sought refuge with them in the sacristy were all consumed in the inferno. "Thus they perished," *The Novgorod Chronicle* says, "giving up their souls to God."

The Mongols fanned out across the city, looting everything of value from palaces, churches, monasteries, and convents, as well as from the shops and private homes. They collected the city's provisions and stocks of fodder, too. And as usual, they sorted out the survivors: children, the aged, the sick, the nobles, and the soldiers were all killed; attractive women and girls were raped, but their lives were spared; and robust young men were also saved from the slaughter.

The Icon of Our Lady of Vladimir

In 1238, days after the Mongol army invaders had moved on, those few citizens of Vladimir who had escaped the carnage returned to their city. Amid the wreckage of the Cathedral of the Holy Mother of God they were astonished to discover that one of their treasures had survived—a much-venerated icon of the Virgin and Child, known as Our Lady of Vladimir. It had been painted by an unknown artist in Constantinople about 1125 and brought to Vladimir sometime before 1155.

The Mongols had ripped off the icon's gold-and-silver sheath and flung the sacred image to the floor. That is where the survivors found it, scorched and battered, but with the faces of the Virgin Mary and the Christ Child virtually untouched. The remaining citizens of Vladimir kept it safe while they rebuilt their city, then installed the icon in its reconstructed church.

In 1395, when another Mongol conqueror, Tamerlane, led his army against Vladimir, the icon was taken for safekeeping to Moscow, where it remained in the Cathedral of the Dormition of the Holy Virgin in the Kremlin until 1918. That year, the Soviet government confiscated the icon and sent it to a laboratory, where layers of paint were stripped off and the twelfth-century original—complete with the damage it suffered in 1238—was revealed. The government installed the icon in Moscow's Tretyakov Gallery, where it is still on display along with thousands of other precious icons.

This battered icon of the Virgin and Child is one of the few artifacts to survive the Mongol destruction of Vladimir. The painting was created by an unknown artist in Constantinople about 1125.

© RIA Novosti / Alamy

THE BATTLE OF THE SITI RIVER

After their victory at Vladimir, Subotai and Batu Khan divided their force. Prince Yuri had collected an army that was marching down from the north—Subotai would deal with them. Batu would head for Novgorod, the last significant city in the region.

On the banks of the Siti River, Yuri camped with his three nephews, Vsevolod of Yaroslavl, Vladimir, and the prince of Rostov, Vasilko. Each had brought armed men, but they were waiting for a major force from Novgorod. While they waited, civilian refugees poured into the camp, telling horror stories of Mongol atrocities. So much bad news unsettled the troops, and as for Prince Yuri, he could hardly bear the loss of his wife and children. Time and again he asked his comrades, "Why am I left? Why do I not die?"

Toward the end of February 1238, Yuri sent out a reconnaissance force of 3,000 men to find the long-overdue army from Novgorod. A few days later, Dorozh, the officer in charge of the reconnaissance mission, returned to report that that he had found no trace of the Novgorod army, but he discovered the Mongol army—and they had Yuri and all his men completely surrounded.

On March 4, Subotai led his Mongols within sight of the Russian camp. It was still winter and the field was covered with deep snowdrifts, yet Yuri ordered his men out of their log-and-earth entrenchments to meet the enemy. Instantly, the Russian infantry became bogged down in the snow, which also slowed the progress of the heavy cavalry. The Mongols, on the other hand, kept their distance and used the firepower of their archers to cut down the Russian troops. When most of Yuri's army lay dead or dying, the Mongols charged in to finish off the survivors. The Russians stood their ground, and the battle ended in brutal, desperate hand-to-hand combat until every Russian was dead, including Prince Yuri and two of his three nephews.

The surviving nephew, Prince Vasilko, was taken prisoner and brought to Subotai. The prince was a handsome young man, and the Mongol commander was in a generous mood. He attempted to show him kindness, but Vasilko would not even put up the pretense of friendship with the man who had murdered so many Russians. He cursed Subotai, calling him "a dark kingdom of vileness." (Of course, the Russian prince and the Mongol commander had no language in common, so there must have been a translator whose unhappy task it was to convey Vasilko's insult to Subotai.) Enraged by what he considered to be the prince's ingratitude, Subotai had Vasilko taken to the middle of the camp and tortured to death.

DROWNING IN BLOOD

Following the destruction of Prince Yuri's army, Batu Khan and Subotai moved toward Novgorod, their rendezvous point. En route, the commanders destroyed more Russian cities—Batu leveled Dmitrov and Tver, Subotai destroyed Rostov, Yaroslavl, and Yuriev. In a matter of about eight weeks, the Mongols had leveled a dozen Russian cities; no one knows how many villages and farms they wiped off the map.

ALTHOUGH THEIR INVASION OF RUSSIA HAD BEEN A TREMENDOUS SUCCESS, IT HAD TAKEN ITS TOLL ON THE MONGOLS. AFTER THREE MONTHS OF ALMOST NONSTOP WARFARE, BOTH MEN AND HORSES WERE ON THE VERGE OF EXHAUSTION.

Batu was about 60 miles (96 kilometers) from Novgorod when he paused to destroy the city of Torzhok. The garrison put up a strong resistance, and two weeks passed before Batu's men captured the city. That delay saved Novgorod. While Batu besieged Torzhok, the weather changed. The first spring thaw melted the snowdrifts and the frozen rivers and streams. Outside Novgorod, Lake Ilmen, fed by the swollen waterways, flooded its banks and turned the land all around the city into a huge, trackless marsh. Unable to fight on such ground and unwilling to risk being caught in a spring flood, Batu Khan and Subotai agreed to pull back.

Although their invasion of Russia had been a tremendous success, it had taken its toll on the Mongols. After three months of almost nonstop warfare, both men and horses were on the verge of exhaustion. Rather than make the long trek back to Mongolia, Subotai and Batu opted to camp for the summer on the steppe west of the Don

River in what is now western Ukraine. Here the Mongols could rest, await the arrival of fresh horses and more supplies from home, and replenish their ranks by training Kipchaks and other captives to fight as Mongols.

The Mongols' route to their summer camp took them close to the town of Kozelsk. As the Mongol advance guard rode by, the town gates swung open and Russian cavalry attacked, killing the entire Mongol vanguard. Russian chronicles claim that the men of Kozelsk slew 4,000 Mongols that day. Once the main body of the Mongol army reached the battlefield, Batu and Subotai called for a halt and besieged the city.

Incredibly, it took the Mongols seven weeks to overpower Kozelsk. The garrison and the citizens united into a single, determined fighting force that repelled every Mongol attack on their walls. Although they were vastly outnumbered—a few thousand defenders against the Mongols' tens of thousands—they made sorties, attacking the Mongol camp and destroying their battering rams. Even when the Mongols finally broke through, civilians grabbed axes and kitchen knives and joined their soldiers in defending their town. The citizens of Kozelsk forced the Mongols to fight for each house and every street. Enraged by such determined resistance, the Mongols succumbed to a kind of killing frenzy; they exterminated every living thing in Kozelsk—men, women, children, livestock, even household pets. The Russian chroniclers tell us that the town's seven-year-old prince, Vasily, drowned in the blood of his own people.

THE FALL OF KIEV

About fifteen months passed before the Mongols made a fresh attack on Russia. They did not spend all that time resting—instead, they subdued more minor tribes that occupied the borderlands along the southern and southwestern edges of Russia.

The primary goal of the Mongols' 1240 campaign was Kiev. This was the largest city in Russia—in fact, with a population of about 100,000, it was one of the largest cities in the Western world. It was the center of Russian Orthodoxy, the ancient capital of the realm known as Kievan Rus, which was the forerunner of both modern Russia and modern Ukraine. The city was famous for its architecture—sublime churches, grand palaces, extensive monasteries and convents, and impressive stone walls that encircled the huge city.

So proud were the Russians of Kiev that they referred to it as "the mother of cities." The Mongols were impressed, too, especially by the gilded domes of Kiev's thirty churches—they called the place "the court of the golden heads."

On December 3 or 4, 1240, Batu Khan sent a delegation to the city. Kiev's prince, Daniel, had abandoned Kiev days earlier, leaving the governor, Dmitri, to defend the city. Batu Khan's envoys urged Dmitri to surrender and save his life and the lives of all his people. Dmitri replied by having the envoys executed.

The next day the Mongols surrounded the city, but they concentrated their catapults against Kiev's obvious weak point—the battlements that flanked the Polish Gate, the only part of the city walls constructed of wood. After enduring hour after hour of assaults with heavy stones, the wooden wall collapsed, the Mongols charged in, and the Russian troops retreated from their places along the walls. But no further Mongol attack followed. It was near sundown, so the Mongols occupied the city walls and spent the night camped there.

SO PROUD WERE THE RUSSIANS OF KIEV THAT THEY REFERRED TO IT AS "THE MOTHER OF CITIES." THE MONGOLS WERE IMPRESSED, TOO, ESPECIALLY BY THE GILDED DOMES OF KIEV'S THIRTY CHURCHES—THEY CALLED THE PLACE "THE COURT OF THE GOLDEN HEADS."

The next day, December 6, 1240, the Mongols leapt down from the parapets and began their drive into the great city. It was a repeat of the fighting at Kozelsk, only on a far larger scale. Foot by foot, street by street, the Mongols drove the Russians back. Hundreds of civilians took refuge inside the Church of the Holy Virgin, where they spent all night fortifying the holy place. Now, as the Mongols drove into the heart of Kiev, those who were still outside pounded on the church doors, begging to be let it. When the doors did not open, crowds of men, women, and children climbed into the bell tower and on to the church's roof—so many of them that the tower toppled over and the roof gave way, crushing hundreds.

When all resistance ceased, a detachment of Mongols discovered Governor Dmitri, badly wounded. They dragged him before Batu Khan. Typically, when his envoys were killed Batu avenged himself on the man who ordered their deaths, but the khan had been impressed by Dmitri's courage, especially compared to the cowardice of Prince Daniel, who had deserted his people. So Batu spared Dmitri's life.

Over the next several days the Mongols worked their way meticulously through every building in Kiev, carrying off everything that had value, sorting out useful captives from useless ones. They broke open tombs, rifling among the moldy bones of the dead for gold and jewels. They ransacked the treasuries of the churches and monasteries, where chests and cabinets were crammed full of gold sacred vessels, reliquaries of the saints, and icons studded with jewels. When they had stripped Kiev bare, the Mongols pulled down the stone buildings, set fire to the wooden ones, then marched west to begin their invasion of Poland and Hungary.

CHAPTER 13

HOW ONE MAN'S DEATH SAVED EUROPE FROM DESTRUCTION

WITH THE CONQUEST OF RUSSIA COMPLETE, THE MONGOL COMMANDERS GATHERED AT BATU KHAN'S CAMP OUTSIDE PRZEMYSL, TODAY A CITY IN SOUTHERN POLAND BUT PART OF RUSSIA IN 1240. TWO OF GENGHIS KHAN'S GRANDSONS NOW NUMBERED AMONG THE COMMANDERS—BAIDAR, A SON OF CHAGATAI, AND KADAN, SON OF ÖGÖDEI. GÜYÜK, BATU'S FIRST COUSIN, HAD ALSO JOINED THEM. BUT THE MAN WHO CONDUCTED THE MEETING WAS SUBOTAI. HIS SWIFT, ALMOST PAINLESS CONQUEST OF RUSSIA MADE HIM THE MOST RESPECTED MILITARY LEADER AMONG THE MONGOLS. HE HAD ALREADY DEVELOPED A PLAN FOR THE INVASION OF EUROPE, AND THE OTHER COMMANDERS WERE EAGER TO HEAR IT.

First, 30,000 Mongol warriors would remain in Russia to administer the country and put down any rebellions. That left approximately 120,000 men for the next stage of the Mongol conquest. Hungary was Subotai's first target, but before they could conquer Hungary the Mongols had to neutralize Hungary's neighbors and potential allies, Poland and Lithuania. Subotai intended to spread out his force along a 600-mile (960-kilometer) front, stretching from the Baltic to the Black Sea. Baidar and Kadan with 30,000 men would sweep into Poland and Lithuania. Batu and Subotai would divide the remaining 90,000 men

---

After the battle of Legnica in southwestern Poland, the Mongols severed an ear from each corpse—
the better to tally up the dead. They filled nine large sacks in all. akg-images

How the Mongols Administered Their Empire

After a country such as Russia had been conquered, the Mongols left a large army of occupation, usually numbering tens of thousands, to snuff out any uprisings. Reprisals against insurgents were severe—rebel leaders were executed, rebel bands massacred, and inhabitants of rebellious towns sold to slave traders.

For all its violence, a Mongol conquest was never a smash-and-grab affair. They were not pirates, they were empire builders, as determined as Alexander the Great or the Romans. Once the initial period of upheaval had passed, the Mongols followed a more or less set routine. The khan in Karakorum appointed a Mongol overlord to govern the new province and provided him with a garrison to keep the peace. The Mongol governor appointed judges and other government officials, usually drawn from the local people. Naturally, the Mongols expected absolute loyalty from these local administrators.

As for the conquered population, it was always at the service of the Mongols. Their most robust men might be conscripted for the Mongol army; their most skilled professionals and artisans could be sent to Karakorum to serve the khan; their loveliest women might be taken from their homes to be the concubines of high-ranking Mongols. And of course, the Mongols collected tribute and taxes.

The Mongols rarely interfered with local laws or customs. They tolerated all religions; in fact, after a Mongol conquest, members of minority religions such as Christians in Muslim countries or Jews in Christian lands suddenly enjoyed full religious freedom.

Like every other imperial nation, the Mongols sought power and wealth, but they were also avid "collectors" of expertise, talent, and information. The Mongol Empire was becoming a vast international marketplace of skills and ideas.

into four columns of 22,500 each and advance through the Carpathian Mountains toward the Hungarian cities of Buda and Pest. Once Baidar and Kadan had crushed the Poles and the Lithuanians, they would lead their Mongols down from the north and rejoin the main body of the army.

A TENUOUS ALLEGIANCE

Western Europe had heard of the Mongol invasion of Russia; in the eastern lands, Poles, Lithuanians, and Hungarians listened in horror as the refugees described the destruction wrought by the invaders. As word of the Mongol conquests spread, the stories became more lurid. One claimed that after raping Christian women, Mongol warriors cut off their victims' breasts and served them as delicacies to their commanders. Another said that the Mongols were a savage race with the heads of dogs; they were so vicious they devoured the corpses of their enemies, and so vile that when they were finished, even vultures would not touch what remained.

Fear of the Mongols spread across Europe, manifesting itself sometimes in odd ways. Danish fishermen refused to put out to sea, afraid they might encounter the Mongol fleet. In fact, the ocean was the one place the Danes would have been safe—the Mongols never did learn the art of navigation.

The Europeans called the Mongols "Tartars," a name they picked up from a Dominican priest, Friar Julian, who regarded the Mongols as a demonic people. He called them "Tartari," or people from hell (*Tartarus* being both the ancient Greek and the ancient Roman name for the habitation of the damned).

THE EUROPEANS CALLED THE MONGOLS "TARTARS," A NAME THEY PICKED UP FROM A DOMINICAN PRIEST, FRIAR JULIAN, WHO CALLED THEM "TARTARI" OR PEOPLE FROM HELL.

The largest group to escape the Mongols were the Kipchaks. In 1240 King Bela IV of Hungary learned that approximately 200,000 Kipchaks had traveled across the Carpathian Mountains into Hungary. In his palace in Pest on the eastern side of the Danube, Bela received the Kipchak khan, Kuthen, who asked the king to accept him as an ally and, as a sign of his friendship, requested priests to instruct his people in the Catholic faith and baptize them. Bela was exultant: Kuthen brought with him tens of thousands of experienced warriors, and he was willing to bring into the church nearly 200,000 new converts.

Unfortunately, the good feelings that had sprung up so quickly between Bela and Kuthen were just as quickly undermined when a letter arrived at the Hungarian court from Batu Khan. He denounced Kuthen and his people as renegades, and demanded that Bela send them back to the Mongols for punishment. If the king of Hungary insisted upon

harboring the Kipchaks, then Batu would bring his army and punish the Hungarians, too.

According to Kuthen, that is how Batu's letter read, but because the letter was written in Uighur, a language no one in Hungary aside from the Kipchaks understood, there was no way to confirm the accuracy of Kuthen's translation. And then there was one passage that made Bela and his advisors uneasy: addressing the Kipchaks, Batu said that when he attacked Hungary, the Kipchaks, who were excellent horsemen, would "find it easy to escape." Then, addressing the Hungarian king, Batu added, "But you who dwell in houses within towns, how can you escape from me?" Some members of the Hungarian court began to suspect that Kuthen and his Kipchaks were a Mongol fifth column, sent to lull the Hungarians into a false sense of security while waiting for the day when Batu invaded and the Kipchaks would join the Mongols in destroying the kingdom. The matter was still being debated among the Hungarians when an Austrian archduke at court decided to settle the question. He killed Kuthen, decapitated the corpse, then threw the head out a castle window.

That outrage severed all ties of Kipchak-Hungarian friendship. The Kipchaks withdrew into the Carpathians, where they became a nation of bandits, robbing travelers, raiding Hungarian villages and farms, and harassing any Hungarian military units that marched through the mountains. And when the Mongols invaded Hungary, the Kipchaks did not come to Bela's assistance.

THE DESERTED CITY

Poland in 1241 was in no position to repel the Mongols. Like Russia, it was a fractured nation. In 1138, King Boleslaw III had divided his country into four quarters, leaving one to each of his four sons. Over the next century these four "kingdoms" had been further divided by the descendants of Boleslaw's sons. As the Mongols rode toward Poland, the country was broken up into nine separate principalities, each with its own nobles, knights, and bishops who were suspicious of their peers in the other Polish principalities.

Previous page: A Hungarian woodcut shows the Mongols marching through Hungary, driving before them Hungarian captives, including women and children. The Mongol Invasion of Hungary in 1241 during the reign of Bela IV (colour litho of an original coloured wood engraving), Hungarian School, (15th century) / Private Collection / Archives Charmet / The Bridgeman Art Library International

The two primary powerbrokers in Poland at the time were Boleslaw the Chaste of Sandomir and Duke Henry the Pious of Silesia. Boleslaw ruled from Cracow, the country's greatest city. Duke Henry had the best army in the country. As it happened, both men had ties to Bela IV: Boleslaw was Bela's son-in-law, and Henry was Bela's cousin.

In February 1241, Baidar and Kadan led their men across the frozen Vistula River into Poland. Because the Poles were not expecting them, no army had been mobilized to meet the invaders. The Mongols sacked and burned the cities of Lublin, Sandomir, and Zawichost; ravaged the surrounding countryside; then divided in order to spread the terror over as wide an area as possible. Baidar led his 11,250 men northwest; Kadan and the same number of Mongols headed for Cracow.

When the Mongols were within sight of the city, Kadan ordered a small detachment to ride toward Cracow. The city's commander, a man named Vladimir, assembled a large force and attacked; the Mongols scattered. Encouraged by this easy victory, Vladimir decided to pursue the enemy. About 11 miles (18 kilometers) from Cracow at a place called Chmielnik, Vladimir and his men galloped into a Mongol trap. From their hiding places, Mongol archers cut down virtually every Pole. A few soldiers managed to escape and reach the safety of Cracow, where they brought news of the disaster to Boleslaw.

The duke collected his family with as many of their most precious possessions as they could carry (and still make good speed) and fled to Moravia in what is now the eastern Czech Republic. Every other citizen followed Boleslaw's example. As they ran to the forests, a trumpeter stood in the cathedral tower, sounding the alarm over and over again until a Mongol archer picked him off.

On March 24, Kadan led his army into a deserted city. After looting it, the Mongols set Cracow ablaze, burning it to the ground.

NINE SACKS OF EARS

Meanwhile, Duke Henry the Pious had marched his army to the town of Legnica (also known by its German name, Liegnitz) on the Kaczawa River in southwestern Poland. With him were a few hundred Moravians and Bavarians, as well as contingents of the three elite military orders founded during the Crusades—the Knights Templar, the Knights Hospitaller, and the Teutonic Knights. Altogether, Henry had about 25,000 men, almost all of them heavy cavalry. King Wenceslaus I of

Bohemia was en route with an army of 50,000, but Henry had no idea when he might arrive. Rather than be besieged by the Mongols inside Legnica, Henry moved his men onto the plain a few miles from town to greet Wenceslaus or fight the Mongols, depending on which army arrived first.

Baidar and Kadan, informed by their scouts that the Bohemian force was a two-day march away, decided to attack Duke Henry before the reinforcements arrived. On or about April 9, 1241 (the precise date of the battle is uncertain), the Mongols formed ranks opposite Henry's army outside Legnica. The Mongol formation was simple—light cavalry in the center, flanked by two wings of heavy cavalry.

Duke Henry's formation mirrored that of the Mongols: light cavalry in the center, with himself leading a contingent of heavy cavalry on the right, and the heavy cavalry of the three orders of Knights massed on the left. Held in reserve were the infantrymen.

Henry himself led a headlong cavalry charge against the Mongols, and the Mongols fell back. Encouraged by what they took to be an indication of weakness, the Poles spurred their horses in pursuit, but as the horses of the Polish cavalry tired, the Mongols changed mounts, wheeled around, and released a deadly hail of arrows into the Polish ranks. Thick clouds of black smoke billowed up from behind Duke Henry's cavalry—the Mongols had again lit pots of pitch to confuse their enemies and keep the Polish infantry

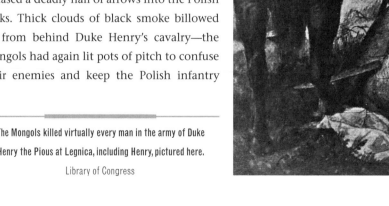

The Mongols killed virtually every man in the army of Duke Henry the Pious at Legnica, including Henry, pictured here.

Library of Congress

from rushing to the aid of the embattled cavalry. Simultaneously, the infantry came under fire as Mongol archers rode in and out of the black smoke, killing infantrymen where they stood.

The Knights of the military orders frustrated the Mongols in one regard—their armor was so heavy the Mongol arrows could not pierce it. So the Mongol archers fired at the Knights' horses. On foot and burdened with their cumbersome armor, the Knights were easy to kill in hand-to-hand combat.

As the pitch pots burned out and the smoke cleared from the battlefield, virtually every man in Duke Henry's army lay dead, including Henry himself.

To make an accurate count of how many men they had slain, the Mongols cut off one ear from each of the dead. When they finished, they had nine large sacks full of ears.

Writing of the disaster to King Louis IX of France, the Grand Master of the Knights Templar did not doubt that soon the Mongols would rampage across the heart of Europe and into Paris.

A BREAK IN THE LINE

In March 1241 Batu Khan and Subotai led their 90,000 men out of the Carpathians and marched south along the Danube to Pest, where, by chance, King Bela had convened a war council. Before the Hungarians had arrived at any decision regarding how best to meet the Mongols, a courier brought word that the Mongol army was only a few miles away. At once Bela sent orders to every nobleman and knight in the kingdom to bring his men and provisions to Pest. Recognizing the dire situation, the Hungarians responded quickly—in two weeks Bela had an army of 100,000 men. As for the Mongols, they kept their distance, making no move to attack or besiege the city.

During the first week of April 1241, Bela IV led his army out to meet the Mongols, but the Mongols retreated, moving slowly in a northeasterly direction. For several days the Hungarians followed the Mongols. On April 10, at a place called Mohi (now known as Muhi), the Mongols crossed a stone bridge that spanned the Sajo River. Subotai left a small detachment of Mongols to guard the eastern side of the bridge, but a party of knights led by Bela's younger brother, Prince Koloman, and Archbishop Hugolin attacked and killed the Mongol detachment and established a much stronger Hungarian presence on the eastern side of the bridge. In the meantime, Bela put his army into what he considered a defensive position—a solid, compact camp encircled by hundreds of wagons bound together with ropes and chains. This arrangement gave his army no room to maneuver, a situation Batu Khan spotted at once. He pointed out to his officers, "They are crowded together like a herd of cattle in narrow stalls, with no room to move about." Then Bela made a second fatal error—he did not send light cavalry and archers along the riverbank to guard against an enemy attack. The Mongols spotted this weakness, too, and after dark Subotai led 30,000 men far downstream. The Mongols threw a wooden bridge over the Sajo and crossed to the other side where they waited for the battle to begin.

At dawn Batu Khan rolled up seven catapults within range of the stone bridge and began lobbing pots of flaming liquid and explosive grenades at the Hungarians. The "shelling" scattered the Hungarians who guarded the bridge and captured the full attention of the Hungarians in the camp. No one in Bela's camp was watching the rear.

Then the Mongols rushed across the bridge toward the Hungarian camp. For two hours Batu sacrificed his men to repeated assaults by Bela's heavy cavalry; it was a necessary expenditure so Subotai could come up behind the Hungarians undetected. Finally, Batu ordered his men to ride toward the Hungarian camp in a thin semicircle as if they imagined they could surround it. The Hungarian cavalry prepared one final charge to break the line and disperse the Mongols, but then Subotai with his 30,000 men suddenly appeared behind the camp. Bela was completely surprised, hemmed in by the Mongols and by his own defense works.

At this point Batu brought up his catapults and began raining firebombs on Bela's camp. Prince Koloman collected a band of heroic knights and attacked the catapults, hoping to put them out of commission, but the prince and his volunteers were driven back. For several hours the Hungarians suffered relentless bombarding until most of their wagons and tents were in flames, their horses were screaming in fear, and the men were looking in all directions for some way to escape. And it was Batu Khan who showed them the way out.

The khan ordered his men to draw back and create an opening through which the Hungarians could escape back to the mountain pass that had led them to Mohi. A few horsemen raced through the break in the Mongol line and reached the pass safely. At that, countless others,

Europe's Failure

As fearsome as the Mongols were, their army numbered only 100,000 men—a fraction of what the kingdoms of Europe could have mobilized if they had worked together. But two important factors got in the way of the Europeans presenting a united front against the invaders: the feudal system, and a new quarrel between the pope and the Holy Roman Emperor.

In the thirteenth century, no European king kept a standing army—it was too expensive. Certainly there were excellent fighting men all across the continent, but they spent their time administering their estates, or serving the king in some official capacity. The only full-time professional fighters were the military orders.

Under the feudal system, when a king went to war he called upon his nobles and knights to conscript men from their private garrisons as well as their household servants and tenant farmers to serve in the king's army. Because feeding and housing thousands of men was costly, wars in the Middle Ages tended to be fought close to home and typically lasted only a few months. After victory or defeat, the army was disbanded.

There were two powers in Europe that could have summoned an international coalition to repel the Mongols—Pope Gregory IX and the Holy Roman Emperor Frederick II. But in 1241 Gregory and Frederick were too busy fighting each other to launch a European crusade against the barbarians from the east. The causes of the conflict are complex, but at its heart was a struggle to determine who would be the ultimate authority in Christendom, the pope or the emperor. Although King Bela IV had appealed to both Gregory and Frederick for help, they ignored him. Perhaps the pope and the emperor were blinded by their obsession with their own quarrel, or perhaps they underrated the Mongol threat. Whatever their rationale, Gregory and Frederick ignored the greatest danger to European civilization since the invasion of the Huns eight hundred years earlier.

Like Russia, the rest of thirteenth-century Europe, as shown here, was disunited, its kings jealous and suspicious of one another, which worked in the favor of the invading Mongols.

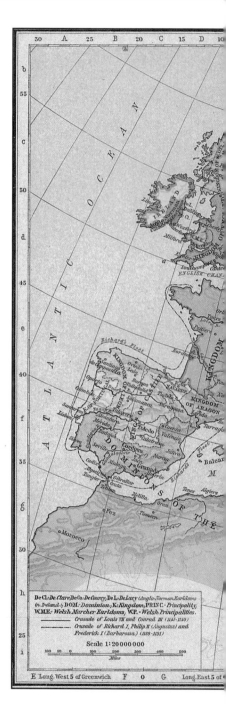

Guelf, Hohenstaufen and Ascanian domains
in Germany about 1176
☐ Guelf ☐ Hohenstaufen ☐ Ascanian
Scale 1:15 000 000
The dark coloring indicates hereditary or imperial domains;
light coloring, feudal territories, and border coloring, suzerainty.

on horseback or on foot, threw off their armor and rushed for the safety of the pass. Only Koloman, Archbishop Hugolin, and the Knights Templar formed up to cover their comrades' disorderly retreat.

Once the camp was cleared and the Hungarians were racing pell-mell through the pass, the Mongols began their pursuit. A few thousand attacked Koloman and his men, slaughtering all the Templars, as well as the archbishop, and badly wounding the prince. A handful of survivors carried him from the field.

ONE NIGHT THE KING SOUGHT SHELTER IN A MONASTERY, WHERE THE MONKS INFORMED HIM THAT THEY HAD ANOTHER ROYAL GUEST, AND THEN LED THE HUNGARIAN KING TO A CHAMBER WHERE THEY INTRODUCED HIM TO THE POLISH DUKE, BOLESLAW THE CHASTE, STILL ON THE RUN FROM THE MONGOLS.

Over the next few days the Mongols hunted down and killed countless Hungarian knights and foot soldiers. The road to Pest was littered with corpses—perhaps as many as 60,000 Hungarian troops. King Bela hid in the forest with one servant, an old man named Vochu. Traveling along forest paths, they headed for Austria. One night the king sought shelter in a monastery, where the monks informed him that they had another royal guest, and then led the Hungarian king to a chamber where they introduced him to the Polish duke, Boleslaw the Chaste, still on the run from the Mongols.

As for Prince Koloman, somehow he reached Pest, where he urged the immediate evacuation of the city. He was carried to the Buda side of the Danube in a boat crammed with frightened women and children. From there the prince had himself taken south to his estate in Croatia, where he died of his wounds.

From their city walls, from clock towers and church steeples, the people of Buda watched as their sister city, Pest, now devoid of inhabitants, went up in flames. They waited for the Mongols to pour into boats and cross the Danube, but the attack did not come. The Mon-

When Bela IV, shown here, fled Hungary, Batu Khan sent 10,000 men to pursue the runaway king.

They were on the verge of capturing Bela when they were called home to Mongolia to elect

a new Great Khan. © INTERFOTO / Alamy

gols were resting after their victory at the Sajo River, and planning the next stage in their conquest of Europe.

A NEW CRUSADE

For the remainder of 1241, the Mongols raided throughout central and eastern Hungary, leveling towns and villages and destroying farms. On Christmas Day they attacked Gran, known today as Esztergom, the ecclesiastical capital of Hungary and a wealthy commercial center. As the Mongols battered the wooden walls with thirty catapults, the citizens of Gran buried their most precious possessions and set fire to the storehouses so nothing valuable would fall into the Mongols' hands. Within a matter of hours the Mongols captured the city, and finding little of value in the churches, monasteries, and homes of rich traders, they suspended priests and merchants over fires until they revealed where they had hidden their treasure.

The military historians Richard A. Gabriel and Donald W. Boose Jr. estimate that in 1241 Hungary lost perhaps as much as half of its population. The Mongols were in control of Eastern Europe from the Baltic Sea to the Danube River. And when winter came and the Danube froze, the Mongols rode across to bring their campaign to Western Europe.

In spite of the threat, neither Emperor Frederick nor Pope Gregory called for a truce in order to unite against the Mongols. Appeals

By chance the Polish duke Boleslaw and King Bela of Hungary both took refuge in the same monastery when the Mongols invaded.

akg-images

from King Bela, Hungary's exiled king, did no good: Gregory said he could not think about the Mongols while the emperor was pressing him so hard, and Frederick replied that given the promising series of victories he was enjoying in Italy, he dare not stop until he had forced the pope to recognize his sovereignty. But both men were willing to make gestures: Gregory granted permission for a crusade against the Mongols to be preached in Germany, and Frederick sent one of his own sons to lead it, Conrad, a thirteen-year-old boy.

THE RETREAT

In January 1242, a Mongol detachment came out of the Alps and was seen outside the town of Udine in northern Italy, just 60 miles (96 kilometers) from Venice. The frightened people of northern Italy were convinced that they were the Mongols' next target, but this was just a scouting party Batu had sent out to track down King Bela. Just as Subotai and Jebe had pursued Muhammad Shah twenty years earlier, Batu Khan sent his cousin Kadan with an army of 10,000 to capture or kill the Hungarian king. By this time Bela was in Croatia, running from one island to the next; he stayed for a time on the island of Rab, then moved to heavily fortified Trogir before scurrying off to the city of Split.

As for Kadan, his pursuit did not go well. At Rijeka a huge Croatian army inflicted a severe defeat on the Mongols. There was not enough grass for the Mongol horses along Croatia's mountainous coastline, and Kadan no longer had enough men to storm any of Croatia's impressively fortified cities. Still, he pressed on, for the son of Ögödei did not have the authority to suspend the search himself.

In Austria, Mongol reconnaissance parties were studying the defenses of Vienna when a courier from Karakorum arrived at the tent of Batu Khan. On December 11, 1241, Ögödei Khan had suffered a seizure and died. The late khan's wife, Töregene, was acting as regent until all the Mongol khans and commanders arrived in Karakorum to select a new Great Khan. Meanwhile, another courier had tracked down Kadan and delivered the same message to him.

As a result, Batu abandoned his campaign against Vienna, and Kadan gave up his pursuit of King Bela. The Mongol armies in Europe broke camp and headed back to Mongolia.

By his death, Ögödei saved Europe from further carnage. How far would the Mongols have gotten if Ögödei had not died? The question is purely speculative, but considering the Mongols' success in Eastern Europe it is not irrational to believe that Batu Khan may have gotten as far as Paris, as the Grand Master of the Templars feared.

Pope Gregory IX, pictured, and Holy Roman Emperor Frederick II could have gathered an international coalition to repel the Mongols, but were too busy fighting with each other to provide assistance.

Getty Images

CHAPTER 14

RIFTS IN THE FAMILY

ON HIS ADVANCE THROUGH EASTERN EUROPE IN 1241, BATU KHAN MAINTAINED A TRADITION ESTABLISHED BY HIS GRANDFATHER GENGHIS BY BRINGING BACK TO KARAKORUM USEFUL MEN SUCH AS MINERS, GOLD-SMITHS, SCRIBES, AND LINGUISTS. IN ADDITION, HE DESIGNATED THOUSANDS OF CAPTIVES FOR SLAVERY IN MONGOLIA. BUT AS THE MONGOLS RODE THROUGH THE CRIMEA, THEY ENCOUNTERED TRADING POSTS OPERATED BY MERCHANTS FROM GENOA AND VENICE, MEN WHO, LIKE THE MONGOLS, KNEW A GOOD BUSI-NESS OPPORTUNITY WHEN THEY SAW ONE.

Rather than have the trouble and expense of herding, feeding, and housing so many captives, the Mongols offered to sell their prisoners to the Italians. The Italians were interested—they knew that in the Muslim world there was a market for fair, healthy young men and women. Although these captives were all Christians, either Catholics or Russian Orthodox, the Genoese and Venetians suspended their religious convictions for the sake of commerce. They bought many of the Mongols' best prisoners, then sold them to slave traders, who auctioned them off in the markets of Egypt. Over the next two centuries, while the Mongols maintained their grip on Russia (a period the Russians refer to as the era of "the Tartar Yoke"), the Italians provided the Mongols with goods from Europe in exchange for fresh consignments of Slavic slaves.

Batu Khan was poised to attack Vienna when he was called home to help elect a new Great Khan after the death of Ögödei. His death saved Europe from a Mongol invasion. Batu Khan Raids Western Europe in 1241, from a series of illustrated chronicles written during the reign of Ivan the Terrible (vellum), Russian School, (16th century) / Russian Academy of Sciences Library Depository St Petersburg / RIA Novosti / The Bridgeman Art Library International

THE FAVORITE SON

It had been Töregene Khatun, the most politically astute of Ögödei Khan's wives, who sent word to all the Mongol princes and commanders that the Great Khan had died. The Persian historian, Ata-Malik Juvaini, tells us that in her message announcing Ögödei's death, she expressed her concern regarding the administration of the empire until everyone arrived in Karakorum and agreed upon a successor. According to Juvaini, the princes asked Töregene to serve as regent during the interregnum.

But Töregene did more than administer the Mongol government. She began to manipulate it so that her son, Güyük, would become the next khan. This would be problematic because, shortly before Ögödei died, he had quarreled with Güyük and exiled him. Early in the 1230s, Ögödei had named his son Kuchu as his heir; after Kuchu's death in 1236, Ögödei had expressed the desire that he should be succeeded by Kuchu's son, Shiremun. Such a wish was not binding on the Mongol princes—that is why they held a *khuriltai* after a khan's death, to decide who would be the best candidate to rule.

To restore her son's standing among the princes and influential men of the Mongol nation, Töregene ingratiated herself by presenting her in-laws—the descendants of Genghis Khan—with rich gifts and showering them with signs of favor and esteem. She did the same with the officers and men of the Mongol army, thereby winning their loyalty and affection.

That a khan's widow should be regent would not have struck any Mongol as odd; Mongol society was ambivalent about the status of women. Mongol women were free to speak out on issues that affected the future of their family, their tribe, and the nation at large—as we have seen in the cases of Genghis Khan's mother Höelün and his principal wife, Börte. When Töregene Khatun became regent, the Mongols accepted it as perfectly normal, which suggests that Mongol women had exercised political power before. Nevertheless, Mongol men regarded their women as property. For example, after the death of Genghis Khan, his wives and concubines (except for his principal wife, Börte) were inherited by Tolui, Genghis's youngest son, which was standard practice in Mongol society.

Töregene's closest advisor and confidante was Fatima, the madam of the most successful brothel in Karakorum. Because Karakorum was essentially a royal city, many of Fatima's customers were members of the Great Khan's court, and it was not unusual that they revealed to her the secrets and scandals of the palace. Soon after Fatima moved to the palace, she began acting as a gatekeeper: no one saw Töregene without Fatima's consent. Töregene shared with Fatima state secrets and details of the activities of the empire's governors. Eventually, Töregene authorized Fatima to exercise real political power. Almost overnight, ministers who had served the Mongol Empire for decades were stripped of office. Henceforth, the highest government offices were restricted to men who were Töregene and Fatima's favorites.

TÖREGENE'S CLOSEST ADVISOR AND CONFIDANTE WAS FATIMA, THE MADAM OF THE MOST SUCCESSFUL BROTHEL IN KARAKORUM. BECAUSE KARAKORUM WAS ESSENTIALLY A ROYAL CITY, MANY OF FATIMA'S CUSTOMERS WERE MEMBERS OF THE GREAT KHAN'S COURT, AND IT WAS NOT UNUSUAL THAT THEY REVEALED TO HER THE SECRETS AND SCANDALS OF THE PALACE.

Ögödei's first minister, Mahmud Yalavach, was among those the women dismissed; so was Yelü Chucai, the Khitan nobleman who had entered the service of Genghis Khan about 1215 during his conquest of Jin China and had served the Mongol Empire faithfully for more than thirty years. The two women only forced Yelü Chucai into retirement, but they sent troops to arrest Mahmud Yalavach. Acting as a gracious host rather than a frightened man on his way to prison, Yalavach spread a banquet before the soldiers and kept the alcohol flowing until he could escape.

One by one, Töregene removed men who had influence with the royal family, replacing them with men who supported Güyük's candidacy. At the same time, she continued to cultivate her in-laws and other powerful elements at the upper levels of Mongol society. She remained regent for almost four years, which suggests that among the Mongol princes and commanders there was no clear favorite to

Pauquet del.

Ch. Colin sc.

succeed Ögödei. In 1245, certain that her son Güyük would be elected, Töregene called at last for the family *khuriltai*.

GÜYÜK KHAN

The *khuriltai* met outside Karakorum, near the source of the Orkhon River. The Franciscan friar, John of Plano Carpini, arrived in time to witness the meeting and has left a detailed account of it. He said the 2,000 dignitaries assembled inside a huge tent made of white velvet. In addition to the descendants of Genghis Khan, the *khuriltai* included tribal chiefs, military commanders, provincial governors, and client kings or their deputies. Friar John estimated that the envoys from every corner of the Mongol Empire numbered 4,000, not counting their retinues. To accommodate all the delegates and their retainers, Töregene had erected a city of tents. And as a sign of her generosity, she drew upon the treasury to cover everyone's expenses.

During the four days of the *khuriltai* the delegates dressed as one: white velvet on the first day, red velvet on the second, blue velvet on the third, and brocade on the fourth. All the leading men of the Mongols had embellished their horses' bits, bridles, and saddles with gold—Friar John estimated that these trappings represented "twenty marks' worth of gold." Establishing a modern equivalency for medieval currency is difficult, but today twenty gold marks would be equal to about eight grams of gold.

As the deliberations progressed, there were three clear contenders for the title of Great Khan: Güyük, his brother Köten, and their nephew Shiremun. Köten was eliminated because his health was poor, and Shiremun because he was considered too young and inexperienced. With no other viable candidate, the *khuriltai* elected Güyük.

He was installed as Great Khan on August 24, 1246. We know the precise date because Friar John observed that the ceremony took place on the feast day of the apostle St. Bartholomew. The crowd gathered around a large tent, the interior of which was hung with brocade, and the wooden beams and columns that supported it were covered with plates of gold. At the beginning of the ceremony all the men removed

Previous page: Thanks to the political machinations of his mother, Genghis Khan's grandson Güyük was chosen to succeed his father, Ögödei Khan. Güyük began his reign by killing family members and their supporters who opposed him. © Mary Evans Picture Library / The Image Works

their hats and draped their belts around their necks—the Mongols' traditional sign of humility—as two of Güyük's male relatives took him by the hands and led him to his throne. Once he had taken his seat, all the Mongol lords and all the foreign dignitaries knelt before him. Next, all the ordinary people present knelt before Güyük Khan.

"Then they started drinking," Friar John tells us, "and, as is their custom, they drank without stopping until evening."

Like every other envoy at the enthronement, Friar John had an audience with Güyük Khan. Friar John described Güyük as being "forty or forty-five years old or more; he is of medium height, very intelligent and extremely shrewd, and most serious and grave in his manner. He is never seen to laugh for a slight cause nor to indulge in any frivolity." The letter Friar John brought from Pope Innocent IV disappointed Güyük—he had expected to receive the pope's submission on behalf of all Christian Europe; instead, Innocent had written to urge Güyük to convert to Catholicism and submit himself to the authority of Rome. Güyük had no intention of doing either thing, and now that he knew the true character of Friar John's mission he simply, politely, ignored him.

In mid-November 1246, when the friar and his party left Karakorum for the return journey home, no Mongol tried to persuade him to stay. The only Mongol who took notice of their departure was their fellow Christian Töregene, who invited Friar John and his party to her tent and gave them velvet-lined fox fur cloaks as tokens of her friendship.

THE END OF TÖREGENE AND FATIMA

During the coronation festivities, Töregene invited one of the guests, Yaroslav, prince of Vladimir-Suzdal, to dine with her in her tent. She served the prince with her own hands, a sign of special esteem. But after the dinner, when Yaroslav returned to his tent, he fell ill. Seven days later, he died. Friar John records, "His whole body turned bluish-gray in a strange fashion," which led even the Mongols to conclude that Töregene had poisoned her dinner guest. Then it was learned that Güyük had sent a message to Yaroslav's eldest son, Alexander Nevsky, inviting him to Karakorum to receive from the khan authority over his family's lands. Alexander delayed making the journey, and Friar John says that a rumor spread among the tent city that if the twenty-six-year-old Russian prince had accepted Güyük's invitation, he would have been murdered, too.

Although the principality of Vladimir-Suzdal had fallen to the Golden Horde like every other Russian principality, Yaroslav and his sons—especially Alexander—had shown themselves to be skillful warriors. At age eighteen Alexander had repulsed a Swedish invasion at the Neva River (it was from this battle that he adopted the surname Nevsky). Four years later, Alexander had his most famous victory, destroying the Teutonic Knights at the Battle of the Ice, when the frozen surface of Lake Peipus gave way and swallowed up the German invaders. Here was a princely family around whom the Russians might rally, and so Töregene and Güyük schemed to eliminate them.

The death of Prince Yaroslav was Töregene's last political act; within weeks of her son's enthronement, she died. Töregene had been invaluable to Güyük—she had essentially made him khan. But from Güyük's perspective, Fatima, Töregene's "enforcer," was another matter entirely. She had spread fear, anger, and resentment among the Mongols and their vassals. To unite the people of the Mongol Empire behind him, Güyük turned on Fatima.

Genghis Khan had outlawed the use of torture among Mongols, but Fatima was not a Mongol; she had been a captive taken from one of the Muslim lands to the west. Technically, she was not entitled to the protections of Mongol law, and Güyük took full advantage of this technicality.

He charged Fatima with witchcraft and had her brought to him, stark naked, bound with ropes. In this condition, she was arraigned before a tribunal in Güyük's tent, where she denied the accusation. Days of torture followed until she confessed to practicing witchcraft. After the execution of Fatima, Güyük sent out his warriors to hunt down and kill all her relatives, friends, and followers.

A BRIEF REIGN

Güyük Khan did not stop with Fatima and her circle. His uncle Temüge, the youngest and sole surviving brother of Genghis Khan, had opposed Güyük's candidacy and had raised an army to pressure the Mongol princes to elect him khan. Güyük had Temüge executed for attempting to seize the title of Great Khan by force.

The Russian Prince Alexander Nevsky ignored an invitation to visit Güyük Khan in Karakorum— the prince suspected the khan planned to murder him.

Then Güyük turned on other members of his family. He pushed aside the rights of Chagatai's widow and seized control of the dead man's property. He forced Sorkhokhtani, the widow of Tolui, Genghis's youngest son, and her four sons to surrender their warriors to him, a demand that lowered the family's prestige while also making them vulnerable. With an army he tried to make a surprise attack on Batu Khan, who was encamped in Russia, but Sorkhokhtani managed to get a message to Batu, warning him of Güyük's treachery.

Tolui's widow may have done more than send a warning to Batu, because while Güyük Khan was on the march he suddenly fell ill and died. He was about forty-three years old and had been in perfect health—at least none of the contemporary sources mention any ailment. He was probably murdered, although by who is impossible to establish—he had made so many enemies in the eighteen months he reigned as khan.

A QUESTION OF SUCCESSION

In imitation of her late mother-in-law, Oghul, Güyük's widow, declared herself regent and attempted to take control of the process that would select a new khan. Unlike Töregene, Oghul met fierce opposition: Sorkhokhtani was keen to regain her late husband's property and put forward one of her four sons as khan. Oghul, on the other hand, did not even have the support of her three sons, each of whom was acting independently of her and of each other in his bid to succeed Güyük.

Sorkhokhtani's strongest support came from Batu Khan. In 1250, before Oghul could act, he called a *khuriltai* near Lake Issykul in the Tian Shan Mountains in what is now eastern Kyrgyzstan. There, Batu and Sorkhokhtani's supporters elected Möngke, the eldest son of Tolui and Sorkhokhtani.

Oghul and her supporters cried foul. The election was illegitimate, they argued, because it had not taken place in Mongolia, let alone anywhere near Karakorum (a city that Oghul and her family controlled completely). So Sorkhokhtani called for a new *khuriltai* in that part of Mongolia where Genghis Khan had been born and where his secret grave was located. This was holy ground to all Mongols, and it was part of Sorkhokhtani's inheritance from her husband, Tolui. Outmaneuvered, Oghul and her family had no choice but to travel to Genghis's homeland to participate in a second *khuriltai*.

The administration of Russia prevented Batu from making the trip to Genghis's home country, but he sent an army of 30,000 to stand in for him and to act as bodyguards for Sorkhokhtani and her family. In July 1251, the delegates, eager to rid themselves of all memory of the despotic Güyük, turned away from his family and confirmed the election of Möngke as Great Khan.

Möngke began a weeklong celebration with a sanctified day of rest, during which neither man nor beast was permitted to do any heavy labor, no animal could be killed, and the Earth itself was left untouched—it was forbidden even to drive a tent peg into the ground on this holy day. Then began a week of feasting in which every day the guests consumed 300 horses, 300 oxen, and 3,000 sheep, all washed down with 2,000 carts of *airag*, the Mongols' beloved fermented mare's milk.

IN JULY 1251, THE DELEGATES, EAGER TO RID THEMSELVES OF ALL MEMORY OF THE DESPOTIC GÜYÜK, TURNED AWAY FROM HIS FAMILY AND CONFIRMED THE ELECTION OF MÖNGKE AS GREAT KAHN.

In the midst of the festivities, Oghul's three sons arrived; they declared their wish to pay their respects to Möngke Khan and swear allegiance to him. The moment they stepped inside Möngke's tent, they were arrested and charged with a plot to assassinate the new khan and murder his guests. Möngke had inherited his mother's political shrewdness and had sent spies among Oghul and her family.

Möngke sat in judgment over Güyük's sons, while Sorkhokhtani presided over the trial of Oghul and her female advisors. The three sons were choked to death, and Oghul was drowned. Before Möngke and Sorkhokhtani had finished, seventy-seven of Oghul's relatives, friends, and political supporters were executed. But the purge did not stop there: Möngke sent out tribunals to every corner of the empire to examine government officials suspected of loyalty to the families of Ögödei and Güyük. It was an empire-wide bloodbath that took countless lives. Once the trials and the killing were over, the

Mongol Empire was firmly in the hands of the descendants of Tolui. Sorkhokhtani had the satisfaction of seeing this before her death in February 1252.

NEW CAMPAIGNS

Töregene and Güyük had burdened the Mongols with heavy taxes; Möngke reduced them. Formerly, Mongol noblemen had collected taxes from the people, and it was not uncommon for some of these nobles to extort more money than was actually due; Möngke abolished this system and created a state agency to collect taxes.

IN ADDITION TO REFORMS AT HOME, MÖNGKE DECIDED TO EXPAND THE MONGOL EMPIRE INTO SUNG CHINA AND ALL THE MUSLIM LANDS BETWEEN PERSIA AND THE MEDITERRANEAN SEA.

In addition to reforms at home, Möngke decided to expand the Mongol Empire into Sung China and all the Muslim lands between Persia and the Mediterranean Sea. In emulation of his ancestor, Genghis Khan, Möngke would lead the invasion of southern China personally, while his younger brother, thirty-nine-year-old Hülegü, would march an army of about 100,000 into Muslim territory. Hülegü would begin in northern Iran, where insurgents were undermining Mongol authority in their Islamic provinces. Specifically, Hülegü targeted the sect known as the Order of the Assassins, whom the local governors blamed for fomenting the unrest.

In 1256, Hülegü and his army arrived outside Alamut, the Assassins' fortress in the Elburz Mountains above the southern shore of the Caspian Sea, in what is now Iran. The Assassins considered this for-

Previous page: Decades after Genghis Khan threatened to attack Baghdad, his grandson Hülegü captured the city in 1258. Ms.Sup.Pers.1113.f.180v-181 Mongols under the leadership of Hülegü Khan storming and capturing Baghdad in 1258 (manuscript), / Bibliotheque Nationale, Paris, France / The Bridgeman Art Library International

The Order of the Assassins

The English word *assassin* comes from the Arabic word *hashishin*, which the Islamic historian Farhad Daftary translates as "low-class rabble" or "people of lax morals," a pejorative applied by orthodox Muslims to a group they considered heretics. The Assassins began as a fringe group of Shi'ite Islam known as the *Nizari*. They combined Islamic mysticism with a puritanical hatred of everything they considered morally corrupt. They emerged in Cairo in 1094 when Nizar, the heir to the caliphate of Egypt, was displaced by a palace coup. Nizar led a rebellion to regain his rights, but he was captured and executed. His followers scattered to what is now Iran, Iraq, and Lebanon, where they built approximately one hundred fortresses and prepared for the day when they would come to power and establish an Islamic utopia.

They addressed their leader as the Imam, although in Syria he was known as the *Elder*, or the *Old Man*, which led the Crusaders and Europeans in general to refer to the leader of the Assassins as the *Old Man of the Mountain*.

The Assassins preferred not to wage full-scale war because they feared slaying innocent civilians. Instead, they sent out the equivalent of modern-day commando squads to eliminate their enemies one at a time. Their targets were Muslims whom they considered greedy, unjust, or in league with foreigners and unbelievers.

The Assassins' method was to strike at night when their victim was asleep, or to attack him in the street. They used concealed daggers and did not leave the scene until they were certain their victim was dead. Marco Polo spread the myth that the Assassins used narcotics such as hashish before they went out to kill, but there is no evidence that during their missions the Assassins were under the influence of any drug.

The Order of the Assassins was destroyed by the Mongols in 1256, but the Nizari have survived as an Islamic sect with large communities in Syria, Tajikistan, Afghanistan, Pakistan, India, and Bangladesh.

tress their greatest stronghold; in preparation for the Mongol assault, the garrison had filled Alamut with supplies of food, water, and weapons, but Hülegü was patient: he rolled up his catapults and other siege engines and waited until they had smashed an opening in the Assassins' defenses. The Mongols massacred almost everyone inside the fortress, but they spared the life of the Imam.

He became a very useful prisoner: Hülegü took him to every other Assassin castle in the region, where he stood outside the walls and urged his followers to surrender. When the Assassins had been subdued, Hülegü sent the Imam, Rukn ad-Din Kurshah, to Karakorum, to Möngke Khan. But Möngke had no interest in receiving the "Old Man of the Mountain"; instead, he had him taken outside the city and executed.

Orthodox Muslims rejoiced at the destruction of the Assassins' stronghold, but their joy turned to dread when Hülegü led his army from Alamut across what is now Iraq toward the city of Baghdad. Mecca was the spiritual heart of the Islamic world, but Baghdad was its commercial and cultural capital. The wealth of Asia and Arabia poured into its bazaars. The greatest scientists and scholars of the Muslim world taught at the city's academies and staffed its libraries. It was a city of musicians, poets, artists, and artisans of every description. The most opulent palaces, the loveliest mosques, and the most sublime gardens were found in Baghdad. As always, the Mongols found such riches irresistible.

Hülegü sent the caliph, Al-Musta'sim Billah, a message rebuking him for failing to send an army to help the Mongols subdue the troublesome Assassins. Yet Hülegü was inclined to be merciful: if the caliph accepted vassal status in the Mongol Empire, his life and the lives of the people of Baghdad would be spared. The caliph replied that if the barbarian Mongols dared to attack Baghdad, all Islam would rise up to defend the city and the Mongols would be annihilated. Al-Musta'sim was indulging in wishful thinking; the days when the caliph of Baghdad exercised any real authority over other Muslim rulers was long past. And in fact, the armies of Islam did not rally to save the city.

As he marched toward his prize, Hülegü called up reinforcements from vassal states in the region, including Georgia, Armenia, and the Turkic tribes—a levy that added approximately 70,000 men to his army. In January 1258, Hülegü had Baghdad completely surrounded. The caliph had only 20,000 troops to defend his city.

Inside Baghdad were many Christians and Jews who chafed under Islamic laws that placed various restrictions upon them and required them to pay annual taxes for the privilege of being permitted to practice their religion. Hülegü selected Christians from his army and sent them into the city to meet secretly with the leaders of Baghdad's religious minorities to urge them not to take part in the defense of Baghdad. In return, Hülegü promised the Christians and Jews complete religious freedom under Mongol rule.

At Baghdad, Hülegü used gunpowder bombs and simple mortars to fire missiles into the city. His artillery concentrated on one section of the walls until, on February 4, 1258, a portion of the battlements collapsed and the Mongols entered the city. As they stormed through the streets they killed 90,000 Muslims, but the Mongols left Christians and Jews, as well as their homes, churches, and synagogues, unmolested.

Hülegü ordered all the Muslim inhabitants to leave their homes and gather outside the walls. For seventeen days the Mongols looted the city, periodically carting the valuables out to Hülegü's camp. Once the city had been stripped bare, Hülegü ordered the execution of the caliph along with all the male members of his family.

Hülegü's next objective was Damascus, and as he approached the city he found that he had new allies: a Crusader army under Bohemond VI, Prince of Antioch, and an army of Seljuk Turks from Anatolia (in present-day Turkey) joined him. Given Hülegü's victories, both the Crusaders and the Seljuks preferred to be the Mongols' friends rather than their enemies. As for the rulers of Damascus, they had learned their lesson, too—they surrendered to Hülegü and thereby saved their city and their lives.

CHAPTER 15

THE RISE OF KUBLAI KHAN AND THE BREAKUP OF GENGHIS KHAN'S EMPIRE

MÖNGKE KAHN'S PLAN FOR THE CONQUEST OF SUNG CHINA IN 1252 DEPENDED ON THE ASSISTANCE OF HIS YOUNGER BROTHER, KUBLAI KHAN. FOR SEVERAL YEARS KUBLAI HAD LIVED IN GREAT SPLENDOR ON THE SOUTHERN SIDE OF THE GOBI DESERT, VERY CLOSE TO MONGOL-CONTROLLED JIN CHINA. BUT KUBLAI WAS NOT A DYNAMIC MILITARY LEADER. LIKE HIS LATE UNCLE ÖGÖDEI, HE WAS ESSENTIALLY A HOMEBODY. HE LOVED LUXURY, AND, GORGING HIMSELF ON RICH FOOD AND FINE WINE, GREW OBESE, BUT HE STILL CLIMBED ONTO A MONGOL PONY TO PURSUE HIS GREAT PASSION FOR HUNTING. KUBLAI'S LACK OF BATTLEFIELD EXPERIENCE MADE HIM CAUTIOUS.

Nonetheless, in 1252 Möngke gave his brother the task of preparing the way for the Mongol invasion of Sung China by conquering the independent Kingdom of Ta-li in what is now Yunnan Province along China's remote western border. It was necessary that Ta-li's independence be sacrificed so that Mongol armies and supplies could pass unobstructed through the territory to the front.

While his other brother, Hülegü, pressed his campaign against the Muslim kingdoms to the west, Kublai characteristically delayed more

A band of Mongol horsemen are shown with their leader, Genghis Khan's grandson, Kublai Khan, crossing a desert region in 1280. Many believe Kublai poisoned his brother and rival for the position of Great Khan, Arik Böge.

than a year after receiving his orders before attacking Ta-li. He left nothing to chance: he was well supplied, his troops were well trained and well rested, and he had recruited as his commander Uriangkatai, son of the great Mongol general Subotai, who had died five years earlier at age seventy-three. During his lifetime, Subotai had, as the historian Basil Liddell Hart wrote, "conquered thirty-two nations and won sixty-five pitched battles." The mere presence of the great man's son would inspire the troops. It may have had an unexpected effect on Kao T'ai-hsiang, the king of Ta-li, too, because no sooner had Kublai's army invaded than the king surrendered. To save face, he tried to run away before he would be obliged to make public obeisance to Kublai, but the Mongols captured the runaway king. Kublai ordered Kao's execution, but spared his family.

KUBLAI'S PLEASURE DOME

Möngke Khan and his generals had decided to invade Sung China from several fronts, so Kublai's easy victory over Ta-li was especially welcome—it gave the Mongols one more secure launching point for their conquest of southern China. As a reward, Möngke gave Kublai the governorship of Henan Province in the north and the region around the ancient Chinese city of Xi'an, all of which had been under Mongol control since the time of Genghis. This gift was particularly agreeable to Kublai, who over the years had shown increasing interest in Chinese culture and Chinese comforts. He surrounded himself with Chinese advisors, but there was one vital facet of Chinese life he disliked—he never warmed to Confucianism, which expected a leader to live virtuously and lead by example; like every other Mongol khan, Kublai ruled by decree.

At a time when more and more of Genghis Khan's descendants were converting to Nestorian Christianity, Kublai was attracted to Tibetan varieties of Buddhism. A Tibetan lama initiated Kublai and his wife Chabi into a Tantric Buddhist sect. Kublai's choice of religion troubled no one—the Mongols were still a religiously diverse nation with no sectarian prejudices.

Kublai was a thoughtful overlord. He opened new land for agriculture and stimulated the economy in his territory by issuing that great Chinese invention, paper currency. He also built a Versailles-like complex for himself 125 miles (200 kilometers) from his formal capital, Beijing. He called the place Changdu, or Upper Capital, to distinguish it from Chungdu, or Central Capital, which was Beijing's name at the time.

Changdu is often referred to as a city, and certainly there was a population of several thousand support staff living within the high earthen walls that enclosed the complex. It is more than likely that Changdu was an elaborate summer residence. To escape the heat of Beijing, Kublai, along with his family and his court, lived there during the summer months.

In the heart of the complex was the palace Marco Polo called Ciandu (the origin of the poet Samuel Coleridge's *Xanadu*). Polo described it as "a very fine marble palace, the rooms of which are all gilt and painted with figures of men and beasts and birds, and with a variety of trees and flowers, all executed with such exquisite art that you regard them with delight and astonishment." All around Changdu was a vast park where Kublai could indulge his passion for hunting wild game.

IN 1257, MÖNGKE SENT A TEAM OF INVESTIGATORS TO CHANGDU TO DETERMINE WHETHER KUBLAI WAS LOYAL, OR WHETHER HE MIGHT BE PLANNING TO SPLIT OFF NORTHERN CHINA FROM THE MONGOL EMPIRE.

Changdu delighted Kublai, but back in Karakorum there were Mongol traditionalists who grumbled that the Great Khan's brother no longer lived as a true Mongol. It was one thing to adopt a few customs or luxuries from the conquered nations, but to his critics it appeared that Kublai was intent on becoming as Chinese as possible. In 1257, Möngke sent a team of investigators to Changdu to determine whether Kublai was loyal, or whether he might be planning to split off northern China from the Mongol Empire.

Kublai was offended that he had come under suspicion. His first impulse was classically Mongolian: he would raise an army and destroy the man who had insulted him. Such a course of action appalled his Confucian advisors, who considered it impious for a younger brother to rebel against the firstborn. The Confucians urged Kublai to defuse the crisis by traveling to Karakorum to reassure Möngke personally of his loyalty.

The Chinese version of the meeting of the two brothers—the only version that has survived—tells how the moment they saw one another they fell into each other's arms and all suspicions and resentments vanished. It's possible. Then again, the brothers may have reconciled because Kublai realized that in a civil war Möngke would almost certainly defeat him, and Möngke realized that in his upcoming invasion of Sung China, the support of Kublai and the Jin Chinese would be essential.

A STALLED INVASION

Almost immediately after his reconciliation with his brother, Möngke Khan began planning the invasion of Sung China. Some Mongol generals opposed the invasion, recalling the disastrous effect that the heat, humidity, and mosquitoes of the Asian subcontinent had had on their armies during Genghis's abortive attempt to conquer India. They suspected they would find the climate of southern China equally unhealthy, but Möngke replied that he could not leave the conquest of China incomplete.

To prepare for the invasion, Möngke returned to Genghis's homeland, where he sacrificed horses to the spirit of his grandfather and made additional sacrifices to Tengri, the Sky God. Although many in his family had become Christians, Möngke had not been converted and still practiced the traditional shamanism of the Mongols. By custom the youngest son of a Mongol family remained at home to guard the hearth; Möngke kept that tradition by appointing his youngest brother, Arik Böge, about forty years old, to guard the imperial hearth at Karakorum and administer the empire in his absence.

In spring 1258, Möngke Khan led his army into China. The exact number of men is uncertain—some sources claim the khan had 600,000 men under his command, and Kublai brought an additional 90,000. Möngke had divided his force into four divisions: one he led personally; the others were led by Subotai's son Uriangkatai, Kublai, and one of the khan's nephews whose name has not come down to us. The armies targeted the western and central portions of Sung China, believing that once these areas were subdued the pressure on the now-isolated eastern sector, the best-defended region of the country, would prove fatal. Better still, it might persuade the Sung emperor, Lizong, to surrender.

Möngke's generals were right—the climate in southern China was hard on the Mongols and their horses. To make matters worse, most of the army came down with dysentery brought on by drinking contaminated water. Despite their physical misery, the Mongols enjoyed victory after victory. Nearly sixty years earlier Genghis had learned how to subdue a fortified city, and by now the Mongols were experts. They still traveled with their Chinese engineers and munitions specialists, who used catapults and primitive cannons and mortar launchers against the cities of the Sung, and one by one, they fell. The Mongols would have preferred to fight their enemies on horseback, as they had done so successfully against the Russians, Poles, and Hungarians, but the Sung Chinese were not about to forsake the security of their walls to take their chances against the world's finest cavalry.

By March 1258, Möngke's Mongols had overrun the province of Sichuan and captured its greatest city, Chengdu, but there the Mongols' campaign stalled. The Sung armies of Emperor Lizong numbered 1.5 million, and they fought ferociously. One year after he occupied Chengdu, Möngke had failed to penetrate deeper into southern China. His generals advised him to withdraw to northern China, reminding him once again of how unhealthy southern China became during the summer months. Möngke rejected their advice and ordered the army to march south.

Heavy rain throughout May and June slowed the Mongols' progress and made day-to-day life miserable. Furthermore, the huge Sung armies kept the Mongols from advancing deeper. And then Möngke Khan fell ill, perhaps with dysentery or cholera. On August 11, 1259, Möngke died, and the invasion of Sung China stalled as the Mongols began to think who should replace their Great Khan.

UNGRACIOUS IN VICTORY

As an escort of Mongol warriors and dignitaries, including Kublai, carried Möngke Khan's body back to Mongolia, the army retreated to Sichuan. Meanwhile, in Syria, Kublai and Möngke's brother Hülegü broke off his successful conquest to attend the *khuriltai* that would elect the next khan.

As the family of Genghis, along with the Mongol generals and the Mongol vassals, gathered once again in Karakorum, it was clear to all that there were two contenders—Kublai and his younger brother Arik Böge. Kublai was intelligent, a proven commander, and an able administrator, and he had a regal aura, but his reputation made other Mongols uneasy. He was too much at ease in cities and palaces, his Chi-

nese tastes were too pronounced, and he did not seem very Mongolian. Arik Böge, on the other hand, was a Mongol of the steppes who did not merely respect the old ways but also lived them. Given a choice between Kublai and the traditionalist Arik, the *khuriltai* that met in June 1260 voted for Arik.

The outcome was a terrible disappointment for Kublai, but once again his Chinese advisors offered him a solution. They urged him to hold his own *khuriltai* in northern China, in the provinces Möngke had given him. Only Kublai's supporters attended, and predictably they elected him Great Khan. But Kublai took matters a giant step further when he also proclaimed himself emperor of northern China. Following the custom of Chinese emperors he adopted a new name, *Zhongtong*, which means "Central Rule." Now he had an army comprised of men from northern China. He had one other significant advantage as well: the farms of northern China had become Karakorum's breadbasket, and the capital relied on regular shipments of food to feed its ever-booming population. Kublai stopped sending food to Karakorum, and he marched his army there instead.

The war between Kublai and Arik dragged on for four years while Hülegü and the rest of the family kept their distance from the fight. Karakorum exchanged hands more than once, but neither army was strong enough to destroy the other. Then, about 1262 or 1263, the standoff shifted in Kublai's favor. Mongol warriors deserted Arik to serve Kublai, convinced that his army was better supplied, and that he was more intelligent and had the will to outlast Arik. The final blow came in 1263, when bad weather ruined the grass of the steppes and the Mongols' horses and livestock began to die of hunger. If the animals died, it would not be long before the Mongols would begin to die, and the greatest stores of food and fodder were in Kublai's China.

With no choice left him, Arik Böge made the humiliating journey to Kublai's palace at Changdu, where he surrendered. In victory, Kublai was not gracious. He received his brother in his audience hall, surrounded by his court. Who was truly the Great Khan? he asked Arik.

As a victorious warrior who kept the old Mongolian customs, Arik Böge appealed to Mongol traditionalists, but in the election for Great Khan, Kublai outmaneuvered his brother. Both were sons of Genghis Khan's son, Tolui. akg-images / Werner Forman

The Silver Tree

If one event represented the end of the Mongol Empire, it was the abandonment of Karakorum. In 1267, Kublai ordered the capital city to be stripped of all its valuables and the palaces and houses pulled down. No one contested the order. Khaidu had moved deeper into Central Asia, perhaps to escape the war between his two brothers; eventually, he would make his capital in Bukhara.

Among the treasures Kublai carried back to China was Möngke Khan's most prized possession—the Silver Tree. William of Rubruck, a Franciscan friar sent as an ambassador to Möngke from King Louis IX of France, saw this marvel in the khan's palace. It had been fashioned by Guillaume Boucher, a Parisian silversmith who was captured during the Mongol invasion of Eastern Europe.

Boucher had erected the Silver Tree in the middle of the palace courtyard. Wrapped around the trunk of the tree were four serpents that were fountains: wine flowed from one, *airag*—fermented mare's milk—from another, rice wine from the third, and mead from the fourth. Standing amid the uppermost branches of the tree was a silver angel with a trumpet at his side. When the khan called for a drink, a servant concealed inside the tree trunk operated a mechanism that caused the angel to lift the trumpet to his lips. As the trumpet sounded, the four beverages gushed out of the open jaws of the four serpents and into large silver bowls. The original tree disappeared centuries ago; today, on the site of Karakorum, the Mongolian government has set up a reproduction of Boucher's Silver Tree.

Before the palace of the Mongol khans stood the astonishing Silver Tree, the work of a silversmith from Paris, which consisted of four serpent fountains that provided wine, mare's milk, rice wine, and mead for Kublai Khan. © Mary Evans Picture Library / The Image Works

In one final flash of pride Arik Böge answered, "I was then, you are now." At that, Kublai insisted that Arik kowtow to him.

Hülegü reproached Kublai for shaming their youngest brother in public, but Kublai was unabashed. He called for yet another *khuriltai* to try Arik Böge. Kublai and his followers escorted Arik back to Karakorum, but the rest of the family would not attend. Necessity compelled them to recognize Kublai as Great Khan, but they refused to participate in a show trial. Rather than risk provoking another rebellion, Kublai became magnanimous and forgave Arik Böge. Many of Arik's support-

ers were executed, and Arik was exiled from Karakorum and Changdu, but he suffered no further punishment. Then, in 1266, he suddenly fell ill and died. Most Mongols at the time, and most historians today, believe Arik Böge was poisoned on orders from Kublai Khan.

THE DISINTEGRATION OF THE EMPIRE

Kublai's seizure of power and his humiliation of his brother Arik Böge divided the family of Genghis Khan, and ultimately shattered the unity of the Mongol Empire. Möngke Temür, the grandson of Batu Khan, governed the Mongols' territory in Russia. Hülegü governed the Mongols' Muslim domains from Afghanistan to the border of modern-day Turkey. Those Mongols who distrusted the influence the Chinese, Persians, Arabs, and Europeans had on their ruling class, and preferred to live in the traditional way on the steppes, rallied to Khaidu, Ögödei Khan's grandson, whose power base was the Mongol heartland. Kublai, of course, governed northern China, Tibet, and part of Manchuria. None of these men had the military strength to force the other three to submit to him, and so the Mongol Empire split into four. From time to time the four men cooperated with each other, but that changed in the years to come: the decade of the 1270s saw increasing independence of action among the four pieces of Genghis Khan's once-mighty empire. Southern China continued to be ruled by the Sung dynasty.

> **THOSE MONGOLS WHO DISTRUSTED THE INFLUENCE THE CHINESE, PERSIANS, ARABS, AND EUROPEANS HAD ON THEIR RULING CLASS, AND PREFERRED TO LIVE IN THE TRADITIONAL WAY ON THE STEPPES, RALLIED TO KHAIDU, ÖGÖDEI KHAN'S GRANDSON, WHOSE POWER BASE WAS THE MONGOL HEARTLAND.**

OVERAWING THE CHINESE

With the dismantling of Karakorum, Kublai Khan made a decisive break with traditional Mongol life; henceforth, he would be a Chinese emperor. To ensure a successful reign, he began to woo his subjects. Historian Jack Weatherford has observed, "For most of its history, China had been a great civilization but not a unified country." Kublai set out to win over the upper classes and the intelligentsia by forging a united China—north and south—under a single ruler—himself. Now that he had proclaimed himself emperor, he announced, in 1271, that he was founding a new dynasty, the Yuan, which means *origins* or *beginnings*. It was customary in Kublai's day to refer to the dynasty as the *Dai Yuan*, or *Great Origins*.

King Louis IX of France sent Father William of Rubruck as an ambassador to Möngke Khan in 1251.
The embassy did not establish permanent relations between France and the Mongol Empire, but Father
William did return with a book of astute observations regarding Mongol life and culture.

To prove to the Chinese that he had the mandate of Heaven, Kublai dressed as a Chinese emperor, learned to perform the religious rites expected of an emperor, and in every way lived like a Chinese emperor. He built a temple to the memory of his ancestors, complete with commemorative tablets and altars on which offerings were made. Just as Kublai had adopted a Chinese name when he became emperor, now he renamed all of his ancestors, going back to Yesügei and Höelün, Genghis Khan's parents.

Such acts were intended to attract China's upper classes. To appease China's great mass of ordinary citizens, Kublai established what he called *Pacification Committees* around the country to rebuild and restore what had been destroyed by war—villages, farmland, roads, and local temples.

Yet in other respects Kublai antagonized the Chinese, especially in his abolition of the civil service exams and the authority of local magistrates. Kublai tried to recast China's government as one immense hierarchy in which government officials at every level were expected to enact the laws the emperor promulgated. To achieve this he placed Mongols in almost all of the highest positions of responsibility. Second in rank came Persians, Georgians, Armenians, and other trusted vassals. The Jin, or northern Chinese, came third. Although Kublai valued the counsel of many Chinese advisors, after he conquered Sung China, he placed the Sung or southern Chinese in the bottom tier.

Kublai may have felt that he had no other option than to elevate the Mongols in China to the highest ranks of society. According to demographic historians Graziella Caselli, Jacques Vallin, and Guillaume Wunsch, there were approximately 8.5 million Chinese in northern China and another 50 million in southern China; the Mongols, on the other hand, never numbered more than a few hundred thousand. Because the Mongols could not outnumber the Chinese, they had to overawe them.

Yet Kublai demanded high standards of performance from his officials. Extortion, bribery, despotism, laziness, or any other form of corruption were not tolerated and were punishable by the humiliation of flogging or even execution.

He established his court on the site of the Jin emperor's capital. Drawing upon a multinational talent pool of architects, artists, and builders, Kublai called for a magnificent city unlike any in China. In place of cramped alleys he wanted broad boulevards and vast open plazas. Instead of haphazard urban sprawl he wanted geometric perfection, with all the streets running either north-south or east-west. This experiment in urban planning was intended to impress, of course, and it brought to the inhabitants the advantages of fresh air and natural light, but the grand squares and wide streets were also ideal for moving armies swiftly into or out of the city. The Mongols called the place *Khanbalik*, or *City of the Khan*; Marco Polo rendered it as *Cambaluc*. The Chinese called it *Dadu*, or *Great Capital*. Today it is known as Beijing.

Kublai made his city a center of international trade, welcoming merchants from throughout the known world (which explains how the Polo family of Venice came to China). To serve the religious needs of this diverse population, Muslim imams, Buddhist monks, Christian priests, and Jewish rabbis moved to the city and opened houses of worship. In keeping with a tradition established by Genghis Khan years earlier, Kublai exempted all members of the clergy from taxation, guaranteed everyone full freedom of religion, and protected all temples, churches, mosques, and synagogues, as well as other religious institutions.

Kublai Khan was fostering a wealthy, cosmopolitan society in his empire, but it paled in comparison to the riches and sophistication of Sung China. And so southern China became the khan's next objective.

CHAPTER 16

THE FIRST MONGOL EMPEROR OF CHINA

■ ■ ■

IN 1260, HAO CHING, A CONFUCIAN SCHOLAR, ARRIVED AT THE COURT OF THE SUNG EMPEROR IN HANGZHOU WITH A MESSAGE FROM HIS MASTER, KUBLAI KHAN. IF THE SUNG EMPEROR LIZONG RECOGNIZED KUBLAI AS THE TRUE SON OF HEAVEN, DESTINED TO RULE AS EMPEROR OVER A UNITED CHINA, HE WOULD BE PERMITTED A DEGREE OF AUTONOMY.

Hao Ching reminded the Sung emperor that the Mongols were a formidable war machine who had conquered everything from Korea to Syria, from the Sung's northern border to Russia. Why invite a war with such people? The Sung had paid tribute to other barbarians—why not acquiesce to Kublai's demands? But Lizong would not give up his throne. In reply to Kublai's message, he imprisoned Hao Ching. When Kublai sent another delegation to plead with Lizong to release Hao, the emperor sent the khan's messengers away.

Although Kublai lost one trusted advisor, fate brought him another. Liu Zheng, a Sung Chinese courtier lured by Kublai's promises of land and other rewards, defected to the Mongols. Liu impressed upon Kublai the necessity of building a Mongol navy. Such a thing had never existed before; since Genghis's day the Mongols had learned siege warfare (thanks in large part to captured Chinese engineers and military tacticians), but sea battles were entirely unknown. The Sung had had a navy for at least one hundred years, but during the 1260s corrupt government officials diverted funds intended for the navy to their own use. Consequently, many of the ships were in poor repair and poorly supplied, the officers were demoralized, and the crews had scarcely any

Kublai Khan completed the conquest of China and founded a Mongol dynasty. Unlike his predecessors, he lived in a palace, not a felt tent, which distanced him from Mongol traditionalists.

training. Liu Zheng persuaded Kublai that if he built his own navy he could defeat the Sung at sea and on the rivers of China.

The Sung had other military problems as well. Rapacious landowners had snatched up virtually all the best farmland in the country and had succeeded, through bribery, to win for themselves exemption from paying any taxes. This strained the Sung's finances severely, so much so that even the military was underfunded.

Convinced by such favorable circumstances that he could conquer Sung China, Kublai recruited shipbuilders and trained crews, most of them Koreans and northern Chinese, in preparation for an invasion of southern China.

THE FIRST CAMPAIGN

In 1268, Kublai sent his army and new navy against the towns of Xiangyang and Fancheng, which stood across from each on opposite banks of the Han River in what is now Hubei Province. Once captured, the towns could be used as a staging place for Kublai's invasion of Sung China. He assembled a general staff comprised of his finest commanders—Mongols, Arabs, and Chinese. The troops were as ethnically diverse as their commanders.

Nonetheless, it took five years of on-again, off-again siege warfare to capture the towns. Xiangyang and Fancheng were both well supplied with provisions and weapons, yet for reasons the sources do not reveal, there were periods during those five years when the Mongols lifted the siege and went back north, which gave the Sung time to reprovision the towns and prepare for the next assault.

The Mongols relied upon a naval blockade of the river to keep fresh men and supplies from reaching the towns. In the case of Fancheng, it was old-fashioned siege tactics combined with a new siege engine that caused the town to fall. A team of Muslim engineers built larger-than-usual counterweight trebuchets that hurled huge boulders with much more force than did traditional catapults. Within a matter of days, the walls were battered down and the Mongols stormed the town.

Across the river, the Muslim engineers built an even larger trebuchet and unleashed it on Xiangyang. After several days of relentless bombardment, a portion of the walls was pulverized and the town's commander surrendered. It was late March 1272 and Kublai Khan had his first foothold in Sung China.

THE NEW GENERAL

After the successful capture of Xiangyang and Fancheng, Kublai prepared to drive deeper into Sung China. One of his Chinese advisers suggested the khan appoint as commander in chief a Turk named Bayan, the descendant of several military men who had served the Mongols. As a young man, Bayan had learned the art of war while accompanying Hülegü against the Assassins and the caliph of Baghdad. In the 1260s, when he was about thirty years old, Bayan joined Kublai's administration, where he established a reputation for wise counsel. Impressed by Bayan's wisdom and experience, Kublai named him commander of the invasion of Sung China.

Throughout 1274 and 1275, Bayan enjoyed a series of victories over the Sung. He mastered the art of deploying a navy as well as land forces, and he learned how to support them with artillery. In January 1275, Bayan's army fought their way across the Yangtze River and inflicted heavy casualties on the Sung army. In mid-March outside Yangzhou, he faced the Sung commander, Jia Sidao. Jia had 130,000 men under his command; the number of Bayan's forces is unknown. We do know, however, that Bayan had artillery and that he used it to great effect, hurling flaming bombs into the ranks of the Sung until the troops fled the field en masse. Afraid he would be captured by the Mongols, Jia and what remained of his army fled the battlefield.

Emperor Lizong died in 1264 and was succeeded by his nephew, Duzong, a hapless alcoholic. After Duzong's death in 1274, his eight-year-old son, Duanzong, became emperor. At the Sung court the advisors of the boy-emperor laid all the blame for their defeats on General Jia. He was stripped of all his offices, his friends and supporters were also demoted in rank, and the general himself was banished. On his way into exile, Jia was murdered by the general who had been sent to serve as his escort.

As Bayan led his army straight for the capital city, Hangzhou, the Sung imperial family, led by the elderly Empress Dowager, tried to turn back the conquerors by promising to make lavish annual payments of silver and silk to Kublai. Bayan rejected these offers. Sung China was within his grasp and he would not return to his khan until he possessed it completely. Recognizing the futility of prolonging a war they could not win, the Empress Dowager and the imperial council informed Duanzong that he must capitulate. In January 1276, the Sung emperor surrendered to Bayan.

Marco Polo

Marco Polo was born in Venice in 1254. His father, Nicolo, and his uncle, Maffeo Polo, were merchants whose quest for riches led them east to the Mongol Empire. In 1260, Nicolo and Maffeo made their first journey to the Chinese court of Kublai Khan, who made them welcome. The Polos spent several years in China, building a fortune and winning the friendship of Kublai. When they returned to Venice nine years later, Marco was fifteen years old. Almost immediately the Polos began planning a second journey to China.

They set out in 1271, but many delays—including an entire year when Marco was too ill to travel—slowed their progress. They did not reach Kublai's court until 1275. According to Marco Polo's celebrated memoir, he made a strong impression on the emperor and almost immediately Kublai sent him on diplomatic missions to the lands along the eastern edge of his empire. Marco visited what are now Myanmar (formerly Burma), Vietnam, and Tibet. He wrote that among other honors, Kublai appointed him governor of the city of Yangzhou in present-day Jiangsu Province. Marco also described being a participant at the fall of Xiangyang and Fancheng.

Unfortunately, Marco was not a consistently reliable travel writer. For example, Xiangyang and Fancheng were captured about three years before he arrived in China. And the sources from Yangzhou do not mention Marco Polo at all, let alone as governor.

There are also curious omissions: although Marco describes jewels and spices and other luxury items in detail, he fails to mention things that were common to China but would have appeared strange to a European, such as foot-binding and acupuncture. Marco does not even mention tea. In explanation, it has been suggested that although Marco was in the employ of the Mongol emperor, he didn't have much contact with the Chinese.

However, his reports to Kublai were clear, concise, and reliable. If they had not been, the khan would not have kept him in his service for seventeen years. The "tall tales" crept into the account of his travels that Marco dictated between 1296 and 1299, while he was immured in a Genoese prison. It is even possible that some of the embellishments were the work of Rustichello da Pisa, his cellmate to whom he told his stories.

In 1324, as he lay on his deathbed, Marco's friends urged him, for the sake of his soul, to retract at least his most extravagant claims about the East. Marco replied, "I have not told half of everything I saw."

Marco Polo, the son of a Venetian merchant, wrote a detailed account of his seventeen years in China in the service of Kublai Khan, yet never mentioned footbinding, acupuncture, or even tea.

Bayan was generous to the Sung. He prohibited looting and insisted that the imperial family be treated with respect. He personally escorted the boy-emperor and the Empress Dowager to Kublai's residence at Changdu, where the khan promised to protect them and their relatives. Kublai confirmed Bayan's order regarding plunder, although he appropriated for himself the imperial robes and regalia of the Sung dynasty. By safeguarding the lives and property of the southern Chinese and treating their imperial family with respect, Kublai won the loyalty of fifty million new subjects.

THE NEW CHINA

Just as Genghis Khan essentially reinvented Mongol society, Kublai took advantage of the dramatic unification of China—the first time such a thing had occurred in the country's long history—to introduce a host of changes and innovations.

Although the Mongol Empire was broken up, there was still freedom of movement among its four parts. Consequently, Kublai could draw upon a talent pool of Chinese, Tanguts, Tibetans, Koreans, Georgians, Armenians, Persians, Arabs, and Turks. Like Genghis, he did not care about a man's social standing, but only about his abilities. When he made rank-and-file appointments to government offices, he named northern Chinese, southern Chinese, and non-Chinese. His empire was multiracial and multiethnic and embraced people of many religions; he would not tolerate cliques. By forcing disparate peoples to work together, he hoped to foster an atmosphere of tolerance and respect.

Under the Jin and Sung emperors, magistrates and local administrators maintained a fiction that they served selflessly, without pay. In fact, they extorted fees and "gifts" from the people who came to them for help. Kublai abolished this system, replacing these venal men with professional salaried government employees.

One of Kublai's most ambitious projects was to create a new alphabet that could be used to write any language. This seemed crucial, because he was often corresponding with Muslim viziers, Vietnamese generals, Hindu princes, and European merchants, each of whom had his own alphabet. Kublai asked a Tibetan lama named Phagspa to tackle the

Previous page: An illustration from Marco Polo's book shows the queen of Quinsai surrendering her city in the province of Magi in South China to one of Kublai Khan's generals in 1271. akg-images

problem. In 1269 Phagspa delivered to Kublai an alphabet comprised of forty-two letters adapted from the Tibetan system. Rather than impose it, Kublai disseminated it throughout his empire, encouraging his people to use it. But this Mongol writing system never caught on. Each of the khan's subjects was too attached to his own alphabet to change. Phagspa's creation lingered on only as long as the Mongols dominated China.

ONE OF KUBLAI'S MOST AMBITIOUS PROJECTS WAS TO CREATE A NEW ALPHABET THAT COULD BE USED TO WRITE ANY LANGUAGE.

Kublai also dabbled in the arts. He encouraged writers to publish in the colloquial language of the people rather than in the formal, classical style of the schools. He enjoyed drama, and so playwrights produced at least 500 new plays during Kublai's reign, about 160 of which still survive. Traditionally, the Chinese regarded performers of all kinds— actors, dancers, singers, musicians—as little better than prostitutes. To show his regard for artists, Kublai erected new theater districts in respectable neighborhoods.

THE DIVINE WIND

Bayan's successful use of naval forces during his conquest of Sung China persuaded Kublai that the Mongols were ready for naval warfare. With his empire stretching now to the East China Sea, he planned to strike the next country in his path—Japan. Since the 1260s Kublai had sent envoys to Japan, attempting to bring the island nation into the Mongol orbit, but Japan's military government, the Bakufu, either refused to receive the Mongol ambassadors, or if they did receive them, they sent them away without an answer. In 1274 Kublai sent 15,000 Mongol and Chinese troops, supported by about 6,000 Korean conscripts, to invade Japan. Korean sailors manned the Mongol armada of about 800 ships.

The Korean-built ships were *kwasons*, or spear vessels. They had been developed as ramming vessels to cripple or destroy Chinese and

Japanese pirate ships that raided the coastal towns of Korea. They were large, flat-bottomed ships equipped with a single mast and a single steering oar. About 300 *kwasons* were built for the invasion of Japan. The remaining 500 were smaller support vessels that transported supplies.

The Mongols and their allies landed on the coast of Kyushu. Japan had a small navy of perhaps 200 ships, but it had not been mobilized. If it had, it is doubtful that it would have been effective. The Japanese had a strange way of fighting at sea; they lashed their ships together and laid down heavy wooden planks to create a fighting platform on

which the samurai could employ the tactics they had developed for fighting on land. The Mongols' catapults and the *kwasons*' rams would have reduced the Japanese ships to splinters.

On shore, the Mongols enjoyed early victories over the Japanese. The Japanese were accustomed to hand-to-hand combat, a form of

During Kublai Khan's second invasion of Japan in 1280, a samurai warrior boards a ship to attack and kill a Mongol officer. History repeated itself when a storm drowned Mongol attempts in 1274 and 1280 to invade Japan. The Art Archive / Laurie Platt Winfrey

fighting at which they excelled, but the Mongols kept their distance, picking off the Japanese troops with arrows and other missiles. In November 1274, the Mongol force was near Hakata when a storm blew up. The Korean sailors insisted that they must put out to sea at once or the storm would smash the moored ships against the rocks. Reluctantly, the Mongol officers agreed, and marched their men onto the ships— but not quickly enough. Before the fleet could get safely to deep water, the storm struck, destroying hundreds of ships and taking the lives of approximately 13,000 men.

KUBLAI KHAN HAD NEVER SUFFERED SUCH A TERRIBLE DEFEAT— IT BOTH SHOCKED AND HUMILIATED HIM. IN JAPAN, THE TYPHOON WAS CALLED A *KAMIKAZE*, A DIVINE WIND, SENT BY THE GODS TO PROTECT SACRED JAPAN FROM HER ENEMIES.

In 1280, Kublai was ready to try again. This time he sent an army of 40,000 men from northern China and an army of 100,000 from southern China to attack Kyushu. Nine hundred Korean ships and 600 ships built in southern China, manned by Korean and Chinese sailors, would carry his army to Japan.

The expedition was troubled from the start. Most of the troops were Chinese, who fought poorly in Japan because they had no interest in seeing the Mongols conquer that nation. Chinese officers quarreled with the Mongol commanders, and their squabbles became more intense once they arrived in Japan, where the defenders put up stiff resistance. Two months into the invasion, the Mongols still did not have the upper hand, nor had they achieved any major victory over the Japanese.

Then, on August 15 and 16, 1280, history repeated itself. A typhoon was blowing off the coast of Kyushu. Once again, the Koreans urged the army to get back onto the ships while there was time. And once again, it took too long to get so many men aboard. About 65,000 of

Kublai's men drowned, while those troops who were still ashore were killed or taken prisoner by the Japanese.

Kublai Khan had never suffered such a terrible defeat—it both shocked and humiliated him. In Japan, the typhoon was called a *kamikaze*, a divine wind, sent by the gods to protect sacred Japan from her enemies. More to the point, these two storms had shattered the idea that the Mongols were invincible. Determined to recover his pride, Kublai planned a third invasion of Japan between 1283 and 1286, but this time the Chinese and the Koreans refused to cooperate, and he was obliged to abandon the idea.

THE UNHAPPY KHAN

Chabi was Kublai Khan's favorite wife, a woman who was as politically astute as Genghis's mother and wife, Höelün and Börte, and as ambitious as Ögödei's widow, Töregene. She was as keen to be empress of China as her husband was to be emperor, but she also understood the importance, from the Mongols' perspective, of Kublai becoming Great Khan. During the succession crisis that followed Möngke's death, Chabi was especially outspoken in urging Kublai to seize the title from his brother, Arik Böge.

Out of his deep love for Chabi, Kublai had named their son, Zhenjin, Crown Prince. There would be no unpredictable *khuriltais* in China; succession would pass according to the traditional method in royal families, from father to son. When Chabi died in 1281, Kublai grieved deeply. He had several wives, but he set up only one memorial tablet in his family temple, and that tablet was dedicated to Chabi.

Then, in 1285, Zhenjin died. Kublai had brought in Chinese tutors to instruct his son in Chinese culture and history, and had groomed him carefully to be emperor; the loss of such a promising heir shattered the khan. Overwhelmed by grief over the deaths of Chabi and Zhenjin, Kublai passed his days overeating and drinking heavily. He became enormously overweight. He lost interest in the administration of his empire. The emperor suffered from gout and other ailments; to find relief he summoned to his bedside physicians and shamans and anyone who claimed expertise in medicine. Yet none of their remedies did Kublai any good.

Early in 1294, General Bayan paid the khan a visit, but even the arrival of an old and trusted friend failed to lift Kublai's spirits. On February 18, Kublai Khan died. He was eighty years old. He was succeeded by his grandson, Temür, the son of the late Zhenjin.

Kublai Khan's tomb has never been found. We know a procession carried Kublai's body into the Kentai Mountains, but where it was laid to rest remains a mystery.

THE FALL OF THE YUAN DYNASTY

Temür, known in China by his "throne name," *Chengzong*, was an effective emperor who kept the peace with the Mongol khanates in Persia and Mongolia and expanded his domain into what is now Vietnam. After Temür died in 1307, the Yuan dynasty was plagued time and again by political chaos. Incompetent, venal emperors burdened the Chinese with crushing taxes. Corruption on the local level, which Kublai had rooted out, returned, adding to the hardships of millions of ordinary Chinese and stirring up their resentment against the Mongol regime. That the Yuan were never fully accepted as Chinese by their Chinese subjects contributed mightily to their downfall.

In addition to the trouble wrought by inept governments, Yuan China suffered a series of natural disasters. In 1331 bubonic plague, known as the "Black Death," erupted in China; by 1351, at least half of the population of China had died in the epidemic. Three times during the 1340s the Yellow River flooded, washing away farmland and bringing famine in its wake.

In 1351, violent peasant uprisings broke out across China. The peasant army, known as the Red Turbans, was led by Zhu Yuanzhang, a peasant who had lost almost his entire family during the famines. Zhu had taken vows as a Buddhist monk, but then left his monastery to become a bandit. The rebellion lasted seventeen years until, in 1368, the surviving members of the Yuan dynasty fled to Mongolia. The Mongols who remained in China were either killed or absorbed into the population. Zhu proclaimed himself emperor, adopted the throne name *Hongwu*, which means "Vastly Warlike," and declared that he was founding a new dynasty, the Ming. The Yuan had not lasted even a century, making it the shortest reigning dynasty in the history of China.

After the premature death of his father, Zhenjin, Temür succeeded his grandfather Kublai as emperor of China. After his death in 1307, Mongol China was plagued by corruption, internal strife, and a series of natural disasters. akg-images

EPILOGUE

I n the 1300s, about thirty years before the Mongol Yuan dynasty was driven out of China, the descendants of Hülegü, Kublai Khan's brother, lost their grip on Persia and the Middle East. The number of Mongols who had made their home in these lands had always been small, and in a short time they were absorbed into the larger population and vanished. In Central Asia, most Mongols returned to their traditional way of life on the steppes, living in *gers*, herding their livestock, consulting their shamans, and feuding with their neighbors. But a Mongol powerbase developed in the cities of Bukhara and Samarkand, where Mongol settlers converted to Islam and adopted the language and many of the customs of the Turks. The most famous of these Mongols was the conqueror Tamerlane, who claimed (incorrectly) to be a descendant of Genghis Khan.

From their capital of Sarai on the lower Volga, the Golden Horde ruled Russia and modern-day Ukraine for more than two hundred years, a period the Russian and Ukrainians recall as the era of "the Tartar Yoke." But over time, the Golden Horde split into at least six petty khanates. In the fifteenth century, as the military strength of the Principality of Moscow increased, Grand Duke Ivan III took advantage of the Mongols' disunity and in 1480 refused to pay any more tribute to the khans. Seventy-two years later, in 1552, Ivan IV, "The Terrible," reversed the tables on the khans by attacking and capturing one of their capitals, Kazan. To celebrate his victory, Ivan built the landmark St. Basil's Cathedral in Moscow's Red Square.

Historians disagree about how many people fell victim to the Mongols—certainly millions, perhaps as high as 40 million. In terms of genocide, to use a modern term, the Mongols had no equal until the twentieth century, when Hitler, Stalin, and Mao slaughtered their enemies by the tens of millions.

But the Mongols were much more than shaggy, bloody-minded barbarians. Out of a handful of rival kingdoms they forged a united China—and that great nation has remained united ever since. They did the same in Persia, which became modern-day Iran. Although it may seem strange that a nomadic people should engage in nation building, it was Genghis Khan who set the pattern when, out of a collection of rival clans and tribes, he created the Mongol nation.

As they extended their empire across Asia, the Middle East, and into Europe, the Mongols established world trade on a level that probably had not been seen since the glory days of the Roman Empire. Like the Romans, the Mongols welcomed not only all manner of goods but also ideas and religions. And then there were the looted luxuries of countless cities, which poured into the Mongol camps, transforming Mongol day-to-day life by introducing lavish, previously unknown comforts, not to mention a host of slaves who liberated Mongol men and women from the most tedious tasks.

Merchants, missionaries, and ambassadors from throughout the known world flocked to the Mongol Empire, but none were as fascinated by the marvels and luxuries of Asia as the Europeans. It can be said that the Mongol Empire, stretching as it did into Eastern Europe, opened Asia up to the Europeans, very few of whom had ventured much farther than Armenia. Once Europeans, particularly European merchants, learned what was available in the Mongol Empire, almost overnight an insatiable market developed in Europe for the spices, silks, porcelain, furs, and other exquisite commodities of the East. It was the desire to find a fast route to the markets of Asia that led to the Age of Discovery. When Christopher Columbus set sail across the Atlantic Ocean in 1492, he carried a letter from Ferdinand and Isabella of Spain addressed to the Great Khan of China. Alas, Columbus never had an opportunity to deliver that letter because the continents of North and South America unexpectedly got in his way.

One component of the Mongols' success was their openness to change. They adapted their way of making war to capture cities and towns, and they sought out engineers, munitions makers, and anyone else who could help them win battles. The Mongols were also adaptable on a personal level. Genghis Khan lived his whole life in a felt tent (although during the last years of his life that tent was very splendid). His sons and grandsons, however, moved from tents into palaces.

Although the Mongol Empire collapsed nearly seven hundred years ago, the Mongol influence is still felt today. In China, Kublai Khan's palace was the origin of the Forbidden City and his capital city is now Beijing.

The Mongols also influenced the course of Russian history. For approximately four hundred years, Kiev in what is now Ukraine had been the political, cultural, and religious heart of the country. After the Golden Horde under Batu Khan destroyed Kiev and virtually every other city in the region, political power shifted eastward to Moscow. Once the Mongol stranglehold on Russia was broken, Moscow became the capital of the Russian nation.

There is no denying the carnage and wholesale destruction wrought by the Mongols. But once the conquest was over, the Mongols set about building a civilization.

BIBLIOGRAPHY

"Ancient Fresco May Show Genghis Khan Funeral." Xinhua News Agency, December 27, 2006.

Asimov, M. S., and C. E. Bosworth, eds. *History of Civilizations of Central Asia*. Delhi: Motilal Banarsidass Publishers, 1999.

Bergreen, Laurence. *Marco Polo: From Venice to Xanadu*. New York: Alfred A. Knopf, 2007.

Boyle, John Andrew. *The History of the World Conqueror*. Cambridge, MA: Harvard University Press, 1958.

Chambers, James. *The Devil's Horsemen: The Mongol Invasion of Europe*. New York: Atheneum, 1979.

Curtin, Jeremiah. *The Mongols in Russia*. Boston: Little, Brown and Company, 1908.

Dawson, Christopher. *Mission to Asia*. Toronto: University of Toronto Press, 1980.

Fennell, John Lister Illingworth. *The Crisis of Medieval Russia, 1200–1304*. New York: Longman, 1983.

Gabriel, Richard A. *Subotai the Valiant: Genghis Khan's Greatest General*. Norman, OK: University of Oklahoma Press, 2006.

Halperin, Charles J. *Russia and the Golden Horde: The Mongol Impact on Medieval Russian History*. Bloomington, IN: Indiana University Press, 1987.

Hart, Basil Henry Liddell. *Great Captains Unveiled*. Cambridge, MA: Da Capo Press, 1996.

Hartog, Leo de. *Genghis Khan, Conqueror of the World.* New York: St. Martin's Press, 1989.

Lamb, Harold. *Genghis Khan: The Emperor of All Men.* New York: R. M. McBride, 1927.

Man, John. *Genghis Khan: Life, Death, and Resurrection.* New York: St. Martin's Press, 2005.

Martin, Henry Desmond. *The Rise of Chinghis Khan and His Conquest of North China.* Baltimore: Johns Hopkins University Press, 1950.

Mischler, Georg, and Chuluun-Erdene Sosorbaram, "Airag." www.mongolfood.info/en/recipes/airag.html, 2005–2006.

"Mongolian History—Online Resources." Compiled by the Indo-Mongolian Society of New York, 2004, www.mongolianculture.com

Morgan, David. *The Mongols.* New York: B. Blackwell, 1986.

Mote, Frederick W. *Imperial China 900–1800.* Cambridge, MA: Harvard University Press, 2003.

Nicolle, David, and Victor Korolkov. *Kalka River 1223: Genghiz Khan's Mongols Invade Russia.* London: Osprey Publishing, 2001.

Onon, Urgunge, trans. *The Art of War under Chinggis Qahan (Genghis Khan).* London: Curzon Press, 2001.

Prawdin, Michael, and Gerard Chaliand. *The Mongol Empire: Its Rise and Legacy.* New York: Free Press, 1967.

Rachewiltz, Igor de. *The Secret History of the Mongols: A Mongolian Epic Chronicle of the Thirteenth Century.* Boston: Brill, 2004.

Ratchnevsky, Paul. *Genghis Khan: His Life and Legacy.* Cambridge, MA: Blackwell, 1992.

Rossabi, Morris. "All the Khan's Horses." *Natural History*, October 1994.

Rossabi, Morris. *Khubilai Khan: His Life and Times.* Berkeley, CA: University of California Press, 1988.

Rossabi, Morris, consultant. "The Mongols in World History," afe.easia.columbia.edu/mongols/index.html.

Saunders, J. J. *The History of the Mongol Conquests.* New York: Barnes & Noble, 1971.

Severin, Tim. *In Search of Genghis Khan.* New York: Atheneum, 1992.

Spuler, Bertold. *History of the Mongols: Based on Eastern and Western Accounts of the Thirteenth and Fourteenth Centuries.* Berkeley, CA: University of California Press, 1972.

Tillman, Hoyt Cleveland, and Stephen H. West, eds. *China Under Jurchen Rule.* Binhampton, NY: SUNY Press, 1992.

Turnbull, Stephen. *Genghis Khan and the Mongol Conquests 1190–1400.* London: Fitzroy Dearborn, 2003.

Turnbull, Stephen, and Wayne Reynolds. *Fighting Ships of the Far East: Japan and Korea AD 612–1639.* London: Osprey Publishing, 2002.

Walsh, John. "Western Xia: Caravaneers, Cattle-Breeders and Empire-Builders." http://east-asian-history.suite101.com/article.cfm/western_xia, May 21, 2007.

Weatherford, Jack. *Genghis Khan and the Making of the Modern World.* New York: Crown, 2004.

Yamada, Nakaba. *Ghenko: The Mongol Invasion of Japan.* Washington, DC: University Publications of America, 1979.

ACKNOWLEDGMENTS

My sincere thanks to my longtime friend and editor Larry Shapiro, whose editorial judgment improved this book immeasurably. My thanks, too, to the generous, helpful, and patient staff of Fair Winds Press, particularly Cara Connors and Tiffany Hill. And finally, my thanks to Will Kiester—a great friend and an inspired publisher.

ABOUT THE AUTHOR

Thomas J. Craughwell is the author of more than fifteen books, including *How the Barbarian Invasions Shaped the Modern World* (Fair Winds Press, 2008), *Failures of the Presidents* (Fair Winds Press, 2008), and *Stealing Lincoln's Body* (Harvard University Press, 2007). He has written articles for *The Wall Street Journal, The New York Times, U.S. News and World Report, The American Spectator, Emmy* magazine, and *Inside the Vatican*. He has been a guest on CNN, the BBC, and the Discovery Channel. In February 2009 the History Channel aired a two-hour program based on *Stealing Lincoln's Body*, in which Craughwell was featured. He lives in Connecticut.

INDEX